BLOOD
TRAIL

BOOK YOUR PLACE ON OUR WEBSITE AND MAKE THE READING CONNECTION!

We've created a customized website just for our very special readers, where you can get the inside scoop on everything that's going on with Zebra, Pinnacle and Kensington books.

When you come online, you'll have the exciting opportunity to:

- View covers of upcoming books

- Read sample chapters

- Learn about our future publishing schedule (listed by publication month *and author*)

- Find out when your favorite authors will be visiting a city near you

- Search for and order backlist books from our online catalog

- Check out author bios and background information

- Send e-mail to your favorite authors

- Meet the Kensington staff online

- Join us in weekly chats with authors, readers and other guests

- Get writing guidelines

- AND MUCH MORE!

**Visit our website at
http://www.kensingtonbooks.com**

BLOOD TRAIL

STEVEN WALKER

AND

RICK REED

PINNACLE BOOKS
Kensington Publishing Corp.
http://www.kensingtonbooks.com

Some names have been changed to protect the privacy of individuals connected to this story.

PINNACLE BOOKS are published by

Kensington Publishing Corp.
850 Third Avenue
New York, NY 10022

All Kensington Titles, Imprints, and Distributed Lines are available at special quantity discounts for bulk purchases for sales promotions, premiums, fund-raising, and educational or institutional use. Special book excerpts or customized printings can also be created to fit specific needs. For details, write or phone the office of the Kensington special sales manager: Kensington Publishing Corp., 850 Third Avenue, New York, NY 10022, attn: Special Sales Department, Phone: 1-800-221-2647.

Pinnacle and the P logo Reg. U.S. Pat. & TM Off.

First Printing: November 2005

10 9 8 7 6 5 4 3 2 1

Printed in the United States of America

ACKNOWLEDGMENTS

I would like to give special thanks to Michaela Hamilton for her belief that this project would come to fruition. The Brown and Nesbit clans in Indiana deserve recognition for welcoming me to Indiana and giving me sources to investigate this book. Thanks to the Lehigh Valley Writers Academy for their constructive criticism. Most of all, thanks to my wife, Kindra, my family, and my friends for putting up with my self-induced isolation while writing.

Steven Walker

Most of the credit for this piece and, in fact, my motivation for writing it, belongs to the family of Ginger Gasaway, the victim. The pain and loss caused to her family could never truly be explained in the short space of these pages, but hopefully some good will come from bringing this true story to light. I would also like to thank the current Evansville Chief of Police, Brad Hill, for giving me the confidence to take this project on.

Sergeant Richard Reed

PROLOGUE

As a newly appointed sergeant on the Evansville Police Department (EPD), Rick Reed had spent most of his working years dealing with violent people. As he worked his way through a banker's box, filled with bits and pieces of the lives of two families, he had to mark the stark differences in the pile of love letters in front of him, and the reality those letters had brought. If you believed the letters, Joseph Weldon Brown and Ginger Rose Gasaway were a couple in love.

They enjoyed simple things, and they fought, like most couples. They even had cute nicknames for each other. He was "Smokey" and she was "Casper," the nicknames referred to their shared cigarette smoking habit. But that was where the cuteness ended.

Literally hundreds of letters, all written to Casper, all ending "Love, Smokey," shared the same theme: one of reconciliation that stopped just short of threats of violence if these overtures were denied. Reed thought perhaps the nickname Casper was a prediction that Ginger would soon become no more than a ghost.

It would become the job of the Evansville Police Department to find out who was responsible for one of the most vicious crimes to take place in the state of Indiana. Who was responsible? Was it Ginger's lover,

Joe Brown? Could it have been her estranged husband, Hobert Gasaway, who also was attempting to reconcile their relationship? Was it someone else that may have been less suspected?

This is a story of abuse, depravity, a love triangle, addiction, murder, mutilation, confession, politics, and a need for notoriety and acceptance. In addition to Ginger's murder, the killer confessed to murdering thirteen other women over a period of five years, resulting in a nationwide search for evidence to prove his statements.

One of those murders remains an open case, and in one statement, a police officer was accused of having been involved with the victim. One of the investigating detectives was also charged with the duty of investigating another murder that involved a former Evansville police chief. *Blood Trail* is a story that unfolds over decades, and although it comes to a conclusion, it also hints at stories that are yet to be unraveled.

PART I

GROWING PAINS

ONE

It is the heartland of America. In the third week of June, tassels already sway at the top of an ocean of cornstalks, giving seed to feed the population of the greatest country in the world.

In a dozen lifetimes, an army of Rumpelstiltskins could not spin the fields of golden thread to equal the amount of shimmering wheat that fills the horizon of southern Indiana.

In some places, the road is walled for miles with towering stalks of corn. At other areas, the horizon seems a million miles away across an endless field of soybean or watermelons. Regardless of what view the southern Indiana roads provide, there is always one thing that stays the same: it is always dark at night.

Except for in the city of Evansville, there are no streetlamps to guide you on your way. The path is not dotted with front-porch lights of nearby houses, and the headlights of passing cars are few and far between. Night falls early in this part of the country, and when it does, it spreads itself as thick as a murky black oil spill across the sky.

One thing that continues to stay light is the skin color of the inhabitants in this heartland. According to the 2002 population statistics printed in *Evansville Visitor* magazine, published by the Evansville Courier & Press, an average of 95.2 percent of the homes in Gibson, Posey, Vanderburgh, and Warrick Counties are owner-occupied by Caucasians.

The city of Evansville, with a population of just over 121,000, contains 85 percent of the population of all four counties put together.

"You may think we're a bit like country folk, but that's only because we are," said Dave York, a resident of the tiny town of Haubstadt.

Duane Brown, Joe Brown's second cousin, and a professor at the University of North Carolina at Chapel Hill, grew up in this southern Indiana farming community. He described the people who live there like this:

"They're just plain folk who like to gossip. Talk about the person down the street who's having an affair is what makes life worth living.

"For the most part, the population is made up of conservative Baptists. There are also a few Methodists and Presbyterians, and not quite enough Catholics to get a bridge party together.

"When people talk, they don't have to conjugate verbs because 'ain't' is the only one used, and the famous Indiana 'Hoosier's nickname came from everyone asking, 'Who's your mother and who's your father?'"

Duane Brown also said that parents don't worry much about keeping their children in school and providing them with a good education.

"What they worry most about is whether or not they make the basketball team. The most important thing to teach them is how to scratch and spit."

Of course, Duane Brown's description was given in jest. He still held a soft spot in his heart for Indiana and was himself a testament to higher education and what could be achieved from a good ol' Indiana boy.

Today, many Indiana parents are intensely proud of the education of their children. It is also true that

Indiana has produced some of the greatest sports legends of our time, including Bob Griese, of the Miami Dolphins, Don Mattingly, of the New York Yankees, and Andy Benes, of the St. Louis Cardinals.

And, of course, Indiana is the home of the country's most famous auto race, the Indianapolis 500.

Indiana know-how also created one of the primary steel-producing industries in the country. In addition to producing agriculture, fishing, forestry, mining, and the production of electrical and electronic equipment made Indiana the eighth highest manufacturing-producing state in the country by the end of the 1970s.

Indiana also produced Joseph Weldon Brown. Because Joe Brown was often described as the apple that didn't fall far from the tree, it's important to describe his father. Gerald "Jerry" Brown was an angry man.

"Jerry was a carpenter, and if he'd hit his thumb with a hammer, he'd tell that thumb that if it was going to hurt him, he'd show it what pain really felt like. Then he'd smash the hell out of it again. 'Damn you thumb for hurtin' me!' he'd say," said local resident James Kincheloe, who knew the Brown family.

James also relayed a story that he had heard about Jerry, who was supposedly an avid raccoon hunter.

"I don't know if you know anything about coon hunting, but usually you let your dog loose and they chase the coon up a tree. The dog will normally stay there and bark until you come up, and can shoot the coon out of the tree.

"Well, Jerry's dog would chase a coon up a tree and then just run off ahead so Jerry wouldn't know which tree it was in. I heard that one day he got so mad at his dog that he took his nail gun and just hung his dog on a tree by his collar."

Regardless of the validity of the stories that captivated the surrounding communities, Jerry Brown had gotten a reputation as a man that you didn't want to associate with, much less cross.

Of Jerry's son Joe, James said, "He was nuts. He came from a nutty family."

Robert "Pinker" Smith worked as a custodian for the North Posey School District for over twenty years, and was considered by many of the locals as the historic aficionado who knew everything about everyone in the surrounding area.

Smith described Joe Brown's grandparents as highstrung, spirited, and quick-tempered individuals. He said that Joe's father, Jerry, was almost a maniac at times.

"One day a guy walked into a bar and saw Jerry. He said to him, 'Hey, Brown, have you stolen any watermelons lately?' and, quick as a flash, Jerry knocked him down on the ground. That's just the kind of guy he was. He didn't take any grief from anybody," Pinker said.

Pinker said that he and Jerry used to hang out together when they were young, and that they sometimes would go roller-skating in Evansville. That was how Jerry met his first wife, Carleen. He bought her a diamond ring in Poseyville, which he never paid for, and, according to Pinker, the couple had a nice wedding reception, which was also never paid for. Throughout their marriage, they endured one hardship after another, and Pinker began to lose contact with them.

"I remember seeing Jerry's firstborn son, Mike, walking down the street with his hands full of empty bottles. He was crippled, and seemed to be having a hard time carrying his load. I hollered over to him, 'Those look heavy, young man,' and he called back, 'Shut your goddamn mouth.' He couldn't have been more than twelve years old, but I could tell that he was a chip off the old block," Pinker said.

"Joey was just messed up. That's about all I can say about him."

A firefighter in the Smith Township Volunteer Fire

Department in Cynthiana, Pinker said that Jerry had three different homes burn down. Back then, small-town volunteer fire companies never investigated the reason for the start of a fire. Everyone just came out and did the best that they could to put the fires out. There was never any thought that a fire could have been the result of arson. Nobody ever questioned whether or not Jerry would have set his own house on fire. Arson just wasn't part of the vocabulary of the residents in southern Indiana at that time.

"I remember Jerry's last fire because I was watching the New Year's Day parade, and I saw smoke in the distance. I was called to the scene, and it turned out to be Jerry's house. Nobody was home at the time, but while we were putting out the fire, Jerry and Carleen came down the street. He was half-carrying her, and she was screaming and flailing around. Nobody paid much attention to them, though. We were more concerned about putting out the fire," Pinker said.

Cynthiana, Indiana, is a very small town. It's not even shown on some state maps. According to the 2000 census, there were 693 residents living in less than 300 households. Most of the people are farmers, landscapers, or contractors. The median household income is $37,589 and 98.6 percent of the population is White/Non-Hispanic.

There isn't much to do in Cynthiana except work all day, and then sit around gossiping over a case of beer at night. If you need groceries, supplies, or are looking for alternative entertainment, you have to drive to another town. Nearby Owensville or Poseyville doesn't offer much more, so that usually means a trip to Evansville, which is at least a half hour away by car.

Cynthiana is the rural town that Joe Brown and his family resided in.

Glenda Houchins also grew up in the tiny village of Cynthiana, and she remembered riding the school bus with Joe and his siblings.

"I knew that there was something wrong with that family from the time that I was a little girl. They always stayed together on the bus, and they never seemed to have any friends. They were quiet, and it was like they had something that they didn't want other people to know," Houchins said.

Alice Kincheloe, James's wife, confirmed Glenda's observation. She said that the Brown children always kept to themselves, but the whole town heard rumors about the abusive way that they were brought up. But it was taboo to talk about things like that, and Jerry had a reputation for being so angry and violent that nobody would have said or done anything anyway. Alice said that everybody would just look the other way.

Another local resident, Bonnie Hendricks, also went to school with the Brown children. She described the boys as bullies and the girls as beautiful, especially Joe's oldest sister, Sue.

Joe's great-aunt and great-uncle, Cecil and Margaret Brown would sometimes pack up their family to visit Joe's grandfather Weldon and the rest of the Brown clan. Margaret said that Joe was the most mistreated child she ever knew. His father, Jerry, would backhand him just for blinking, and knock him flat. Margaret and Cecil believed that it would have made matters worse if they tried to intervene because Jerry had such a violent temper. Still, they discussed trying to adopt Joe when he was about twelve years old because they felt terrible for him. As they expected, Jerry wouldn't have anything to do with it.

During one visit, Jerry and his brothers chased each other around the property with loaded guns. Fearing for the safety of their own children, Margaret and Cecil stopped visiting them.

Two

Joseph Weldon Brown was born in 1954, and he was raised in the rural Indiana town of Cynthiana. His parents, Carleen and Jerry Brown, were not well off financially, and like many people in the area, they struggled to get by. Jerry worked as a contractor, and Carleen was a stay-at-home mother.

There were a lot of mouths to feed in the Brown family. In addition to Joe, Carleen had given birth to two other sons and two daughters as well.

The Browns had a history of excessive drinking, and Carleen also kept a continuous flow of medication in her bloodstream to fight off her bouts of depression.

According to Joe Brown, when he was eight years old, a local boy twice his age would visit the house and sexually molest him. Young Joe looked toward his mother for protection from this abuse. He said that she knew what was happening but did nothing to stop it. Instead, she would take another pill, have another drink, and disappear into the bathroom, pretending that nothing wrong was going on.

According to Cindy Byrd, a schoolmate of Joe's oldest sister Sue, there were many unsettling problems in the Brown family. When Sue couldn't stand it any longer, she decided that she would end her life.

"Sue and I were in tenth grade together in 1965. She wasn't as much of a loner as her brothers were, but she didn't have many true friends. I remember that she invited me to stay overnight at her house one time. They seemed like a fairly normal family, but I knew that Sue was a troubled girl.

"One morning at school, Sue told me that she had taken a lot of pills. I don't know if she stole them from her mother or not. I didn't know what to do, so I told the school nurse. I heard that they had to induce Sue to vomit, or maybe pumped her stomach, I'm not sure.

"She never really told me why she did it or gave any specifics, but I knew that she had problems at home. I don't know if she really intended to kill herself, or if it was just an attempt to get attention. I do know that she had a lot of responsibility because her mother wasn't quite right. Their house looked like it was in pretty good order, and that was probably because of Sue.

"We were in high school when I found out that Sue had a crush on my boyfriend. Our friendship kind of fell apart after that," Cindy said.

Sue was afraid of what might happen to her if she told anyone the real reason for her attempted suicide, and the horrors of life at the Brown family were never uncovered. At that time, and in that town, domestic problems were not investigated as thoroughly as they would be today.

Joe's other sister, Jennie, said that their father used to physically beat up Joe on a regular basis, and continuously humiliated him.

She related a story of one particular Christmas when Joe had begged his parents to buy him a guitar. On Christmas morning, Joe was practically drooling when he came into the room and saw a guitar case lying on the floor beside his father. He ran to the case and dropped to his knees to open it. It was full of rocks. His father could barely breathe from laughing so hard at the sight of his son's disappointment.

Joe was not a particularly bright student. He also had a difficult time with the other students, and he was often involved in fights with the other boys in school. By the age of twelve, Joe began to spend more time in juvenile correctional facilities than he did in school, and so he never graduated.

In a letter written on June 18, 2004, Joe Brown wrote, "Now that I'm older, I can look upon my childhood and see it for what it really was. My father beat me practically every day until I reached fourteen years old. As long as my father took his anger out on me, at least it gave my mother the opportunity to protect the other four kids from getting physically abused.

"You can basically say that my mother sacrificed me to protect the other kids. It worked, and at times I was probably a rotten little kid, but no kid deserves to be beaten like I was."

Brown expressed satisfaction that he was able to protect his brothers and sisters by becoming the target of his father's anger, and yet he still harbored feelings of resentment, and even hatred toward his siblings.

Brown said that his family used to live in California until his oldest sister was raped, although there are no police records to verify the incident.

"I guess that my mother was afraid that my dad would kill [the guy] so we moved back to Indiana around 1959. My parents decided to sweep that incident under the rug. That was the easiest way to deal with that," Joe Brown wrote.

He barely remembered his grandparents, except that they died within six months of each other in the early 1960s.

"From what I've been told, my father's mom beat him and his brothers. I learned from an early age that if I done something wrong, I would get a beating from my father. That was my way of getting his attention. There's no doubt that the physical abuse I received from my father influenced the way that I grew up. From way back as I can remember, I was mistreating our dogs and cats, picking fights with all the kids in town and more."

Brown said that a turning point in his life took place in 1962 when his family's house burned down. Joe claimed that it was during this time, while his father was building them a new house, that another family member began molesting him.

"Every time that happened, I would be threatened that if I said anything, my father would be told, and I would get a whipping," Joe said.

He claimed that the molesting went on for the next five years. Joe also claimed that an older boy named Ronnie, who lived next door, also began molesting him.

"He would bribe me with being allowed to ride his new Stingray [*sic*] bicycle and then afterwards, he would say that if I said anything about it, that he would tell my dad and I would get a whipping," Joe wrote.

"Every time that I was molested, I would always cry afterwards. Something was telling my young brain that this wasn't right, but on the other hand, I didn't want no more beatings.

"This was the time that I really started mistreating animals, and I was getting into fights every other day at school. I done really poor in school and flunked the first grade. I can remember basically not caring about anything."

Brown said that he would try to avoid that family member at any cost, and that when nighttime came around, he would try to find a safe haven by hiding in his closet.

"During this time in my life, I felt like I was different from everyone else. I wetted the bed until I was twelve years old. My parents kept calling me a sissy, and said that they would make me wear diapers if I didn't quit wetting the bed."

Joe claimed that he would urinate in his bed to deter the alleged molestation by another member of his family.

"Ronnie finally quit molesting me when I was about eleven years old. I don't really know why he quit. I guess he could sense that I didn't like it. I always felt that if people knew about what happened, they would think I was queer or something. Today I realize that I was just a little kid back then."

During a 2004 interview, Joe's childhood neighbor, Ronnie, denied having ever molested Joe.

"You have to take everything Joe says with a very big grain of salt. Everyone in that family was a half a brick off," he said.

Ronnie said that if Joe claimed that a neighbor boy twice his age molested him, he might have meant his (Ronnie's) older brother, Tom, who was now deceased.

"Like any kid at that age, we used to play doctor. It was just a curiosity kind of thing, but I definitely wouldn't call it molesting. It was more like 'show me yours and I'll show you mine,' and there might have even been a little bit of touching involved, but nobody was molested. My younger sister, Debra, once told me that Joe offered her some cookies to look at her body. That doesn't mean that she was molested," Ronnie said.

Ronnie said that there was one time when his mother walked into a place he called the "smokehouse" and she caught him, his brother, Tom, and Joe with their clothes off. He said that it was a very embarrassing moment, but he was too young to know any better at the time. He said that his parents sat him and his older brother down that evening to explain the facts of life.

Ronnie said that he was closer to Joe's oldest brother, Michael, than any other member of the Brown family.

They used to ride bikes together, and they played baseball and basketball.

"I knew something wasn't right with Michael the first time that I saw him, but despite his problems, we still hung out together and became friends. The rest of the family was way the hell out there. Nobody in the neighborhood would go near their house because of Joe's father. People knew that if he'd go off, he might kill you. He loved his dogs more than his kids, and he treated his dogs badly. You could always hear screaming and yelling coming from the house. Michael was on the shit list more than Joe ever was. Because of his disability, he wasn't what his father was looking for in a son," Ronnie said.

Ronnie's family moved to the other side of Evansville in 1964 and Ronnie didn't associate with the Browns after that. Most of the kids in the neighborhood would hang out at Cappy's restaurant, next to Harold Gee's gas station, to play pinball or pool, and listen to the jukebox. Ronnie went back there once and saw Michael. By then, the older Brown child had already quit school and spent his time cruising the area on his motorcycle.

Brown said that in 1967 he began sneaking out of his house at night and would stay out until three or four o'clock in the morning. He would spend his time playing pinball and hanging around town. He said that he would then sneak back in.

"It was during this time of my life that we had another neighbor, who had a daughter named Kara Washington. She was a couple years younger than I was. Me and Kara would sneak off together all the time, and just take our clothes off and stare at one another.

"One day, in the early part of 1967, my sister, Jennie, caught us naked out in a cornfield. She ran home to tell mom. That was one of many times that I didn't ever want to go back home," Joe said.

Despite his apprehensive feelings, Brown said that he got dressed and went back home, expecting to get a beating from his father.

It was at this time that Brown said he told his parents about being molested but they didn't do anything about it.

It was then that he began completely to keep to himself. The people in town viewed him as an outsider, and now he became an outcast within his own family.

"I guess my mother and father decided to bury all of this under the rug and go on. But for me, I was so confused. Throughout my entire life, every time I did something wrong, I got my ass beat. This automatically placed in my mind that what had been done to me wasn't bad or wrong," Joe said.

Despite the fact that Joe felt alienated from his father, and claimed that his father regularly abused him, he also thought that, in some way, his father was trying to live his childhood through him. Joe claimed that his father made him join the Little League team and forced him to practice pitching every day for hours without even taking a break to eat.

Whether Joe's memory was valid or not, his schoolmates remembered that he threw a mean curveball, and that batters had a hard time connecting to anything that the left-handed pitcher threw over the plate.

Sue Brown got married in 1968, and although Joe Brown despised his siblings, he said that after Sue left, his family life went downhill.

His mother, Carleen, began taking large quantities of prescription pills every day. People who knew her weren't sure what to expect from her anymore. She would be depressed and melancholy one time, and then exuberant the next. Carleen's weight fluctuated as much as her emotional state. At one point, she weighed nearly 180 pounds, and at another time, she became a frail and bony woman who barely tipped triple digits on the scale.

After Sue got married, Brown said, he turned his attention to his other sister, Jennie, who was just two years older than he was.

"One night, I had a really bad nightmare and got out of bed at about one or two o'clock in the morning. I took a paring knife and sneaked into Jennie's bedroom. I squatted alongside of her bed and just stared at her for a couple of hours.

"For some reason or another, I dropped the knife on the floor and went back to my closet to hide until the next morning. Jennie told Mom that she thought she saw me leaving her bedroom when I dropped the knife on the floor. We were sitting at the supper table when my mother told my dad. All he ever said was that if I ever touched Jennie, he would cut my dick off," Joe said.

Joe said that sneaking out of the house led him to something that helped him to keep from having nightmares and night sweats. That thing was gambling.

"I started out playing pinball machines, but gradually I started playing pool, and then cards for money with other kids at the town's pool hall. Yep, gambling was my escape from all my problems."

Joe Brown's problems were just beginning, though. It wasn't long before his mother would be found dead.

THREE

On February 16, 1970, there were only two people inside the modest Brown dwelling—Joe and his mother. Carleen was taking a warm bath to relax. Joe reported that was where he found the naked, lifeless body of his mother and he called the police.

When they arrived at the scene, Brown told the police that his mother had passed out and hit her head on the tub.

"It was an accident," Joe said, even though nobody was accusing him of being responsible. The official coroner ruling was asphyxia due to drowning, brought on by pentobarbital intoxication.

Sergeant Rick Reed, of the Evansville Police Department, said that he believed that Joe might have been responsible for his mother's death, but no proof to support that suspicion had ever been uncovered. Locals who knew Carleen described her as a very modest woman who would most likely have locked the door while bathing. If that was true, Joe wouldn't have been able to enter the room, but the door was not locked when police arrived, and there were no visible signs of forced entry.

Ronnie Fields described Joe's mother as someone who was "way out there" and he said that she would always be hyped up on caffeine, drinking twelve RC Colas a day. Fields joined the U.S. Air Force a few months before Carleen was found dead in her bathtub, but he said that he wasn't surprised to hear that she had killed herself.

Twenty-four years after his mother's death, Joe Brown wrote, "I can't even remember talking to my mom as I grew up. Like I said, I was the one that she tossed to my father to abuse. I guess that I had a lot of inner hate and anger towards my mom and dad."

Jerry had a problem adjusting to having to take care of himself and three children; so just three months after Carleen's death, he married another woman, Imogene Stallings.

"I rebelled against my father remarrying, especially so soon! My stepmother had three kids of her own, so our house was very full," Joe said.

Joe was accustomed to getting a beating from his father if he did something wrong, and although he hated it, he also thrived on being able to gain his father's attention. He began to do things like steal his father's car to go on joyrides, knowing that he would get caught. As much as Joe blamed the physical abuse that he endured in his childhood for his later actions, he also admitted that he craved the attention that he received, and even provoked it.

Finally, in December 1970, Joe was arrested for stealing cigarettes from the pool hall that he frequented. He was ordered to State Hospital in Evansville for psychological examinations, and then he was sent to the Indiana Boy's School until March 1971.

When he was released, he found out that his family had moved into his stepmother's house. His sister Jennie had stayed at their old house. Joe never got along with Imogene and it didn't take long until they got into a big argument.

When Joe's father came home from work that

evening, Imogene gave him an ultimatum. Either she or Joe had to go. Jerry told Joe to leave the house. He told him to go live in their old house with his sister Jennie until he was able to sell it.

"So here I am, sixteen years old with no job, no diploma, no money, and no food. I did not have the slightest idea how to make it until I was eighteen years old.

"During that time, I didn't get involved with any girls. I didn't trust any women. I learned early in life that by visiting a prostitute, I didn't have to worry about getting emotionally involved. Most importantly, I didn't have to worry about them hurting me inside again," Joe said.

After Joe turned eighteen, he enlisted in the U.S. Army in November 1972. He said that he went to Fort Ord, California, for his basic training and then was shipped to Fort Hood, Texas, for Advanced Individual Training, where he learned how to drive a tank.

"While I was in the service, my gambling habit went rampant. I gambled on anything and everything. After a long night of gambling in Fort Hood, Texas, I started to become homesick. It had been a couple of years since I had talked to my father and I caught a Greyhound bus back to Cynthiana, Indiana," Joe said.

Joe was afraid that he wouldn't be welcome at his father's house, and he couldn't find anywhere else to stay, so he stole a car and lived in it for about two weeks until the police caught him. Joe was charged with auto theft, but he was given an opportunity to have the charge dropped if he would return to the army. Joe was so afraid of being sent to Vietnam that he chose to face the charges against him instead. He was sentenced to one to ten years, and sent to the Indiana Youth Center.

Joe was soon transferred to the Indiana Reformatory. While there, his oldest brother, Michael, passed away in 1974 because of a brain tumor. Joe didn't find out about his brother's death until two months later because his father didn't want him to attend the funeral.

Jerry drank heavily, and his brothers, Roger and Robert, told police that he often talked about killing himself. Robert Brown said that Jerry had actually attempted suicide once during this tumultuous period in his life.

On November 12, 1975, Jerry was found inside an orange Ford pickup truck, sitting alongside County Road 350 East, about two miles northwest of Stewartsville, Indiana. He died of what was determined to be a self-inflicted gunshot wound to the head.

Ronnie Ellis, of Poseyville, drove along the rural road every day. He was used to seeing the orange truck pulled over on the shoulder, because Jerry had taken to the habit of pulling over near the same vicinity, to sleep off his increasingly frequent bouts of drunkenness.

Ellis drove to his friend's house and brought John Webb back to the scene before Webb called the police.

At the time of his death, Jerry was separated from his second wife, Imogene, and had moved to Stewartsville. Joe was allowed to attend his father's funeral. When he was released from prison on May 19, 1976, Joe was officially on his own, although he had already been living that way for most of his life.

"The only good thing that Gerald Brown ever did for his son was to put a bullet between his own eyes," said Evansville police detective Rick Reed.

Uneducated and poor, Joe Brown kept looking for an easy way to make money without actually having to work for it. The possibility of getting a big payoff made gambling an addictive behavior for Brown.

Always thinking that he was smart enough to beat the odds, and having a desire to hold a winning hand, Joe Brown fell further and further into debt. It did not take long before he dug a hole that seemed too deep to pull himself out. Still, the excitement of laying down his hand of cards was more than he could resist.

After being released from prison, Jerry's youngest brother, Roger, and his wife, Sharon, took Joe into their home. They also helped him to get a job at a construction company that was owned by Joe's other uncle, Bill.

In June 1976, Joe met a young redhead named Donna Kay Graham. They fell in love, and they got married just one month later. The young newlyweds began having marital problems almost immediately because Joe continued to gamble, and caused them to fall further into debt. Donna's repeated pleas for Joe to quit gambling fell on deaf ears. On March 14, 1977, Donna gave birth to daughter Jamie Leigh Brown. Even that added responsibility did not hinder Joe's gambling habit. In fact, it had gotten worse.

Unable to deal with the responsibility of a family, Joe would disappear for weeks at a time. He practically lived in Shelly's Pool Hall in Petersburgh, where a poker game was held around the clock, every single day. Brown couldn't remember how much money he lost there, but he said, "I lost my soul."

Until this point in his life, the most serious crime that Joe had been convicted of was stealing a car. But now, he had lost his job, run his credit cards into the ground, and ran out of relatives from whom he could borrow money.

He felt desperate and decided that his only way out of debt would be to commit robbery in order to get some fast cash. He borrowed a gun from someone. He never said from whom, and the EPD never followed up on tracking down where the weapon came from. His intention was to rob a grocery store, but at the last minute, he couldn't get up the nerve to do it.

Four

Star Wars was a smash hit at the box office. Those who hadn't served time there already forgot about the Vietnam War. Led Zeppelin continued to rock our socks off, but disco was reaching its apex. Polyester leisure suits were the fashion rage, and twenty-two-year-old Joseph Weldon Brown took a gamble that would change the course of his entire life.

There were a lot of addictive things available in the 1970s, but Joe avoided most of them, choosing gambling as his vice. He wasn't very good at it, and soon he was in debt well beyond his capability to pay it off.

The solution that he chose to solve his financial problems was to place another sure bet.

He lost.

He needed to pay off his gambling debt before it took complete control of him. Joe Bender was his next alternative. He thought that his worries were over, and didn't think much about Bender or what the consequences of robbing him would bring. Within three months, society would have complete control over every aspect of Joe Brown's life, and life was the sentence that he would receive for kidnapping and armed robbery.

"I went to Joe Bender's house. He was a friend of mine who had loaned me money before. I was desperate at this point so I begged Bender to loan me some money. I never went there with any intention to rob or harm him. But when I pulled into his driveway, I left the gun in my back pocket," Joe Brown wrote.

"Me and Joe (Bender) sat out on his carport for about an hour and he told me that he couldn't loan me any more money. I asked if I could at least get enough cash to buy some gas for my car. He said that I should pull my car up to his gas pump and that he would fill my tank up.

"That's when he saw the gun in my back pocket and I guess that he thought the gun was meant for him. He tried wrestling me to the ground to get the gun away from me but he didn't succeed. Instead, I pulled the gun out and pointed it right at his face. I told him that he fucked up. Anyway, we both went into his house and he told his wife Dorothy to go get me all of the money they had stashed away in their house. She picked up a bible and removed $775 in cash.

"Afterwards, I turned the gun over to Bender to prove to him that I wasn't there to harm him or his wife. As I started to leave, I asked him to go with me. He didn't want to but he did. After we left his house, I had to slow way down to make a left-hand turn. When I did, Bender bailed out of the car and ran across the road to his brother's house.

"I panicked and floored my car. I was going to Lakeview Truck Stop to get gas but before I got there I ran out. I should have filled my tank at Bender's house before I left. I hitched a ride to Lakeview and as soon as I got there, a State Trooper pulled in, got out of his car and threw down on me. I took off running across Highway 41. How I got away, I'll never know, but I did.

"The following day, I caught a taxi cab to Princeton, Indiana. I bought me a new set of clothes, spent a night with a prostitute, then caught a Greyhound bus to Las Vegas, Nevada. It took me three days to get there, and by the time I did, I only had three hundred dollars left," Joe penned.

"I went to the first casino that I came to, the Stardust Hotel, and managed to blow all of the money in a couple of hours.

"After that, I started hitchhiking back to Indiana to turn myself in. I made it to Salina, Kansas before I was picked up by the Kansas Highway Patrol. I was extradited to Indiana the next day.

"My attorney said that he could get me a ten year sentence but I wouldn't plead guilty. After it was all said and done, I ended up with a life sentence. I got to spend a couple of hours with my wife and daughter before I was transferred to the Reception Diagnostic Center to begin serving my time. After that, I was sent to the Indiana Reformatory to finish my sentence," Joe wrote.

Court records show a slightly different version of Joe's story. On July 13, 1977, prosecuting attorney George J. Ankenbrand filed cause number CR-77-52 in Gibson County, Indiana, against Joe Brown.

It stated, "On or about the twelfth day of July, Joseph Brown did unlawfully, feloniously, and forcibly by violence, and putting Joe Bender in fear, take from the person and possession of the said Joe Bender, money of the value of $520 which the said Joe Bender then lawfully held in his possession."

During the trial, it was revealed that Brown demanded a total of $1,700 from Bender, and when Bender could only come up with $520 in cash, Brown demanded that Bender write a check for another $1,200.

Joe Bender signed an affidavit stating that Joe Brown came to his residence in Owensville, Indiana, and demanded money. Bender also testified that Brown threatened to shoot both him and his wife on several occasions, and that after they gave him all their money, Brown waved a gun at Bender and motioned for him to get into Brown's car.

When Brown slowed to take a corner, about $2\frac{1}{2}$ miles from the house, Bender jumped out of the car and ran to his brother's house, where he called the police. Bender stated that at no time did he accompany Brown willingly, but that he was afraid that if he did not do so, Brown would shoot both him and his wife.

On July 13, 1977, the state of Indiana found sufficient evidence to proceed with a trial and set Joe's bail amount at $25,000. Thirteen days later, Joe filed a petition stating that he was of unsound mind at the time when he allegedly committed the offense.

In a letter dated August 12, 1977, psychiatrist Charles H. Crudden, of the Southwestern Indiana Mental Health Center, wrote that he conducted a psychiatric examination on Joseph W. Brown on August 2, 1977.

In addition to conducting personal interviews with Joe Brown, Crudden also reviewed a social services report done on December 11, 1970, a report of a psychological examination performed on December 18, 1970, as well as the discharge summary of Joe's brief stay at the Evansville State Hospital at that time.

Crudden also studied the findings of another psychological examination of Joe Brown performed on July 28, 1977, by psychiatric social worker William Seymour.

In the letter, Crudden concluded that Joe was competent to stand trial, understood the nature of the charges against him, and could distinguish between right and wrong.

"I can find no reason to believe his state of mind (at the time the crime was committed) basically was any different than when I examined him," Crudden wrote.

On September 21, 1977, Joe Brown was found guilty

of armed robbery and kidnapping. By order of Gibson County circuit judge Walter H. Palmer, he was sentenced to ten years for armed robbery and issued a life sentence for kidnapping. Joe Brown was twenty-two years old.

At the Reception Diagnostic Center, Brown was given another psychological evaluation and a revised Beta Intelligence Test. His range of intellectual functioning was rated at above average, and he was determined to have an IQ of 115.

Behavioral clinician Charles Ware and psychologist Jack E. Thomas signed off on Brown's evaluation. The evaluation stated that he was cooperative and aware of his surroundings. He answered questions pertinently and didn't seem to be suffering from any psychotic or neurotic processing.

Ware and Thomas wrote that Brown believed that the jury was paid off and that he felt that he should have only been given a couple of years for this offense.

"There is suspiciousness, a tendency to be worrisome, confused, restless, withdrawn, and socially inept," they wrote in their evaluation.

Ware and Thomas also stated that Joe Brown harbored a great deal of hostility, feelings of alienation, and inflated self-worth. They concluded that he had few intellectual resources, would resist intervention, and that he might be a security risk inside a correctional facility.

In November, Joe Brown wrote Judge Palmer pleading for a lesser sentence. In return, Brown promised that he would drop all appeals.

"My wife came up to see me at the Indiana Reformatory in November 1977 and again in March of 1978. On the last visit, she brought my one year-old daughter up. That would be the last time that I seen either one of them again.

"My wife put my daughter up for adoption. Donna

didn't want or allow any of my relatives to adopt my daughter. I was faced with the hardest thing I ever had to do in my life, and that was to sign a form releasing all of my parental rights.

"I never thought I'd ever be released from prison, so the least that I could do for my daughter was to give her a chance at having a family. I signed away my rights. I think Donna did that to get back at me," Brown wrote.

On June 18, 1979, attorney William J. Marshall entered an appeal on behalf of Joe Brown. In the appeal, Brown contended that all of the evidence against him should have been excluded because it was obtained from him without a knowing and intelligent waiver of his Miranda rights.

The appeal read, "The evidence at trial showed that following occurrences on July 12, 1977, appellant (Joe Brown) fled by bus to Las Vegas, where he gambled away the money taken from the Benders. In an effort to return to Indiana, appellant was arrested for hitchhiking in Salina, Kansas.

"The Indiana authorities were notified of appellant's arrest and State Trooper Zickmund and Gibson County Sheriff Emmert traveled to Kansas to pick him up. In Salina, Zickmund and Emmert orally advised appellant of his Miranda rights but did not obtain a waiver because they did not have a form with them at the time.

"During the return trip to Indiana, appellant was reminded that he did not have to say anything to the officers. The three engaged in general conversation concerning the weather and scenery until they approached Gibson County.

"At this point, Officer Zickmund asked appellant if he would show them the location of the gun. Appellant responded that he would do so on the condition that he be allowed to see his wife that evening. Appellant then directed the officers to a truck stop where he retrieved the gun used in the offenses from some weeds. Appellant was then transported to the police station in Princeton, Indiana, where he signed a waiver of rights form and made further statements to police. The gun thus recovered, and four bullets contained therein, were introduced at trial along with the waiver of rights form over appellant's objection.

"Appellant contends that all of this evidence should have been excluded as it was obtained in violation of his Miranda rights. He argues that since he did not sign a waiver form until after he had led police to the weapon, that there was therefore no evidence establishing a voluntary relinquishment of the right to counsel and the right not to incriminate himself."

Brown's appeal was defeated.

"From then on, I basically forgot about society. It was the only way that I could deal with a life sentence," Brown wrote.

Local residents speculated about the supposed friendship between Joe Brown and Joe Bender. Brown was a poor and troublesome youth, while Bender was an older man who was very prominent and wealthy.

"They had nothing in common. There was no reason for them to have any kind of relationship at all, unless there was something queer going on between them," Pinker Smith said.

He went as far as to suggest that Brown may have had a homosexual relationship with Bender, and that he might have been blackmailing him to keep it quiet, but there is no proof that such a thing was true.

In a letter dated July 28, 2004, Brown wrote that there was no blackmail involved, but he also wrote that Bender did make sexual advances toward him.

"He said that he could do lots of things for me. I always did think Bender was a queer. Just mentioning his name leaves a bad taste in my mouth," Joe Brown wrote.

In a statement given decades later, one of Joe Brown's

ex-wives, Mary Lou Seitz, also hinted at the possibility that Brown and Bender may have been more than just friends.

"I wouldn't be surprised if Joe and Bender were intimate with each other at some point. He (Joe Brown) did tell me about a boyfriend that he had while he was in jail," Seitz said.

Repeated attempts to get Joe and Dorothy Bender to talk about the situation were returned with a refusal to comment.

"It was a horrible time in our lives and we just want to let it go," Dorothy said.

Brown had pretty much given up on the idea of ever becoming a free man, and on several occasions, he mentioned that he was adjusting well to his life of confinement. He had a roof over his head and three steady meals a day. He enjoyed his job working at the prison kitchen, and was able to relate to his fellow inmates. Most of all, he enjoyed the fact that he was still able to play cards and gamble every day.

Despite his desire to be in control, Joe Brown conformed well to the life of incarceration. To Brown, prison was just a different environment that was not far from the reality of life. It provided him with an opportunity to become someone who was desired, and yet, at the same time, feared.

Never having practiced oral hygiene, Brown suffered from severe tooth decay, and while in jail, he opted to have all of his teeth removed. He later confessed that he did so in order to make money in prison, by being able to better service the inmates through oral gratification. At the same time, Brown made it clear that he did not condone homosexuality.

Thinking that he would never see the outside world again, Brown felt that he had nothing left to lose. So, in February 1980, when a fellow inmate made sexual advances toward him in the kitchen, Joe Brown took a heavy, five-pound, steel, commercial-grade can opener and used it to beat the man nearly to death.

"The guy's nickname was 'Wolfman.' He hit on me sexually, and I told him I wasn't interested. He tried to pursue it further, but I busted his head wide open. He left me alone after that," Brown said.

An additional five years were added to Brown's life sentence for the battery charge.

On May 7, 1987, Institutional Release Coordinator Jerry Adank filed a petition for clemency on Brown's behalf. Despite his unstable state of mind, his addictive behavior, and his capacity for a violent reaction to those who did not conform to his ideas of right and wrong, Brown became eligible to appear before a parole board in December 1987.

Judge Palmer responded by writing, "I defer to the prosecutor."

Prosecuting attorney Ankenbrand's response was "I object strenuously to any clemency for kidnappers and armed robbers."

Brown's clemency was denied, but that did not mean that his life sentence would be fulfilled.

"I had basically forgot all about society. I had only received one visit during the years that I was locked up, and that was when Jennie came to see me in 1990. I think she came up more out of guilt than anything else," Brown wrote.

"Sue hadn't had anything to do with me since 1975 and even my youngest brother David didn't have anything to do with me. Why, I don't know.

"I passed my time raising a cat at the Indiana State Prison. We were allowed to have cats at this particular prison. I had 'Brownie' my calico cat for fourteen years. She was a female . . . helped me to grow up a lot. Brownie and gambling passed away all those years behind forty-foot walls.

"I also saw several women therapists, which they

helped me to get over the trauma of being molested. Even back then, I didn't trust any women. I just basically played with them for amusement . . . let them think they were helping me. But I finally did get out of prison. I had to parole to the Evansville Rescue Mission. I had no other place to go," Brown wrote.

On June 16, 1995, Joe Brown was released from prison.

PART II

MURDER

FIVE

Handling white-collar crime was definitely a change from the Violent Crime Unit (VCU), where Evansville, Indiana, police detective Rick Reed had worked for the previous thirteen years. For one thing, this type of perpetrator seldom, if ever, resisted. Reed blamed his new desk job position for the fact that he had gotten soft and was gaining weight.

It was a beautiful summer day when a call came from a friend at Old National Bank. Reed's assistance was needed to look into a financial crime. Reed took advantage of the opportunity to get some exercise by walking the few blocks along Main Street from Police Headquarters to the main branch of Old National Bank.

It was sad how the face of Main Street had changed over the years. Some shop windows stood vacant, some boarded over to prevent further vandalism, and it seemed like every other business was empty. This was supposed to have changed when riverboat gambling came to Evansville, Indiana. The increased revenue, extra taxes, and attraction of people seeking food and entertainment was supposed to revitalize the Main Street businesses. But these promises, like so many other promises of politicians, proved to be just more rhetoric used to line the city's pockets.

Reed was old enough to remember a different face of downtown—one where people happily shopped and crowds were not just the "lunch bunch." He nodded at the regulars that he knew: some homeless, others disabled, and smokers, who were condemned from their workplaces as the last group of people who were allowed to be prejudiced against.

The Old National Bank building on the Main Street Walkway was the tallest building in the downtown area. Although the customer service area and executive offices of Old National Bank occupied most of the building, there were still numerous other business offices located among the eighteen floors. The top floor sported an exclusive private club and restaurant called the Petroleum Club.

Reed was headed for the fifteenth floor and the office of Gerry Gorman, the vice president of corporate security for Old National Bank. Reed had only been in the Bunco-Fraud Unit of the EPD for about two years, but had made many friends in the banking community because of the shared problem of financial crime.

While the more sensational crimes—murder, robbery, and even motor vehicle accidents involving a death—drew the attention of the news media, violent crimes only cost the public a fraction of what was lost every year monetarily to white-collar crime.

Gorman's recent promotion gave him control of security for all Old National Bank holdings in multiple states. Because Gorman had been promoted and "booted upstairs," Reed was surprised to hear from him again. These weren't the type of matters that Gorman was directly involved with anymore. It turned out that the information Gorman had not only involved a large loss at Old National, but there were also substantial losses at three or four other banks in the Evansville area involving the same suspect.

Gorman told Reed that a white male named Joseph W. Brown had been cashing and depositing checks into his Old National Bank account from a Fifth Third Bank account, and that these checks were nonsufficient fund (NSF) checks. Between July 7, 2000, and August 3, 2000, numerous checks on the account of J. W. Brown Masonry had run this account $2,659 into a negative balance.

Reed obtained the original checks that Gorman currently had in his possession and took a police report from Gorman naming Joseph Weldon Brown as a suspect in fraud against a financial institution. Gorman would have one of his people track down any other checks that were still floating around in the bank system, and would then contact Reed with the additional information that was needed for this type of case.

This was such a standard routine for Reed that he spent some additional time catching up on news from his friend before making the walk back to Police Headquarters. After all, there was no hurry. The damage had been done, and no one was physically harmed or threatened. As soon as Reed got back to his desk, he put out a bank alert via computer e-mail, warning all the financial institutions in Evansville about Joe Brown and his scheme. Reed then expanded the alert area to include surrounding counties in Indiana, and in some surrounding states that shared the same con artists and "paperhangers." Paperhangers are criminals that make their living by forgery, or just passing bad checks.

Having done that, he would just have to wait for the banks to research their losses and contact the police about filing criminal charges.

The checks that Joe Brown had been depositing into his Old National Bank account were written on a Fifth Third Bank account also belonging to J. W. Brown Masonry.

So the next logical step was to contact Fifth Third Bank vice president of security, Ramona Burns.

Fifth Third Bank was only a few blocks away, and the extra walk would be a blessing on a day as beautiful as this one had been. So Reed turned west on SE Fourth Street and hoped he would find Ramona in her office when he got there. She was used to the Bunco-Fraud detective just dropping by, and always had access to hot tea or coffee. Reed thought that the public would be surprised to know how much police work is actually done in the break room of a business, or during a lunch meeting. (Television police work was seldom like the real thing.)

Burns was Gerry Gorman's counterpart and, like Gorman, she was responsible for a wide geographic area and numerous branches of Fifth Third Bank. She started at the bank many years before as a teller when it was Citizens Bank. She was promoted to branch manager, before it became Civitas Bank, and ultimately, she became vice president of security. The bank had recently been sold to Fifth Third Bank, out of Ohio, and Ramona was kept in her position, which wasn't the case for many employees.

Burns was already aware of Joe Brown's troubled bank account with them because almost immediately after it was opened, it had gone into a negative balance and had to be closed. Her research showed that Joseph Brown had opened a Fifth Third Bank account with money obtained from a woman named Ginger Gasaway. Burns said that Ginger was reportedly Joe Brown's girlfriend, and that she had used a large sum of money from her 401K retirement account to open the J. W. Brown Masonry account for Joe just a few months earlier. Burns had intended to see if Ginger was aware of the loss of the money, but the bank had been unable to make contact with her since the problem was discovered,

There had only been one deposit made into the J. W. Brown Masonry account before it became overdrawn, but Joe Brown was still depositing and cashing NSF checks from this account at other financial institutions. Old National Bank was only one of several other banks involved.

Reed groaned at this information. The paperwork on this case would be an accountant's nightmare, and Reed was no accountant.

It was not yet known if Brown had been trying to deposit checks from other sources into the J. W. Brown Masonry account because Fifth Third Bank had promptly closed it, and Joe Brown would not be allowed to reopen it.

Reed took his second police report of the morning. This one from Burns named Fifth Third Bank as a victim of fraud on a financial institution. This type of fraudulent activity is called "check-kiting" in police talk. That means opening multiple bank accounts at multiple banks, and then moving the checks around in these accounts to give the appearance that there is money in all of them. But, in fact, none of the accounts have any money except for a small initial deposit, usually less than $20. By the time the banks find out that the checks are not going to be honored, the culprit has obtained several thousand dollars and is on his way to another city, where he can start the process all over again.

Before it was over, Reed would find that Brown had fraudulent accounts at Integra Bank, Diamond Valley Credit Union, and Warrick Federal Credit Union, in addition to the other two that reports had already been taken from. At one point, Joe Brown had accounts open at every banking institution in the Evansville area, and had stolen more than $40,000 with this fraud, and with the forgery of checks on Ginger Gasaway's personal bank accounts.

While this sounds like a large theft, it was a routine case for the police department's Bunco-Fraud Unit, where yearly losses were counted in millions of dollars, and not thousands.

In the year 2000 alone, Bunco-Fraud investigators averaged over 150 cases each, while other detectives in units, such as Violent Crimes, rarely carried more than fifty cases a year. The loss for that year alone topped more than $5 million.

Detective Reed had jokingly coined a motto: "If you can't do the time . . . do white-collar crime." This facetiously referred to the fearless attitude that white-collar criminals had toward the courts and their total lack of concern at being prosecuted.

In most cases, Reed would simply call suspects and get a confession over the phone. Then a warrant would eventually be issued for the suspects, and they would sometimes turn themselves in. It was no wonder that from a victim's point of view, the police and prosecutors seemed to have no zeal for going after the perpetrators of white-collar crimes. After all, these crimes were often referred to as victimless.

But in actuality, these crimes are pursued and prosecuted vigorously. The sheer abundance of cases each year was overwhelming, but prosecutor Stan Levco had a good record of punishing these criminals.

SIX

The name Joseph Brown didn't come to anyone's attention again until August 31, 2000. For twenty-one days, it had been quiet on the financial-crime front. But that morning, Reed received a telephone call from Old National Bank branch teller Rachelle Lutz.

About ten o'clock that morning, upon the advisement of branch manager Steve Millay, himself a retired Evansville police officer, Rachelle called for Detective Reed. She had seen the alert circulated by the banks regarding Joseph Brown, and she now advised Reed that Joseph Brown had come into her branch as soon as the bank opened that morning.

She almost hadn't made the connection with the alert, and, in fact, hadn't remembered the alert at all, until Brown had already exited the bank. It was the way he left that finally made her suspicious enough to check on his attempted transaction.

Lutz said that Brown didn't try to cash any of the J. W. Brown Masonry checks that the Fraud Unit had listed on the alert. Instead, he had tried to pass an Old National Bank check written on an account owned by a Ginger R. Gasaway, and made payable to Joe Brown for $360. This check purportedly bore the signature of Ginger Gasaway.

Lutz was apologetic because she wasn't sure the

detective wanted this information. Reed assured her that she had made the right decision to call him, and that he was very interested in any checks that Joe was passing because they were probably fraudulent. He questioned her further.

Although Rachelle Lutz sounded very young, she had been around the banking business long enough to know when something was wrong. She now told the detective that what first caught her attention wasn't the fact that Brown had come in the bank so early, in fact only minutes after they opened their doors, but it was the way he left the bank that made her suspicious.

Lutz said Joe had seemed confident enough in his actions that he didn't look out of place or nervous, as so many check forgers do. Joe handed Lutz a check that was made out to himself. He also gave her an Indiana driver's license that identified him as Joseph Weldon Brown. It took her a few minutes to look the check up in her system. There didn't appear to be anything wrong with the account, but he was standing so stiff by this time that she decided to check with her manager. Lutz was a very conscientious teller, and she wanted to make sure someone else saw this customer. She could only explain to her manager that something didn't feel right.

Lutz said that while she and branch manager Steve Millay were looking at the check, Brown's confidence must have broken. He approached them and took the check and driver's license from her, saying that he would cash the check someplace else. He then exited the bank.

Reed asked her if Brown had run out, or if he seemed angry at them for not cashing the check. She said that she and Millay thought Joe acted pretty cool about the whole thing.

"He took the check from me and said, 'I'll just take this to my own bank'; then he walked out the door very nonchalantly," she said.

Reed knew that Steve Millay was a retired police officer and that he was astute at spotting a problem. The check hadn't shown as "stolen" on the bank's computer system, and the account appeared to be a legitimate one. But if Millay had told Lutz to call about this, there was probably more to it. It would have to be checked out further.

Reed knew from experience that just because a check looked all right on the surface, it could still be stolen or forged. It was always possible that the victim of the stolen check didn't know it was missing, or that it had happened so recently that the check owner hadn't been able to notify his bank yet. Given Joe Brown's burgeoning file with the Bunco-Fraud Unit, this check was probably stolen.

Lutz didn't have any further information, but she promised to get a copy of the bank's security video. If the check turned out to be stolen, at least there would be a film to show Brown trying to cash this one. Reed hung up the phone and pulled out his thickening file on Joe Brown.

Brown had left the bank several hours earlier, so it was not extremely urgent to go to the bank branch. But a quick check of the computerized records showed that Joseph Brown victimized Ginger Gasaway several times in the past. This was now the second time her name had come up in this investigation. First as someone that Joe Brown had obtained financial aid from in the past, and now as someone who might be a victim instead.

One of the criminal charges shown on the computerized files involved Joe Brown stealing and forging some of Ginger Gasaway's personal checks. But it was some other criminal charges that caught Reed's attention. And these were far more distressing.

In 1999, Ginger Gasaway, age fifty-three, had filed a battery charge against Joe Brown, and there were several other police reports taken for domestic violence–

related incidents. Ginger had also filed for several protective orders against Brown.

Brown's police record showed an FBI number that indicated he had been in prison, or at least had other felony charges filed against him in the past. Additionally, Brown had a misdemeanor warrant outstanding for his arrest. This appeared to involve Ginger Gasaway as well, and was related to one of the domestic-battery charges.

Reed decided he had better make a strong effort to contact Ginger Gasaway. First of all, to make sure that she was not the victim of Joe Brown in a physical sense; second, to find out if her checks were stolen again. If either case was true, and Ginger would sign a police complaint, it would give Reed something current to use to arrest Joe Brown. But Reed had already decided that whether she signed a complaint or not, he was going to find and arrest Brown. It was obvious to Rick Reed that Joe Brown was not going to stop committing crimes until he was behind bars.

SEVEN

When Reed recruited Detective Loren Martin for assistance, the task of locating Ginger Gasaway had sounded simple enough. Find Ginger. Ascertain if her check was stolen. Then find Joe Brown and arrest him. Even if her check wasn't stolen this time, the banks had provided more than enough evidence of fraud on a financial institution to charge Joe Brown with numerous felony charges. Brown was already looking at about thirty years.

As a general rule, when a crime has occurred more than two days in the past, the detective will go to the prosecutor and request an arrest warrant. In that case, the arrest process would have started with the detective preparing and filing a case with the Vanderburgh County Prosecutor's Office (VCPO). The prosecutor's office then prepares a filing affidavit, which is a document that spells out the exact nature of the crime and the reason for requesting the warrant. This affidavit is then taken by the detective to a judge who reads the document, has the detective swear that it is the truth, and then signs the affidavit, thereby issuing the arrest warrant for the individual named.

When an arrest is needed more immediately, it is not uncommon for the detectives to make the arrest, and then take the perpetrator in front of a judge at the earliest opportunity. This is known as a probable-cause arrest. In either case, by warrant or by probable cause, the final decision on the appropriateness of an arrest lay with the judge.

Martin and Reed decided that, given the circumstances, they would easily be able to make the arrest of Joe Brown based on probable cause alone. This probable cause was based on Reed's previous conversations with Old National Bank and Fifth Third Bank. If Ginger's checks were stolen as well, that would just be icing on the cake. The charge of fraud on a financial institution is a Class C felony in the state of Indiana. Class A felonies are for the most serious crimes, such as murder, while Class D included the least serious, such as theft.

A Class D felony could be reduced to a misdemeanor charge by the prosecutor or a judge, which would mean the difference between doing a minimum of two years in prison or getting probation and a fine. However, a Class C felony could not be reduced. That meant that Joe Brown was facing several counts of a crime that could net him prison time. In fact, each count of this charge could net Brown an additional eight-year stay in an Indiana prison.

Detective Martin was new to the Bunco-Fraud Unit, the white-collar-crime arm of the Detectives Unit, and new to the Detectives Office as well. Having spent his first nine years in motor patrol duties, and most of that on the graveyard shift, coming to day shift for Martin was as much of a culture shock as trying to learn the system in the Bunco-Fraud Unit. The work was very different between motor patrol and detectives, and there seemed to be different sets of rules for working shifts as well. Reed had spent more than half of his career on the graveyard shift, and that was how he had come to meet Martin.

Reed had asked for Martin to be assigned on this case with him because of Martin's tenacious manner and aggressive work ethic. He was one of the police department's martial-arts instructors, and he held a black belt in judo. At five feet eight inches tall, he was 225 pounds of muscle. But he wasn't just another muscle head—he was smart and quick-witted as well.

Judging by what Reed had seen out of Martin in the couple of months he had been in the unit, he considered Martin to be every bit as aggressive on a case as he was in a judo match, and just as effective.

Reed and Martin left the police station at about 2:00 P.M. and drove to Hatfield Drive in the Embassy East Apartments to locate Ginger Gasaway. Reed had already called T.J. Maxx, a warehouse on the north side of Evansville, where Ginger drove a forklift on the day shift. He was told that Ginger had failed to show up for work on Wednesday, Thursday, and now for her Friday-morning shift as well.

T.J. Maxx's human resource manager also said that Ginger had worked for them for more than fourteen years, and had never been guilty of this type of unexcused absence. However, she stated that Ginger had planned to move from her present apartment at Embassy East Apartments into a new one on the east side of Evansville. She believed it was Village Green Apartments, and gave the detective both the old address on Hatfield Drive and the new one that Ginger was moving into.

Because of the fear of lawsuits or work actions resulting from right of privacy issues, obtaining information over the telephone was never easy. Most human resource departments within companies will not even give you the time of day, policeman or not. The fact that the human resource manager herself was talking to him—much less giving this much information—was an indication to Reed just how worried these people were about Ginger's absence.

The two Bunco Unit detectives decided to go to her current apartment first. The Embassy East Apartments sprawled over an area about the size of four city blocks and boasted 248 one-bedroom units. Being one of the older apartment complexes, it had been built on the outskirts of town until the city had grown around it. And since most of the apartment complexes in that area were tenanted with underemployed and economically disadvantaged people, the businesses that had moved in catered to the needs of people with limited mobility and transportation.

Just to the south of the complex, across a large field grown thick with thistles and weeds, a Buehler's Buy Low grocery store bustled with activity. The Osco Drugs pharmacy was attached to the grocery, and shared part of the spacious parking lot. Catty-corner from the drugstore, and located on the same parking lot, the Golden Buddha Chinese restaurant faced toward Vann Avenue. A vacant and boarded-up building that had once housed a National City Bank sat on the far corner of this parking lot completing a perfect square. It was rumored that the vacant bank building would be torn down to make way for a new Kuester's Hardware store—a sure sign that times were getting better for the neighborhood.

The large field standing between the apartment complex and the Buy Low was sometimes used to park empty semitrailers, but it now sat empty. A large blue BFI Waste Company Dumpster sat on its westernmost edge, just behind the vacant National City Bank building. Both Reed and Martin were very familiar with the area, since both had worked several off-duty security jobs for the businesses.

The second-floor apartment belonging to Ginger Gasaway was easy enough to spot from the big parking lot, and the detectives parked their unmarked vehicle out of sight. If Joe Brown was staying there, he might be savvy enough to recognize an unmarked police car, and possibly would not answer the door or try to flee. Reed didn't cherish the idea of a foot pursuit, but Martin always looked forward to a good chase. That was another reason that Reed had requested his assignment.

Ginger's apartment had that lived-in look. On her balcony, white plastic lawn furniture sat on either side of a wooden spool that might have onetime contained telephone cable at one time, but now was being used as a table. A brightly painted yard gnome stood watch on top of the makeshift table, next to a small *Chlorophytum comosum* plant, commonly known as a spider plant because of its long shoots that extend away with bunches of leaves at the ends.

A humming air-conditioning unit jutted slightly out from the large front-porch window with tightly drawn curtains. Several other units along the upper porch had lawn furniture, but Ginger's seemed homey. In fact, something about the whole environment made the detectives believe that someone was home.

Detective Martin started to knock, but then he noticed several notes stuck to the front door. A cursory inspection showed the notes to be from family members, mostly confirming that someone or other would be by to help her move on Saturday. This also confirmed what the human resource manager at T.J. Maxx had told the detectives. Apparently, Ginger was indeed planning to move that weekend.

Martin knocked politely, but there was no answer. He knocked again, a little harder this time, while Reed watched the curtains and the peephole in the front door for signs of movement. Nothing. The detectives decided to try the Village Green Apartments address.

The lady at T.J. Maxx gave an address on Effingham as the apartment that Ginger was preparing to move into. The detectives knew this was in Village Green

Apartments on the far east side of Evansville. These apartments were spacious and the buildings were new by Evansville standards, which meant they were only about twenty years old. Three hundred and eighty-four 1-, 2-, and 3-bedroom units and town houses spread over a parklike setting near the river. The grounds were beautifully landscaped.

The Village Green Apartments were as good an example of a melting pot as you would find in Evansville. The occupants were primarily blue-collar workers, but with a liberal dash of both federally subsidized lower-class and middle-class professionals thrown in. Not much ever happened at Village Green of a criminal nature and the management was professional and caring.

Detective Martin called the office of Village Green Apartments and was told by the bookkeeper that the property manager was out showing an apartment. She would be gone for an hour or more. The detectives decided to head that direction, maybe just drive by the new address. If they were lucky, they would find Ginger moving in her things. If they were really lucky, Joe would also be there to help her.

Less than ten minutes later, Reed and Martin were parked in the parking lot, facing the Effingham address. The apartment was vacant, with absolutely no sign of activity. Even the floor-to-ceiling curtains of the double patio doors were open, and not a thing sat on the floor or counters. Martin knocked anyway. There was no answer. That left the investigators with only one other place to check for information.

Before they had left Police Headquarters, they had run a rap sheet on Joe Brown—that is, a computerized version of all of Joe Brown's contacts with Evansville police. They had printed out a copy of this list and Detective Martin checked it for the last address that both Joe Brown and Ginger Gasaway were known to have lived.

Prior to moving to Ginger's address at Hatfield Drive, Joe Brown and Ginger Gasaway had occupied an apartment together at the Fairmont Apartments. That address was located on Tippecanoe Avenue.

Martin and Reed now headed toward the Fairmont Apartments, which were at the opposite end of Greenriver Road from their present location, but only about a fifteen-minute drive. While Reed negotiated the speed bumps leaving Village Green Apartments main drive, Martin filled him in on the police information that went with the next address.

The Tippecanoe address was connected to a police report that Gasaway and Brown had filed against each other on November 29, 1998. In that incident, a neighbor called police to report a domestic violence in progress; Officer Keith Whittler had arrived at the apartment complex and saw a 1993 red Mustang attempting to leave the parking lot. A second responding officer, Paul Jacobs, stopped the vehicle and spoke to the lone occupant, Joseph Weldon Brown. The story he was told by Joe Brown—and again by Ginger Gasaway—was one he had heard hundreds of times, a typical story of domestic violence.

Officer Whittler wrote in his report, "Both subjects live at this address. The female was leaving the male so that she could return to her husband. She called police because he (Joe Brown) was attempting to leave in her vehicle. Both agreed to part ways without destroying any property."

Whittler made another entry in that report that would later be echoed by Hobert Gasaway as a warning of things to come. "The female's husband (Hobert Gasaway) has a restraining order against the male living at this address."

Detective Martin read another of the police reports. This one for theft, filed by Ginger Gasaway on April 21, 1999, while both she and Joe were apparently still living at the Tippecanoe address. In this report, Ginger stated that she had let Joe take her Mustang to go to work, and that after he left, she discovered some checks missing from her checkbook.

On May 7, 1999, Ginger Gasaway called the Evansville Police Department and spoke to Detective Dan Winters of the Bunco-Fraud Unit. She asked Winters not to file the theft charges against Joe Brown, and stated to the detective that Brown had made arrangements to pay her back. This charge was not filed.

The routine of domestic violence was becoming clear to the two detectives. But what wasn't clear was that Ginger Gasaway appeared to be self-supporting, unlike so many other victims of domestic violence who rely on the abusive partner for their financial existence. The two men couldn't figure out what was driving her to stay with someone that abused her both physically as well as emotionally. On top of that, Joe Brown was stealing her blind.

At least they had the misdemeanor warrant from the original battery charge, where Brown had beaten Ginger senseless in the laundry room of Embassy East. That would be enough even without Ginger's cooperation.

Neither Reed nor Martin could know how important that small warrant would become, or how big a part it would play in the progressing investigation.

EIGHT

The Fairmont Apartments were approximately two miles north of the detectives' present location on Greenriver Road. They drove north as quickly as the pre–Labor Day Weekend traffic congestion would allow.

Reed had been planning a family reunion for most of that year. The weather was beautiful and the temperature had dropped to a pleasant number somewhere in the low seventies. Unusual for that time of year, but not unheard of.

The detectives discussed how the clear skies and good weather projections would spawn a hoard of traffic accidents and arrests for driving under the influence. What the detectives didn't have to discuss were the high number of natural deaths and suicides that holidays seemed to precipitate. Statistically speaking, it was a safe bet that someone in the Violent Crime Unit would be busy this weekend.

In Evansville, there seemed to be a rule that said, "Where you find a major thruway, you will find orange barrels." That rule was accurate as usual, and the detectives bumped over patched spots, braked suddenly for confused drivers, and found that they "couldn't get there from here." Detective Martin knew a shortcut that ended up adding an additional fifteen minutes to what should have been a three- or four-minute drive.

Turning east on Tippecanoe Avenue from Greenriver Road, the men drove past a now-defunct adultentertainment club called Baby Dolls. Before the club had been closed, liquor was not allowed to be served to the underage patrons and dancers. But since it was touted as a private club, police were not allowed to enter to check on the venue. This still didn't keep Baby Dolls from being raided regularly by Vice cops, and eventually the place was shut down.

To the north of this establishment, the Signature Inn Motel had almost gone out of business, causing them to sell off some of their holdings, including what was once their main office. The main office was large enough to house conference rooms and a fully equipped kitchen. This building was sold to Oakland City University, and it was turned into an extension campus.

The Fairmont Apartments were tucked in between the Signature Inn Motel, to the north, and the Shamrock Apartments, to the south. The buildings were mostly brick and were lined up in neat rows, two buildings across and four buildings deep. Altogether the complex contained 140 single-bedroom units that rented for less than $400 monthly.

Directly south, on the other side of Tippecanoe Avenue, the Shamrock Apartments sprawled. Both apartment complex parking lots were filled with junk vehicles and "gang banger" rides, some of which were backed in to hide the fact they hadn't been registered for years.

For such depressing surroundings, the upbeat and professional management staff at the Fairmont Apartments pleasantly surprised the detectives. Trudy Molt, the manager, offered the men a seat as they advised why they were there. She immediately remembered Joe Brown.

Going to a file cabinet, she pulled the old lease for where Gasaway and Brown had lived. Ginger had originally rented the apartment, but Brown was listed as living there for a while. There had been numerous complaints from neighbors saying that the couple fought constantly, and not just verbally. She remembered that police had been called several times, both by her staff and by Ginger.

Molt had a faraway look in her eyes as she recounted one incident occurring shortly after Ginger Gasaway and Joe Brown had moved in. In that incident, Ginger had tried to leave one night after a particularly loud furniture-smashing type of fight. She made it to her car with Brown hot on her heels. Brown grabbed Ginger, and he tried to drag her back to the apartment. Someone drove into the parking lot and slowed down to see what was going on. The manager thought Brown must have been scared by the presence of a witness, and he let Ginger go. Ginger left for a while, and then the police showed up.

Reed asked if Brown had gone to jail over that incident and Molt gave a short laugh. She advised the detectives that Brown was gone for a few days, but eventually was living there again with Ginger.

She flatly stated that she was glad that Joe Brown no longer lived there. On the other hand, she said, Ginger was a very pleasant woman that would do anything for her neighbors.

When asked if she had any other information that might help the detectives locate Ginger Gasaway or Joe Brown, she stated that it had been almost a year since they had both moved out. She added that she hoped never to see Joe Brown again.

"He scared me to death," she said.

As the detectives left the Fairmont Apartments office, they exchanged meaningful glances, but didn't speak until they were back inside their unmarked police car.

"What do we do if we don't find her today?" was the immediate question in both men's minds. They were white-collar-crime investigators. The police department would never approve the overtime to allow them to continue looking for Ginger Gasaway.

"I guess we can call Sergeant Davis and see if he'll authorize the overtime," Martin offered. Overtime was paid at time and a half, and had become a precious commodity. Given no more information than they possessed about Ginger's disappearance, they knew that the likelihood being granted overtime was slim. And even if overtime was approved, they would probably not be the detectives assigned to work the case. They were white-collar-crime investigators, and not Missing Persons or Homicide detectives.

Martin started the car and headed south on Greenriver Road once again. They would try a few more places before giving up for the day, and then they could worry about calling their sergeant.

"They won't even let us keep working on our own time if they know about it," Reed said, more to himself than to Martin. He was referring to the fact that police work, or the actual performance of police work, is an act that is governed by rules and laws. Unlike on television, policemen are not allowed to run about town questioning people during off-duty time. The rules are there supposedly to protect the public from overzealous policemen.

Reed had another problem on his mind—his family reunion. He had about seventy relatives coming from all over the country, and they would all want to meet the family member who had put this together. What would he, or his wife, tell all these people if he didn't show up for his own family reunion?

As Martin pulled back onto the main road running through the Village Green Apartments, their private thoughts were replaced with one overriding question: where was Ginger Gasaway?

Martin and Reed entered the main office and the lady at the front desk said that Tonya Gaddis would be with them momentarily. The men barely had time to look around the spacious room before a young woman with a smart business suit approached them.

Tonya Gaddis looked to be in her early twenties and was strikingly attractive. With a disarming smile, she motioned the men to sit at one of the sofas that lined the wall. When the detectives explained their situation, she checked her records and found that Ginger had been there over the weekend of August 26, had filled out an application for one of the apartments, and was to pick up her keys at 4:00 P.M. that very day.

Gaddis said that Ginger actually wasn't scheduled to move into the Effingham apartment until Saturday. She then offered the men coffee and asked if they would like to wait. It was almost 4:00 P.M.

At 4:30, when Ginger didn't show up, Reed asked the petite lease manager if she would call them as soon as she heard from Ginger. She promised that she would call. He left several telephone numbers, and they were off again for Embassy East Apartments.

Ginger had not been heard from for far too long, and after talking to people that knew her, the detectives didn't believe this was normal behavior for the missing woman. They decided they would stop by her current apartment at Embassy Apartments, and this time they would make an entry to check on Ginger's welfare. It was late and there was a good chance the manager had already left, but the men were determined. If checking on Ginger Gasaway meant breaking down a door, then so be it.

The detectives decided they had better call ahead due to the lateness of the hour. Martin spoke to Carol Blair, the apartment manager, and she reluctantly agreed to meet them and allow the investigators to look inside Ginger's apartment.

When Martin hung up, he advised that the manager said she was getting ready to leave for a Labor Day Weekend vacation. She had made it plain that she was unhappy about the inconvenience.

Given the manager's reluctance to cooperate with officers, Reed called dispatch and had a uniform officer sent to Embassy East Apartments. He was to make contact with the manager and to make sure that she didn't leave early for her vacation.

Martin and Reed found it difficult to believe that Blair could have such a callous attitude toward another woman, especially one that had been the victim of a domestic battery while living at the apartment complex that she managed. But as the detectives would find out later, this manager had sent a letter to Ginger Gasaway after Joe Brown attacked her in the laundry room of the complex. Not a letter of sympathy, but rather, it was a demand that Ginger clean her blood up from the laundry room area, and warned that this type of incident could get her evicted. When the detectives arrived, Blair was almost in a rage, and she demanded to see a search warrant.

Reed explained to her that it would take several hours to get the warrant, and that she would have to stay nearby so she could open the apartment when they finally obtained it. The manager reluctantly gave permission for the policemen to enter Hatfield to see if Ginger Gasaway might be either injured or dead.

NINE

Officer Wayne Hunt was already waiting at Embassy East Apartments when Martin and Reed arrived. In police work, it is usually preferable to have a uniformed police officer make these type of entries. There is less chance for someone to mistake a uniformed officer for a burglar.

Officer Hunt took the key from the apartment manager and lead the way to Hatfield. He opened the door and the three policemen went inside. There was a note stuck to the front door from Ginger's daughter Lisa, saying that she would meet her there on Saturday morning to help her move. Just inside the door were numerous boxes packed and stacked. This was the living room. It definitely looked as if Ginger had packed in preparation to move.

Hunt went toward the single bedroom, loudly announcing, "Police. Is anybody home?" Reed and Martin stayed in the living room until Officer Hunt came back from the bedroom and just shrugged his shoulders. He'd drawn a blank. Reed then went with Hunt back to the bedroom to see for himself. He asked Hunt to look under and behind the bed, and while this was being done, Reed looked in the bathroom and the closets. The only thing that might have been out of place was the fact that the shower curtain was missing. But Reed believed that this could have already been packed. Almost everything else had been.

The police officers went back to the living room and kitchen area to discuss their findings. They had nothing. Ginger was not there. They didn't recognize any evidence that she had been forcibly taken from her apartment, or that she wasn't coming back. Even the coffeemaker was still turned on. Reed turned this off, and the three men reluctantly left the apartment.

The investigators were walking to their car when a neighbor came up to them and identified himself as Steve Sparks. He told them that he hadn't seen Ginger for a few days and that wasn't like her. He said that she was driving a green Taurus, but he hadn't seen it for a few days either. Sparks identified himself as the president of the neighborhood watch for the area, and further remarked that Ginger had been very active in that group. That was the reason he thought it was highly unusual for her to be gone for so long without telling him or another resident. He said they always looked after each other's apartments, watered plants, and brought in mail when one of them was going to be gone for more than a day.

Sparks stated that Brown had seen Ginger with her ex-husband, Hobert Gasaway, over the previous weekend. He said that Brown was jealous and angry about that. He didn't think that Brown had talked to Ginger that day, because he hadn't seen her that day, or since.

Sparks lived in the same building as Ginger, and he said that Ginger had never indicated to him that she was afraid of Joe Brown. He told the detectives that on the Saturday before Ginger went missing, he had spoken to Brown.

"I was coming up one day, one afternoon, getting out of the car, coming up the steps and Joe was sitting downstairs on the end apartment in the lawn chairs out front," Sparks stated.

Sparks related the conversation he had with Joe Brown that Saturday. He said that Brown asked him if he knew that Ginger went on vacation with her ex-husband. Sparks told Brown that he wasn't aware of that and asked how he knew if that was true. Brown pointed to a car in the parking lot in front of Ginger's apartment and stated, "That's his car. I just saw them leave."

Sparks said that he didn't want to have this conversation, but Joe wanted to talk and continued by saying, "I'm tired of this. I'm going to quit trying. I'm just going to move to North Carolina."

Sparks said then he asked Brown if that was where his family was from, and Brown told him that there was just a lot of work there. Brown told him good-bye and Sparks thought that he was leaving for North Carolina.

Sparks went back to his own apartment, and he didn't think any more about it until he ran into Hobert Gasaway in front of the apartments.

Sparks said that Hobert told him that on Saturday he had come back to the apartments with Ginger, after looking at her new apartment, and Joe Brown was waiting for them in the parking lot. Hobert told Sparks that Brown gave him the middle finger as he drove past, and then followed him for a distance in Ginger's red Mustang.

Sparks also told detectives that on Thursday, August 31, he saw Brown again at the apartments. He wasn't sure if it was Wednesday or Thursday, but he thought it was Thursday. He said it was early evening when Brown knocked on his door and wanted to know if he had seen Ginger. Sparks told him that he hadn't.

Sparks said that Brown then told him that he called Ginger and that her phone had been disconnected, so he assumed that she had already moved. He said that it seemed as if Brown was trying to get Ginger's new address. Sparks said he pointed out to Brown that Ginger's lawn chairs were still on the porch, and that she might not have moved yet. He asked if Joe Brown had tried knocking at her apartment.

Brown told him that he had spent the night with her on Tuesday, and that she gave him money to get his own apartment. Sparks told the detectives that Ginger was the type of person who would have done exactly what Joe Brown said—that is, she would have given Brown money for an apartment. He did think it was a little strange because they were no longer living together, and it appeared that Ginger was trying to get on with her life.

Sparks said that Brown left without trying to find Ginger at her apartment, and he just assumed that Brown was going to North Carolina to get an apartment with the money that Ginger gave him.

Sparks also gave another piece of information that would be vital when they interviewed Joe Brown. He said that Ginger had told him that she was still in love with her ex-husband, Hobert Gasaway. Sparks thought that eventually they would get back together.

Apparently, on the same day that he had talked to Brown and had been told that Joe was moving to North Carolina, Sparks's daughter and her boyfriend had seen Brown near the abandoned National City Bank building, about a block from the apartments.

They said that Brown saw them watch him as he parked his car, and then started walking toward the apartments. He stopped beside their car and stuck his head inside. He told them, "Don't worry. I'm not going to do nothing stupid. I'm not going to hurt her. I learned my lesson." Sparks also told detectives that Brown would often park his car out of sight like that when he and Ginger were not getting along. Brown would then stand somewhere near her apartment and watch her.

Steve Sparks advised Reed that he would call if he saw Ginger or found out where she was. Carol Blair also said that she would keep an eye out. She advised the investigators that she might have spoken with Ginger on Wednesday morning, but she wasn't sure if it was earlier in the week.

It was two hours beyond the end of their regular shift, but the two detectives still felt too uneasy to stop the search. Reed contacted Sergeant Howard Davis at home and explained the situation to him. Since there was no concrete evidence of any crime other than the financial crimes committed by Joe Brown, it was decided that the investigators should go off-duty and return home to their families. It was, after all, the long Labor Day Weekend holiday.

The detectives did as they were ordered and they went back to headquarters to turn in their equipment, get their personal vehicles, and go home. Reed decided to make a few phone calls before he left.

The first call was to Village Green Apartments, where he again spoke with Tonya Gaddis, the rental manager. Tonya advised that there was still no word about Ginger, but the office would be open until 6:00 P.M. She advised that she would call Reed at home or on his department cell phone if Ginger came in. She said that Ginger had come on a Saturday last time, and that they would be open from 10:00 A.M. until 5:00 P.M. this Saturday, and then noon until 5:00 P.M. on Sunday. She said that Ginger could possibly come on one of those days.

Reed obtained the telephone number that Ginger had listed with Village Green as an emergency contact number. This telephone number was for Ginger's daughter Lisa Thompson, who lived in Rockport.

The second call was to Embassy East Apartments, but only the answering service would pick up. Carol Blair had apparently left on her vacation.

The last call Reed made was to a friend in the Crime Scene Unit. CSU officer Ben Gentry promised Reed that he would go by Hatfield and put crime scene tape over Ginger's apartment door with a note to contact Detective Reed. This done, Reed finally went home. But the feeling that something was wrong would not leave him, and it would turn out to be a premonition of things to come.

TEN

On Saturday morning, September 2, 2000, Reed called Village Green Apartments. They still had not heard from Ginger. Reed decided to call Ginger's daughter Lisa at her home. He asked if she had seen her mother recently. Lisa said that she worked at T.J. Maxx with her mother. She thought her mother may have been at work on Wednesday, but she wasn't sure. She said her mom was in the process of moving to Village Green Apartments.

Reed advised her that he had been in contact with the apartment manager, and that her mother had not been there to get her keys. He then asked Lisa about Joe Brown, explaining that he was looking for Brown in reference to some bad checks. He explained that Brown had been trying to cash one of her mother's checks on Friday at Old National Bank.

Lisa said Joe Brown had been dating her mother for several years, and had lived with her, off and on. But Brown wasn't presently staying with her mother. She said her mother was afraid of Brown, and that he had beaten her up very badly last year.

She also revealed that Brown had stolen her mother's checks and cashed them in the past. She said she didn't know where Joe Brown might be staying now.

Reed asked her about the note he had found on Ginger's apartment door. Lisa said her mother had asked her to help her move this coming Sunday, September 3, and that she was concerned because her mother had not contacted her for almost a week to verify this. She said she had gone by her mother's apartment to confirm the moving date, but Ginger wasn't home. That was when she had left the note. She confirmed that her mother drove a '95 green Ford Taurus. She also said that Brown might still have a red Mustang convertible that belonged to her mother.

Reed assured Lisa that he would continue to look for her mother, and he gave her his home number. He asked her to start contacting family members, and to call him if she found any information. He also apprised her of the possibility that she may have to file a missing person report for her mother.

Reed contacted the Police Dispatch Center on Saturday, September 2, and had them put out a BOLO (be on the lookout) and an ATL (attempt to locate) on Ginger Gasaway, the 1995 green Ford Taurus, and also on Joe Brown. In it, he requested all subjects be held until he was contacted.

The Fraternal Order of Police (FOP) campground and reception hall had been rented for the Reed family reunion, and it still needed to be readied for the large crowd expected to come in on Sunday. Reed's wife was doing this alone, under the circumstances. She was used to the unexpected demands of her husband's job.

At 3:45 P.M. that day, Reed received a call from dispatch on his cell phone. Officer Doug Kemmerer had located the Taurus. It was abandoned in the parking lot of a Buehler's Buy Low grocery store on Vann Avenue.

Reed called Kemmerer and learned two things. The car was locked, but the keys were still in the ignition.

Secondly, the car had a security keypad by the door locks. That meant the owner should have been able to gain entry to their car if they accidentally locked themselves out. However, the most significant fact to Reed was the location of the vehicle. It was parked less than a block from Ginger's apartment, and just across a grassy field. It could almost be seen from her porch.

It was possible that Ginger had left the car there to avoid a confrontation with Joe Brown. In Reed's experience, it wasn't uncommon for a person to hide their vehicle somewhere close to their residence in order to avoid unwanted visitors. But this didn't explain why the keys were in the ignition.

Reed also wondered how long the car had been there, since pedestrians heavily travel that area on their way to the grocery store and the adjacent Taco Bell. It was not uncommon for windows to be smashed, and cars stolen in that same area. This thought made Reed wonder if that was the reason the vehicle was left there. With the keys in plain sight in the ignition, it would make a tempting target for a juvenile joyrider.

Once again, Reed contacted Sergeant Howard Davis at home, and he told him that the car had been found. He was advised to contact Lieutenant Terry Brooks, commander of the Bunco-Fraud Unit.

When contacted, Lieutenant Brooks told Reed to have Motor Patrol officers check the vehicle for signs of any forced entry, or evidence of any type of other crime. This was not considered significant enough to warrant Reed coming into work on a holiday. The city was trying to keep the overtime pay down, and holiday pay is double time. Reed decided to go into work anyway, and not to turn it in for overtime.

Reed told Officer Kemmerer not to let anyone touch the car, and to call a wrecker to open the trunk. Nothing else was to be disturbed to preserve evidence. Reed prayed that Ginger would not be in there. If she was, she might need immediate medical attention. If not, the idea was to preserve evidence.

Reed then contacted Crime Scene technician Ben Gentry. Gentry sped toward the location of Ginger's car, and agreed to see if he could place the car in the CSU garage until it could be determined exactly what they were dealing with.

Reed had almost arrived at Police Headquarters when he received a call on his cell phone from Gentry. The car had been opened by the wrecker service without any damage, and the keys were then used to open the trunk. Ginger was not in the trunk. Gentry advised that the car was being towed to the Crime Scene garage, where it could be processed with greater detail.

Gentry and Officer Kemmerer met Reed at the CSU garage. They examined the car and concluded that there was no sign of any violence inside the Taurus. In fact, it was extremely clean. The only thing noted by the detectives was a small piece of beige-colored carpet lying inside the trunk. This was close to the same color as the vehicle's carpet, and at that time it had no meaning for Reed.

Officer Kemmerer canvassed the area where the vehicle was located, and had talked to a Buehler's Buy Low assistant manager. He learned that the Taurus had been parked there since Friday night, but had not been noticed before that. Reed made a note to obtain the video from Buy Low, and would later learn that the outside cameras had not recorded the vehicle being driven onto the lot.

Reed decided to leave the vehicle in the CSU garage until he could find Joe Brown or Ginger Gasaway.

Back at home, Reed called Lisa Thompson again to tell her that her mother's car was found. Lisa said that Joe was probably driving a red 1993 Mustang with a black vinyl convertible top. Her mother had purchased the Mustang a year or so earlier, and she let Joe use it to get back and forth to work. Ginger had tried several times to get this car back from Joe, but he refused to return it. Ginger had recently told Lisa that she was going to get the car back from Brown on Wednesday, August 30, and she threatened to file charges against Brown for auto theft if he didn't return it this time.

Lisa didn't think her mother would have parked at Buy Low, but she explained that her mother had been hiding from Joe lately. Ginger would not even go outside without looking out the peephole and windows first. She said it was possible that her mother had left the car there to keep Brown from knowing when she was home.

Lisa said she had talked to family members and that none of them had heard from her mother. She was sure her mother hadn't shown up for work on Wednesday either. However, she said that her mother had met Joe through Gamblers Anonymous (GA), and that she couldn't be 100 percent sure that her mother hadn't gone somewhere with Joe for the Labor Day Weekend of her own free will. She said it wouldn't have been the first time that they had split up and then gotten back together.

Reed advised her that they would have to get a missing person police report from one of the family members to continue to look for Ginger. He also explained that he had put out bulletins on the radio to alert other policemen to contact Reed if the car was located. He would now have to add the red 1993 Ford Mustang to the alerts.

Reed drove back to police headquarters, where he ran an Interstate Identification Index check on Joseph Weldon Brown. That is a computerized check of records from any law enforcement agency in the United States. Reed discovered that Joe Brown had been in prison from 1977 until 1995 for armed robbery and kidnapping. He also found the 1999 report where

Joe had beaten Ginger severely enough to send her to the hospital.

Reed contacted Police Dispatch Center again, and this time added the 1993 red convertible Mustang, including the registration and license information. He couldn't put out a missing person BOLO without a police report from one of Ginger's family, but at least this would get other agencies involved. Reed instructed dispatch to put this information out to surrounding states, as well as in Indiana.

Lisa Thompson's comment that her mother may have left voluntarily with Brown to go gambling, or on an extended holiday, put a different light on the case. If Reed left the BOLO in place, and Brown and Ginger were stopped, they would be upset because of the police interference. If the BOLO were rescinded, and Ginger was in danger, or kidnapped by Brown, or even worse, if she were dead . . . Reed didn't want to think about that possibility. Up to this point, his supervisors had shown little interest in this case, and seemed to think that it was something that could wait until Tuesday. Then, if necessary, it would be assigned to a VCU detective. After all, this wasn't exactly a Bunco-Fraud issue anymore.

He had done all that he could do, and Reed finally went home. The rest of that day was uneventful. Reed and his wife made preparations for the family reunion, and spent the remainder of the day cleaning and decorating for the crowd expected on Sunday. But even with all that activity, Reed couldn't get the missing woman off his mind. The nagging feeling that he should do something more to find Ginger grew as the night fell.

An attempt at sleep proved futile. Reed's mind raced with thoughts about Ginger and Brown. He got out of bed at around 11:00 P.M. and went to his small office in his home. He dialed Lisa Thompson's phone number. When she answered, he quickly apologized for the late call, but explained what he wanted her to do. She couldn't sleep either and agreed to make a trip to the Evansville Police Department.

Lisa drove from Tennyson, Indiana, to the EPD records room before midnight on Saturday, and filed a missing person report on her mother. She also brought a couple of recent photos of Ginger with her.

Reed called the records room and asked them to hold the photos for him. He also advised that he needed all of this information entered into the computer systems of the National Crime Information Center (NCIC), and into Indiana Data and Communication Systems (IDACS). These two systems would allow the information to be available over the entire United States, Canada, and through INTERPOL. Once the information was entered, if Brown or Ginger was stopped, or if their license plates or vehicles were found by police anywhere, they would be detained until Reed was contacted.

In addition to the regular missing person information, Reed had police dispatch add the caution that Ginger may have been abducted by Joe, and that there was an outstanding warrant in Evansville for failing to appear on a domestic-violence battery charge against him.

Sunday morning came bright and beautiful. The weather cooperated nicely for a family reunion. A place for playing horseshoes had been set up outside the reception hall at the Fraternal Order of Police Camp, and people were starting to arrive. The FOP Camp also had a lake stocked with fish, several outside picnic tables, and a playground for the young children. Reed continually called police dispatch and the two apartment complexes to check for updates on Ginger.

One of the first people to arrive was Joe Reed, Reed's

brother, who was a deputy chief on the Evansville Police Department. Reed told his brother of the situation he was investigating regarding Ginger Gasaway, and it was suggested that he go to a higher-ranking supervisor with the information. Joe Reed suggested that his brother contact Captain Clayton Grace or Deputy Chief David Fehrenbacher.

Captain Grace was not home, but Deputy Chief Fehrenbacher answered immediately. Reed apologized for calling him at home, and after explaining the situation, Reed asked permission to go back to headquarters and contact the news media. He wanted to use a news conference to alert the public about Ginger's disappearance.

Fehrenbacher fully supported the idea, and gave Reed his cell phone number. He wanted to be kept apprised of the situation. For the first time since this case had started, Reed felt that something was being accomplished.

Reed left the reunion and drove to headquarters, where he contacted every local television station, radio station, and newspaper, informing them that he was sending a news release to their fax machines. He requested from each of them that they send someone to the police station at four o'clock that afternoon. He would give them photos and a plea for public assistance at that time.

ELEVEN

The news conference was held at 4:00 P.M. in the front lobby of the police department. Although the media hadn't been given much notice, there was a good turnout. Every local television station and newspaper was represented, but a reporter from only one radio station attended.

Though few details were released, the fact that the information was being released as a possible abduction had stirred their interest. Packets of information, including photos of Joe Brown, Ginger Gasaway, and a description of the red Mustang, along with the license plate information, were given to every media representative. Each packet included a plea to the public to call with any information. Reed's cell phone number and the telephone number for the Detectives Office was listed. Reed confided to a television news anchor that he hoped that Ginger would call and "chew him out" for embarrassing her. Somehow he didn't really believe that would be the case.

A half hour later, the lobby was empty again, but the word had been put out. Both the law enforcement community and the public had been informed now, so all Reed could do was sit and wait. The hardest part of any case is the waiting.

Reed's next stop was the FOP Camp, where the family reunion had all but wound down.

Reed received a call at his home at about 8:00 P.M. from Deputy Chief Fehrenbacher. A woman named Susan Geiselman had called the Detectives Office from Somerville, Indiana, a little town located about an hour north of Evansville. She had information and wanted to speak to Reed.

Back at headquarters, Reed called the number he had been given. Susan Geiselman said her husband, Harold Geiselman Jr., was Joe Brown's cousin. Reed learned that about the same time he was giving his information to the media, Joe Brown was pulling into Geiselman's driveway in Gibson County.

Susan said she had seen the six o'clock news on Channel 14 asking for information about Joe Brown, and after the way Brown had acted, she knew she had better call right away.

Brown was driving the red Mustang when he pulled into her driveway, but he parked at the very far end near the street. Her driveway is fairly long and she couldn't see if anyone else was in the car. She didn't think that was strange by itself, but then Brown was acting very hyper, kind of shaking, as if he couldn't stand still.

She said that Brown had only been to her home a couple of times since he got out of prison, and that it was always to borrow money. This time was no different. But what he said scared her, even before she heard the television report.

Brown looked around nervously when he told her he was desperate and broke. He needed money to get gasoline so he could go see his brother.

Susan said she told him that she didn't have any money, when, in truth, she did have $100. She didn't want to give that to Brown. But what he told her next made her change her mind, and she would have given him anything to get him out of there.

Brown told her, "Me and Ginger had a real bad one this time. I've got to get out of town quick."

Susan said that the way Joe Brown said it was so creepy that he "scared the bejesus" out of her. That, and the thousand-yard stare in Brown's eyes. She described it as "the lights are on, but no one's home" kind of look.

Susan called her husband at work and told him Joe Brown was at their trailer asking for money. She hadn't seen the television news report yet or she would have been even more afraid. She said her husband told her to give him $20 and not to let him in. Brown told her he didn't think $20 would be enough to get him to Ohio. She only had the $100 bill, so Joe had suggested that she go with him to get change for it.

She didn't even want him in the house, so there was no way she was going to leave with him in the Mustang. She told Brown to wait a few minutes on the porch and she rushed to a neighbor's home to get change.

Reed asked her if she had given Brown any money, and Susan said, "I gave him forty dollars to get rid of him."

Susan didn't know Brown's brother, David, who lived in Ohio, but she was pretty sure that he was younger than Joe, and that he was a big shot with the Colgate Company. She also said that Joe was going to Ohio to find him. She didn't know where in Ohio, and at that time she didn't care. She just wanted him far away from her home.

Reed wasn't sure where Colgate was located, but he believed it was in Cincinnati, Ohio. If Joe was going to that area, he would most likely travel the interstate highway system.

The detective placed another call to police dispatch, this time asking them to send a special type of message called a point-to-point bulletin. This kind of bulletin is a computer message that can be sent to one agency, to a group of agencies, or even routed along a certain highway in a particular direction. He directed police dispatch to route a point-to-point bulletin along interstate highways I-64, I-70, and I-71, between Evansville, Indiana, and Cincinnati, Ohio.

The point-to-point bulletin gave all the necessary information needed by any agency that might come across Joe Brown, Ginger Gasaway, or the red 1993 Mustang convertible. It stated that Brown was a suspect in the disappearance and possible abduction of Ginger Gasaway. The missing person portion of the information had a line added urging that any agency that came into contact with any of these subjects or the vehicle should use extreme caution. To give these agencies the authority to detain Joe Brown, it also contained information about an outstanding warrant against him.

The one thing that was most unnerving for the detective at this point was the fact that the warrant was only for a misdemeanor charge. Since that information was required for the point-to-point bulletin, it was possible that an outside police agency, especially one in another state, might not honor the warrant.

Reed contacted the prosecutor's office and they had assured him that this warrant would be sufficient, so there was nothing else he could do. He was a detective, not an attorney, so he would have to trust in their judgment.

Joe Brown only had a few hours' lead on the investigator now. The net was closing, thanks to the news media, and to Susan Geiselman.

The news release yielded several more calls in response to the plea to the public for information. One call came from Tony Boyer, who owned a small masonry business and had employed Brown for a short time. Brown ended his employment with Boyer to open his own company, and Boyer was kind enough to refer some work to Brown.

Boyer turned out to be a wealth of information regarding not only Joe Brown's work record, but also his relationship with Ginger Gasaway. He said that Brown had borrowed a large sum of money from Ginger to open his own masonry business, but had spent all of the money gambling. By a large sum of money, he meant over $20,000. Joe Brown's gambling habit had been a huge problem for Joe, and was one of the major reasons that he and Ginger fought, according to Boyer.

He also confirmed that Brown had a brother living in or near Cincinnati, Ohio, although he didn't know the brother's name. Tony said he thought that there was "bad blood" between Joe and the rest of his family due to his gambling addiction and his prison record.

Boyer also said that Brown had a daughter living somewhere in the southern part of the country, but he didn't think Joe had ever met her. He thought her name was Jamie.

The last piece of information that Boyer gave the detective was unsettling, though not unexpected, and would become a common theme in the relationship between Ginger Gasaway and Joe Brown. Boyer said Brown had beaten Ginger several times in the past and that he had a very explosive temper. He described it as the kind of temper that could become physical in an instant, and it was usually over something insignificant.

Brown's ex-wife Mary Lou Seitz would later confirm Joe's quick temper. She had seen Brown in action many times when he felt that he had been wronged. She said that Brown's anger would jump to the surface for something as slight as being bumped into at the grocery store.

The next call was from Tom Stallings, of Wadesville, Indiana. His mother, Imogene, was Joe's stepmother. Stallings was able to provide the name of Joe's younger brother. He said that David Brown was a few years younger than Joe, and that he lived and worked in or near Cincinnati, Ohio.

He also said that Joe had two older sisters. The oldest, Sue, lived in Georgia, and he didn't know much about her. His other sister, Jennie, was married and lived in Terre Haute, Indiana. Her husband's parents still lived in Cynthiana, Indiana, where the Browns had grown up.

Stallings also remembered Brown having a daughter by his first marriage to a woman named Donna Graham. He said Brown had given the girl up for adoption in 1977 when he went to prison for kidnapping and armed robbery. Stallings thought the girl would have been an infant at the time.

He said that Brown's father, Jerry, had committed suicide when Joe was still a teenager, and that his mother, Carleen, had died several years before.

"She drowned accidentally in the bathtub, and Joe was the one that found her," Stallings said.

Shortly before Brown's father committed suicide in 1975, Stallings's mother had divorced him.

The next call came from Roger Reisz, another masonry business owner for whom Brown had worked as a bricklayer. Reisz said that he last saw Brown around August 28, 2000, when Brown had come to his home to ask about a nearby house that was vacant. This house was located on South Craig Street, and Joe was thinking that he could use it to sleep in at night. He didn't know if Brown had actually stayed there.

Reisz thought Brown had been taking Prozac, an antidepressant, but he didn't know if it was prescribed. Reisz had seen the news report and wanted to tell police that Brown was very abusive to Ginger. He believed it was possible that Joe Brown might kill her.

Reisz said that Brown had told him of several occasions when he had beaten Ginger. He also said Brown told him the Mustang was his, and that it was the only

thing in the world that he owned. Reisz was unaware
that the Mustang was owned by Ginger, but it didn't surprise him when he found that out. He suggested that
Sharon Brown should be contacted. Reisz said that
Sharon was Joe's aunt, and that she would have the address and telephone numbers of Joe's family members.
Reisz was able to supply Reed with Sharon's telephone
number.

The call to Sharon Brown was informative. This was
where Joe had briefly stayed in 1995 when he was released from prison. It was Sharon's son, Bryan, who
gave Joe his first job when he was released on parole.

Sharon and her husband, Roger, lived in a trailer
court on the north side of Evansville. She confirmed
that David was Joe's younger brother, but she said that
David lived in Zanesville, not Cincinnati. She gave
David's address and telephone number to Reed. It was
also from Sharon that Reed learned the name and
telephone number of Joe's sister Jennie. She said Jennie
and her husband, Mark, lived in Terre Haute, Indiana.

TWELVE

Jennie was very apprehensive when she answered the telephone. She hadn't seen the news broadcasts about her brother, and she didn't subscribe to the Evansville newspaper.

While Detective Reed explained what he was investigating, Jennie seemed hesitant to speak about Joe Brown. But after he told the tale of his search for Ginger Gasaway and the information related to him by Susan Geiselman, she became less resistant to speak, although it was apparent to Reed that talking abut Joe was painful for her.

Jennie painted a picture of a man who had lived with a history of family violence. She described Joe's troubled past and brushes with the law as a means of explaining his violent temper. She also told of the time when Joe beat Ginger so badly, in September 1999, that he thought he had killed her.

On that day, she and her husband had gone to Evansville on business. While they were in town, they received a phone call from home. Her teenage son and daughter were there alone, and her son was almost in a panic.

Brown had come to her house looking for a handout. There was nothing unusual about that because Joe had a reputation within the family for always needing money. But his demeanor and appearance on this occasion had her children scared.

Joe told Jennie's son that he had killed Ginger, and Joe wanted money to get out of town. The excited boy told his mother that they had given Joe what money they could find.

After hearing that, Jennie and her husband had looked for Ginger, but were unable to find her for several days. She said she was frightened to death that Joe had really done it this time, that he had actually killed Ginger. But then Ginger turned up, and they found out that she had gone to a friend's house to hide from Joe.

After what Susan Geiselman had related earlier about Brown's need for money, and his hurry to get out of town, Reed felt a chill run up his spine. Obviously, Joe hadn't killed Ginger last time. But had he done it this time? Or was she just beaten up and hiding somewhere like before?

Jennie went on to say that her husband's parents also live in Cynthiana, just behind the park. She was afraid for their safety, and made Reed promise to call the Posey County sheriff to check on them.

Jennie said that Joe might be going to Ohio to try and find his younger brother, David. She said Joe hated David because while Joe was in prison, David and his wife had refused to write or communicate with him. She said that David was living in Zanesville, but she didn't think Joe could find him because he had just moved again not long ago. David had asked everyone not to tell Joe where he was.

Jennie also advised that there was an older sister, who lived in Marietta, Georgia. She hoped that Joe wasn't going there. She promised to call her sister, and pleaded with the detective to contact her again if Joe or Ginger was found. Reed promised that he would, and had every intention of keeping in touch with her.

He had a feeling that her insight into Joe's personality might be helpful if or when Joe was found.

It was almost ten o'clock at night. The phones in the Detectives Office were silent. There was nothing to do now but wait. Wait, and hope that Joe Brown was found somewhere between Evansville and Ohio. Reed left contact phone numbers with the Detectives Office, police dispatch, and central records. Then he went home.

Reed missed his family reunion, but he wasn't lucky enough to miss the cleanup detail afterward. It was after one o'clock in the morning before he got to bed and fell into a restless sleep. It felt as if he had just dozed off when a noise woke him with a start. The clock on his side of the bed read 6:30 in red glowing numbers. For a second or two, he was dazed and couldn't imagine who would be calling at that time of morning. Then he remembered Ginger, and he jumped out of bed to grab the telephone.

Deputy Chief Fehrenbacher wasted no time with preliminaries. No "good morning" or "did I wake you?" He said Brown had been found in Lebanon, Ohio, and that Ginger wasn't with him. Reed hoped the deputy chief was done speaking because Reed had already hung up and was pulling on some clothes. There was no traffic on the short drive to headquarters, which was a good thing because the detective's mind was on anything but driving.

He arrived and went immediately to the Detectives Office. Fehrenbacher sat behind a desk. He nursed a steaming cup of coffee as he brought Detective Larry Nelson up to date on the case.

Reed didn't find out until much later that the case had almost been assigned to Detective Nelson, and that there was some question as to whether Reed would even be allowed to continue on the case. The Violent Crime Unit had argued that Reed was a Bunco-Fraud detective, and this was a possible homicide.

It didn't matter that Reed had worked in the VCU for almost twelve years prior to transferring to the white-collar-crime section of the Detectives Unit, or that Reed had successfully worked numerous other homicides.

Police departments are like any other large corporation. Within the police department, there is an unwritten hierarchy. Many detectives feel that they are a step above uniform patrol officers, and the VCU feels they are a step above the other Detective Units. So, it wasn't a surprise that the VCU would oppose him working this case. To them, he was encroaching on their turf. At least that was Reed's impression.

Most detectives abhor the violence and senseless loss of life at a murder scene, but paradoxically these are exactly the types of cases that they want to work the most because they are high-profile, exciting, and possibly even career-making. The deputy chief had already made the decision for Reed to remain on the case, or he wouldn't have received a call to come in.

Sergeant Kennard, of the Warren County, Ohio, Corrections Complex, was called. Kennard said that Brown was being held on the Indiana warrant, and, in addition, they had tacked on a charge of fugitive from justice. The charge of fugitive from justice was fairly standard whenever a prisoner was arrested for another state, but it surprised the detective that Ohio had done this, since all they had was a misdemeanor warrant.

Fugitive from justice meant that Joe could not pay a bond and be released before the Evansville detectives could get to him. It also meant that Joe would go to an extradition hearing on Tuesday morning, September 5, 2000.

The purpose of an extradition hearing is to guarantee the constitutional right to any accused person that the government will only arrest on a warrant that is obtained with probable cause, and sworn to by a law enforcement officer in front of a judge. The idea is to protect people from unreasonable seizures. At the hearing, Brown would be given an attorney if he wanted one. He would also be allowed to fight extradition back to Indiana.

If Brown decided to fight extradition, Indiana would then be required to obtain a governor's warrant. This amounts to an official demand for the prisoner's return to Indiana to answer the charges filed against him there. This whole process could take as long as three months for the courts in Indiana and Ohio to decide if Joe Brown should be sent to Indiana.

If, however, Joe waived his right to fight the extradition, he would be transported to Evansville immediately after the hearing in Ohio. Reed had never met Joe Brown and couldn't know what Brown had in mind.

Sergeant Brian Kennard gave Reed the telephone and contact information for the Ohio State Highway Patrol (OSHP) barracks in Lebanon, Ohio.

Sergeant James Ertel answered the phone at the barracks. Both he and Lieutenant Kelly Hale had been dealing with the Joe Brown matter since almost six o'clock in the morning. He said that Trooper Randall Adams had read the BOLO off the teletype that morning, and had intended to make the rounds of all the rest areas along I-71.

Trooper Adams had pulled into a Warren County rest stop when he spotted the red convertible Mustang. The windows were fogged up, as if someone were inside. Trooper Adams switched on his forward-facing video camera and approached the car. Inside, he spotted a man sleeping in the driver's seat. Adams quietly returned to his cruiser and called for backup.

State Trooper Timothy Hall and Sergeant Ronald Adams (no relation to Trooper Adams) arrived at the scene to find a sleepy but angry Joe Brown. The Ohio troopers swiftly took him into custody.

Brown was uncooperative and insisted on knowing

why the state troopers were "messing with him." Hall decided that due to the serious nature of the BOLO he had better read Joe the Miranda rights before he said too much.

Trooper Hall promised Brown that he would answer all his questions as soon as he got some other matters taken care of. He then placed Brown in the back of the original trooper's marked cruiser and turned the video camera around to face him.

As Hall read the Miranda rights, Brown had gotten better control of his temper. He had been awakened from a sound sleep, and the full consequences of his arrest hadn't had time to sink in. When Reed later viewed the videotapes of Brown's arrest and subsequent Mirandizing, it was apparent that it didn't take too long for Joe to grasp his predicament.

Fehrenbacher had advised Sergeant Ertel that two Evansville detectives would be coming to talk to Joe Brown. Reed now explained to Sergeant Ertel that they had another matter to take care of before coming to interview Brown. A warrant would have to be obtained to search Hatfield Drive. It would be important to ascertain if there was other evidence to be collected from Joe Brown before making the long trip northeast. Sergeant Ertel promised complete cooperation.

THIRTEEN

Deputy prosecutor Jonathan Parkhurst was contacted, and with his help a search warrant was obtained for the apartment on Hatfield Drive. Ginger had been missing almost a week at this time.

Minutes later, the detectives were at the Crime Scene garage and had the keys to Ginger's green Ford Taurus. One of the keys looked as if it could be an apartment key, and this was what they were after. A few minutes later, they were back where they had started, at Hatfield Drive. Only this time, there wouldn't be any uncooperative rental manager. This time, they had a search warrant in hand.

As he approached Ginger's apartment, Reed felt more than just apprehension. He found himself hoping against any logic that Ginger might still be alive. Injured maybe, but alive.

As the investigators walked toward the steps leading up to the apartment, that hope was crushed. Crime Scene technician Tony Walker found what he described as small droplets of blood on the sidewalk. He took a piece of white chalk from his pants pocket and began to circle the droplets. A distinct trail emerged, which led from the parking lot in front of the building to Ginger's doorway.

Walker began to lead the detectives up the concrete stairway toward Ginger's door just as a young woman approached them with her dog.

Nancy Kleczka lived in an apartment next door to Ginger for about a year. To Reed's embarrassment, she asked if the officers had found blood on the steps. Apparently, she had been listening to the Crime Scene technicians teasing the detective about missing this clue on his earlier visit.

Reed told her that they had found something, although he was still unsure that the spots were blood. They looked more like grease stains.

Kleczka crouched down on the walkway and rubbed her dog's head like a proud parent. She said her dog, a registered basset hound, had been stopping on those stairs for the last few days and was licking at the spots.

It made Reed feel a little more vindicated when she admitted that she couldn't see anything there either. But she continued, saying that her dog would always sniff on the steps and then lick at something. The detectives thanked her for the information and took a statement from her.

Kleczka was a full-time student at the University of Evansville. She lived next door, directly to the north of Ginger's apartment. She said that she had known Ginger for less than one year. Kleczka said that she moved into her apartment shortly after the incident when Joe Brown had caught Ginger in the laundry room of the apartment complex and proceeded to beat her unconscious. She said, however, that she wasn't aware of that incident, and Ginger never spoke to her about it.

Of Ginger, Kleczka said, "She was always upbeat. She never let on that anything was going wrong in her life. Everything always seemed perfect. She was always cheerful."

Kleczka did say that Ginger once told her how afraid she was of Brown. She said that in April 2000, Ginger asked her to call if she ever saw Brown hanging around the property.

"I left my apartment to take my dogs out and Joe was pounding on Ginger's door. When she didn't answer, he left, but then returned three more times. The last time he was gone for about two or three hours before he returned again. Ginger peeked out her door and told me that she did not want him at her apartment, and that I should phone her if he returned," Kleczka said.

Kleczka told the detectives that she thought she had last seen Ginger at the apartment complex on Tuesday or Wednesday.

Kleczka stated that she owned two dogs, and that one was a basset hound, which she kept in her apartment. She stated that on Wednesday or Thursday morning she had taken her dogs for a walk, and that her basset hound kept stopping every foot or so along the upstairs porch, and down the stairway that she shared with Ginger's apartment. She told detectives that she had found dark brown spots leading down the porch and stairs, and she thought that maybe someone had cut their foot because of the way the dog was attracted to the spots.

Outside the door of the Hatfield apartment, Reed and Nelson waited while Crime Scene officers went inside to photograph and take video. Once that was accomplished, the two detectives were given a careful tour of the inside, and they were watched closely to make sure that they didn't move or disturb anything. This was routine procedure.

Reed pointed out the coffeepot he had turned off. He also told the Crime Scene investigators about everything that he or the other police officers had touched when they were there earlier. Except for the possible trail of blood on the outside walkway, nothing inside appeared to be out of order in the combination living room/kitchen/dining area.

The boxes were still packed and stacked near the door in the living room. The cable television box was unplugged and disconnected from the cable. Packing materials were laid out. There were stained outlines on the walls where pictures and mirrors had recently been taken down. These were all obvious signs of someone in the process of moving.

They proceeded in single file to the bedroom. A few days earlier, Reed had looked in the closet and in the bathroom, while Officer Hunt had been on his hands and knees looking under the bed. This time, as he looked into the empty room, something jumped out at him that was so obvious, it was embarrassing.

On the floor, at the foot of the bed where Officer Hunt had been crouched, lay a cheap woven throw rug. It was a small rug and barely covered a sunken outline beneath it. One of the CSU team lifted the corner of the throw rug, and Reed felt his face getting hot. Bare concrete peeked up under the wall-to-wall carpeting. A curved section of carpeting was missing all the way to the base flooring, which in these apartments appeared to be concrete board.

Wanting to move on quickly, Reed explained to Walker that Lisa Thomson said her mother took several medications daily. She also said there was no way her mother would have left the apartment for very long without taking them with her. Reed hadn't known to look for these items before, but they looked now.

Several bottles of medication were in the medicine cabinet. These were left undisturbed for CSU to collect. The shower curtain was also missing from the bathroom. Most likely, if Ginger had already packed it, she would have been ready to leave that same day. But obviously she had not left—at least not of her own free will.

Nelson and Reed had seen all they needed. They were led outside again, where they intended to help other detectives do a more thorough neighborhood check. Before this could be started, Reed was advised by one of the assisting uniform patrol officers that he was needed at headquarters.

When Reed returned to his office, a message was waiting for him from Mary Ellen Ziliak, an old high-school friend that he hadn't seen for years. She said that she saw the news release in the *Evansville Courier & Press* and recognized the picture of Joe Brown as someone she had recently seen.

Ziliak said that she had become a nurse, and was on her way to work at St. Mary's Hospital on Thursday or Friday morning. She thought it was about ten-thirty when she was driving south along Vann Avenue, toward Covert Avenue. What made her remember this subject was that he looked nervous, and was pacing back and forth on the sidewalk by the Dumpster.

Reed asked what Dumpster she was talking about. The entire area was dotted with apartment complexes and businesses, and most of them had their own garbage Dumpsters.

Ziliak described the one next to the Buy Low at Covert and Vann Avenues. This was almost the same location where Ginger's green Ford Taurus had been abandoned.

She described the man she saw "lurking near the Dumpster" as a white male with dark hair, parted on the side. She recalled he was about five feet ten inches, or maybe taller, and was thin. She was positive this was the same subject that she had just seen photographed in the local newspaper.

Joe Brown had already been in custody for eight hours before Detectives Reed and Nelson left for Lebanon, Ohio. But before they did so, Reed contacted his partner, Detective Martin, and asked him to put together a case file charging Brown with check kiting on the local banks. Reed wanted a solid charge to hold Joe Brown, and didn't want to trust an out-of-state agency to keep Brown in custody very long on the misdemeanor charge.

FOURTEEN

The 250-mile drive to Lebanon, Ohio, takes about four hours in good traffic. In "orange barrel" miles, it is closer to six hours. The city of Lebanon is about thirty miles northeast of Cincinnati, but the OSHP office was a little closer. Nelson and Reed filled the time on the long drive by catching each other up on developments, and discussing possible approaches for the anticipated interview with Joe Brown. Nelson had been assigned from the Violent Crime Unit, and although he had worked with Reed before, they had very different styles for interviewing suspects.

Reed was willing to talk to a suspect for as long as it took, all day and night if necessary. Sometimes, Reed would not even talk about the case at hand for the first thirty minutes to an hour. This type of interviewing can drive some other detectives crazy.

Reed considered interviewing a suspect to be similar to a negotiation. His philosophy was similar to dealing with a barricaded gunman or a hostage taker.

"You give a little, you get a little. Given enough time, you will get it all. Patience is the key," Reed would say.

Nelson was brought up in the old school, and he believed that interrogation, not interviewing, was the key to a successful case. Interrogation is more confrontational, more direct in its questioning; so, by its nature, it can be very intimidating. Sometimes that was what it took to get a confession, though. But the problem with interrogation was that it could end a conversation very quickly. Once the suspect had been pushed enough, he often became tight-lipped and rode his lawyer down the road.

Reed's method of discussing rather than interrogating might be effective, but it was also time-consuming. The problem that the detectives faced was that time wasn't on their side. If Ginger was still alive, but severely injured somewhere, every minute might be precious. And Reed could feel the clock ticking while on the drive to Lebanon. He'd promised Ginger's daughter, Lisa, that he'd find her mother. He wasn't sure that he would be able to keep that promise.

It had been raining intermittently during most of the drive, but the sun came out of hiding just as they reached the turnoff for Pee Wee Valley Correctional Facility, a medium-security prison for women.

The detectives rounded the portion of I-70 where the city of Cincinnati suddenly comes into view. On the left side of the highway stood a towering wall of rock that marked where the road was cut through the edge of the mountain. On the right, and straight ahead, a lake stretched out toward the horizon. Beginning from somewhere behind the city, and seeming to empty into the lake, a rainbow had formed, and was reflected in the misting rain.

The two men drove on silently, each with his own private thoughts, but the appearance of the rainbow served as a reminder that no matter the result of this trip, the world would continue. The beauty of the countryside calmed them and, at the same time, prepared them for the darkness that was yet to come.

This was the first time either man had traveled

through this part of the country. And though the view was breathtaking, it wasn't quite enough to pull their minds from the task they were there to perform. Soon the city of Cincinnati was behind them and they were once again deep in conversation about how to approach Joseph Weldon Brown.

Nelson and Reed arrived at the OSHP barracks in Lebanon about six o'clock that evening. They were immediately introduced to Sergeant James Ertel and Lieutenant Kelly Hale. They were told that Joe had been read his Miranda rights on the trooper's car video, and that they would be allowed to view this. The videotape was then signed over to Detective Reed.

Lieutenant Hale explained what the two Evansville detectives were watching as the tape ran. The first view from the video was filmed from Trooper Adams's car windshield as he approached the red Mustang parked in the rest area, then of Trooper Adams returning to the vicinity of his car as he waited for backup. Seconds later, Sergeant Adams arrived and both troopers approached the red Mustang.

One trooper knocked on the window of the Mustang while the other trooper pointed his weapon in the direction of the man sleeping inside. A figure of a man could be seen behind the steering wheel. His face turned first toward one trooper, then the other. Finally the driver's window was rolled down.

A few words were exchanged and then Joe Brown emerged from the vehicle, rubbing his eyes. He was handcuffed, and the trooper returned his duty weapon to its holster.

Trooper Adams was very respectful but firm in his initial questioning, demanding to see identification. He explained to Brown that they had a bulletin on the Mustang from Indiana. Brown actually froze in place at these words. The tactics of the two Ohio lawmen preempted any thoughts of fleeing that Joe Brown may have had. Reed was very impressed by their professionalism and calmness.

On the video, Joe Brown agreed that he understood his rights, and in almost the same breath, he demanded to know why he was being stopped.

Brown was asked to come back to Trooper Adams's car, where he was advised that there was a warrant for his arrest out of Indiana, and that he was going to be taken to jail until Indiana police could be contacted. Brown didn't resist, but he became more stiff and deliberate in his movements. It was clear that this wasn't what he had planned for the morning.

Sergeant Adams then turned the car's video camera around to view Brown in the backseat. In the frame, Brown was read his Miranda rights and stated that he understood those rights.

"Do you know where Ginger is?" Sergeant Adams asked.

Brown turned his head to the side, his face turned up slightly and away from Sergeant Adams.

"Last time I saw her was at Caesar's Casino last Friday," he answered.

"You mean Caesar's in New Albany?" Adams asked.

"I don't understand why you're holding me," Brown said without answering the sergeant's question.

Sergeant Adams changed his tactics and asked how they could contact Ginger to verify that she allowed Brown to drive her car, but he denied several times even knowing where Ginger lived. The impression he tried to give was that he was only a casual acquaintance of hers, and was not her live-in boyfriend for almost three years. Adams didn't push the questioning.

For the remainder of his time in the custody of the Ohio State Police, Brown remained reticent, answering just the most basic questions. He gave his name, last address, date of birth, and not much else. The look in his eyes on the video was that of an animal trapped in a cage. Brown finally said that he wasn't going to talk any longer. The remainder of the video showed Joe Brown sitting with his back straight as he stared defiantly into space.

Nelson and Reed were then shown a second videotape of Brown's transport from the state police barracks to the Warren County Detention Center, in Lebanon. In that video, a constant frown creased Brown's features as he cast an occasional furtive look at the camera. When the videotape was shut off, Sergeant Ertel advised the Evansville detectives that no one had attempted to speak with Brown since he had been incarcerated at the Warren County Jail. Joe Brown had not yet asked for an attorney.

FIFTEEN

Lieutenant Hale and Sergeant Ertel acted as liaisons for the detectives and led them through the countryside to the Warren County Corrections Facility. Like most newer lockups, it was not called a "jail" anymore. The term jail must have offended someone, and as a result of countless lawsuits of overcrowding and abuse in county lockups across the country, the term was changed to "corrections facility." Even though it had the same steel bars, the name had a kinder and gentler feel to it.

But there was nothing soft or gentle about the Warren County lockup. Steel and concrete, and a full staff of professional corrections officers, made for a formidable site. From the outside, it was landscaped and designed to be aesthetically pleasing, but on the inside, it was all business. Joe Brown wasn't going anywhere without permission.

The four men were relieved of anything that resembled or could be used as a weapon, and then they were escorted to a room that was sometimes used by attorneys to talk to the clients they defended. The concrete wall and thick steel door made the twelve-foot by twelve-foot room almost soundproof. Because it was used for legal matters between defense attorneys and the inmates, there was no video capability.

The last thing Lieutenant Hale had told Reed before entering the room was that Joe Brown had not said a word to anyone since arriving at the jail. But he had not asked for an attorney, which meant that no matter how much he protested, Joe Brown legally had not invoked his right to silence.

Sergeant Ertel asked Reed how he intended to get Brown to talk. He confided that Brown pretty much had told everyone to "go stuff themselves."

Reed thought about that for a moment, then decided that he would try to use Brown's anger to get the conversation going. Anger was a good motivator, and people that are emotional will sometimes say the darnedest things.

"I'm going to negotiate with him. He's got something I want and I'm gonna get it," Reed told Ertel

By coincidence, Sergeant Ertel was also a crisis negotiator. He chuckled slightly at the idea of using negotiations to do an interview of this type, but he admitted that it made sense in a way because of Brown's hostile demeanor. Both he and Reed had faced that type of anger countless times while negotiating with some suicidal or scared type. In fact, this type of tactic seemed to work best with angry people.

Sergeant Ertel and Lieutenant Hale asked if they could be in the room while the interview took place. Reed and Nelson readily agreed. Normally, you would not want more than two investigators involved in this process, but this wasn't a normal situation. Reed thought that he could use Brown's animosity toward the Ohio State Police to his advantage, so their presence might act as a catalyst. Brown had not met these men yet, but if he became angry, they could always ask the Ohio lawmen to leave.

As the four detectives entered the room, Brown's

gaze ran from one man to the next, and then settled on the two Ohio officers.

"I already told you assholes, I ain't talkin' to no one," he said.

Reed quickly introduced the four of them, ending with the fact that he was with the Bunco-Fraud Unit of the Evansville Police Department. Brown seemed surprised at that, but didn't rise to the bait.

"We're not with these guys, Joe," Reed said as the Ohio officers pulled two chairs to the back of the room and sat down quietly.

"Detective Nelson and myself are from Evansville. I just want to be sure that you understand what your rights are."

"They read my rights to me." Brown fixed Reed with a stare. "Look, I know my fuckin' rights. I already told these guys and I'll tell you, I got nothin' to say. You might as well fuckin' go home."

Reed forced himself to grin. "Nice mouth, Joe," he said, chuckling, and was rewarded with the shocked look on Brown's face that he was hoping for. He hurried on to keep the momentum going.

"I just drove over four hours to see you because I need some help, and you go and cuss me like that." This was delivered in a serious tone, but with a teasing grin on his face, the way he would tease a friend.

Brown started to grin, but stopped himself. "You can talk all you want, but I ain't saying nothing."

"Okay. That's fair," Reed said, and pulled up a chair close to Brown.

Detective Nelson pulled a seat off to Brown's right at the far end of the table. His job at this point was to listen carefully and take notes. Reed would not be writing—not unless Brown expected him to. Sergeant Ertel and Lieutenant Hale made like statues. So far, Joe Brown hadn't insisted that they leave, nor had he made any further remarks to them.

"Let me tell you why I'm here, Joe," Reed began. "Like I said, I work in the Bunco-Fraud Unit . . . that's the financial crime section, you know." He paused long enough to get an acknowledging nod from Brown.

"I got a call from Old National Bank that you were trying to cash a check belonging to Ginger Gasaway . . . your girlfriend."

Brown was listening, but true to his word, he didn't speak.

Reed forged on. "So I started by trying to find her because you've been hanging paper all over Evansville."

"All over Evansville?" Brown asked.

"Well, pretty much. The Fifth Third Bank, Old National Bank, National City Bank," Reed said.

"I didn't do any fucking checks at National City Bank."

"Well, maybe it wasn't National City."

Brown leaned back in his chair and a slight grin passed over his face. He was enjoying this. Reed was also pleased that he had already gotten Brown to participate in the conversation.

Reed explained for a few minutes how the banks had called about some of Brown's checking accounts being overdrawn. Brown explained that he had a business and was planning to straighten it out. Then the two men talked about Evansville, and the masonry business, and how the city had changed over the last several years. Brown talked about having been in prison before. He asked where Reed had gone to school and they both discovered that they had been in the army at about the same time, and both had been stationed in California— Brown at Fort Ord, and Reed at the Presidio of Monterey Language School.

For about thirty minutes, they had both avoided the subject of Ginger Gasaway—Joe, because he didn't want to talk about her; Reed, because he was trying to judge what a truthful answer looked and sounded like. The only way to do that was to ask numerous nonthreatening questions.

Reed finally decided it was time to broach the subject of Ginger.

"Joe, I need some help to find Ginger," he began. "You were probably the last one to see her."

"You're asking the wrong guy." As Brown said this, he turned his head away and looked at the floor. "You need to talk to Hobert."

Hobert Gasaway was Ginger's estranged husband. They had divorced shortly after Brown and Ginger met at a Gamblers Anonymous meeting. Hobert was as worried about Ginger as anyone. The divorce had not been an angry one. In fact, Hobert and Ginger had been talking about reconciliation. Reed knew this because he had already talked to Hobert. But if Brown wanted to blame this on Hobert, that was fine. At least he was still talking.

"I've already talked to Hobert, Joe. I didn't care for the man too much. I got the feeling that he didn't care what happened to her."

"Well, if anyone knows what happened to her, it'd be Hobert."

Detective Reed knew from a conversation with Steve Sparks outside Ginger's apartment that Brown had exhibited some jealousy over her continued contact with her ex-husband, Hobert. Brown showed some enthusiasm about talking for the first time.

Although Joe Brown initially claimed to have virtually no knowledge of Ginger, he was now full of slanderous insinuations that he espoused as firsthand information. Brown smiled and stated, "There are a lot of things that Ginger's family don't know about them two."

He claimed that Hobert and Ginger were "swingers" that were into wild sex with multiple partners at the same time. He said that the reason he was invited to live with them was so they could all have sex together.

When Hobert was questioned about this, he claimed that Brown's insinuations were preposterous. He said that he was still recovering from an open-heart surgery that was performed in the summer of 1998, and he was not in good health when Brown moved in six months later. His inability to keep up with Ginger's desires may have played a role in her decision to initiate a romantic relationship with Brown.

This was not the first time that Hobert's health was in jeopardy. He had his first heart attack in 1993, and he said that his relationship with Ginger had never been the same since that time.

"There was a breakdown in communication between us. After thirty years together, we had a discussion about the possibility that one of us might be left behind at some point. I think that the thought of being alone scared her, and that was what caused problems in our relationship," Hobert said.

Hobert said that he and Ginger agreed to let Brown move in with them because they felt sorry for him because he was down on his luck. He said that it was just their way to try to help out others who were less fortunate than they were. The real circumstances behind how or why Joe Brown moved in with the Gasaways would never be discovered, but Hobert's statements about his ill health were verified.

It was clear that Brown intended to deflect the suspicion that now lay on him by turning it toward Hobert. Brown lowered his voice conspiratorially and continued the story of how he had met Ginger, and the life they had lived, sometimes as a threesome: Joe, Ginger, and Hobert.

Brown intimated that he had a bad gambling problem for most of his life. He admitted that sometimes he had to resort to less than legal means to support that habit, and that he discovered that he was successful at passing bad checks. He described gambling as an addiction, stating that it was as bad as a drug habit. He added that he had just gotten out of prison in June 1995 after doing twenty-five years of a life sentence, and the first thing he wanted to do was go to a casino and gamble. Investigators would later learn that Brown actually had been in prison eighteen years, and that he had a tendency sometimes to stretch the truth.

Brown said that when he was released from prison, he wanted to clean up his act, and although he wanted to go and gamble, he decided to go to Gamblers Anonymous instead. He would make an effort to go straight. The gambling, according to Brown, was the root of all his other problems. He added that Ginger had a problem with gambling too, and was even more addicted than he was.

He explained that he had met Ginger at a Gamblers Anonymous meeting and that she had then asked him to go for coffee after the very first meeting. Hands tucked shyly between his legs, Brown smiled almost embarrassedly as he bragged that he'd always been attractive to the women. He said Ginger wasn't the prettiest woman he'd ever seen, but he hadn't been with a woman for quite some time because of being in prison. He agreed to go for coffee with her.

Going out for coffee after GA meetings became a regular thing for Brown and Ginger, and Brown said that they hit it off right away. Ginger told him that her husband was an alcoholic, and that he was abusive to her, both physically and emotionally. Whether or not Ginger truly related any of these statements to Brown was questionable, because investigators never verified any abuse of Ginger at the hands of her ex-husband. In fact, Ginger's friends and family members indicated that she did have a gambling problem, but that Joe Brown was the only person who ever abused her. Whenever Brown talked about any woman he was involved with, a common theme emerged: one of abuse, drugs, and/or alcoholism.

Joe was childlike when it came to life experience. Much of his time after the age of sixteen was spent in Boy's School (Indiana Reformatory), or in prison, so he had not developed even the most basic of social skills. This made him prone to becoming dependent on anyone with whom he had a relationship. Ginger was tailor-made for Joe in this respect. She was seven years older than he was, held down two jobs, raised two children, and was more than capable of maintaining a solid relationship.

Ginger was a rock. But the constant battering of a determined and needful predator—such as Joe Brown—can crush even a rock.

According to Brown, it was Ginger who made the first move. At one of their coffee meetings, Ginger asked Brown if he would move into the home that she and her husband, Hobert, shared. Brown said it surprised him that she even wanted him to visit her house, much less move in. After all, he had not even met her husband yet.

Ginger corrected that problem the next time they had coffee—she brought Hobert along to meet Joe. At that particular time, Joe was staying at the Rescue Mission in downtown Evansville.

Brown asked Reed if he knew about the Rescue Mission, and was assured that Reed had been there numerous times.

"Then you know what it's like inside there. There's no privacy at all. No way to protect your things," Brown said.

This was the reason that he agreed to move into the Gasaway home, according to Brown. It afforded him some privacy and gave him the company and attention that he craved.

Brown said it wasn't long after he moved in that Ginger made moves on him, and they became sexually involved. Brown became uncomfortable being with Ginger sexually, while Hobert was living under the same roof. Brown told her he was going to move out— that was when Ginger decided to get an apartment. She was going to let Joe move in with her.

SIXTEEN

It was discovered that Ginger and Joe had stayed in the Alpine Motel for about a week in 1999, and then Ginger rented a one-bedroom apartment on Tippecanoe Avenue in the Fairmont Apartments. They weren't in this apartment long before Ginger filed for a divorce from Hobert.

Brown said that although he and Ginger dated for about three years, they only lived together periodically. Her gambling habit was as bad as his, if not worse. He said he could go to the casino and still leave with some money in his pocket. But Ginger would gamble away every dime she brought.

During the course of the interview, Brown stated that Ginger took a strong antidepressant drug called Prozac. He was soon taking her pills and abusing the drug. Brown said that he had been taking about three pills a day for a long time, but he had quit using the drug for the last three days.

Reed wondered why Brown was telling him about this, but then remembered hearing that defense lawyers claimed the usage of Prozac as a defense in criminal cases. This seemed to be where Brown was taking the conversation now. If he was building a defense, maybe he was going to confess, Reed thought.

Brown was asked if he knew what he was saying, and if he felt in control of himself, or if he thought his Prozac usage had affected his thinking. Brown grudgingly admitted that he knew what he was doing, but that he would like to get back on the medicine, if it was possible.

Questions to Brown about past fights he'd had with Ginger were met with short, almost monosyllabic answers. So a picture was painted for Brown in words, describing the view from the front of the apartment at Hatfield the way Reed had seen it earlier that morning. It was suggested to Brown that he and Ginger had probably sat on that porch many nights, just people watching, drinking coffee, and enjoying each other's company. Brown's quiet acquiescence was taken as a sign that the remarks were probably close to the truth.

Brown was also reminded that for the last several years, he was the one person who was the closest to Ginger. It was his responsibility to protect her and care for her.

Brown admitted that he had hurt Ginger in the past, and told of a stormy relationship in which he had beaten her badly at times. He added that he hadn't done anything to her recently, and that he didn't know where she was at the present time. He again suggested that Reed should talk to Hobert about that.

"Like I said, I've already talked to Hobert. I told you, I didn't like him much. Do you think he did something to Ginger? Do you think she's with him?" Reed asked.

Brown again clasped his hands and stuck them between his knees, as if he were afraid they would give something away.

"I don't know where she is."

Brown looked at the floor and shuffled his feet.

"I ain't seen her."

He looked up again, but wouldn't keep eye contact with the detective.

"Who knows what a guy like Hobart would do. I mean, a guy who'd do things like he done already," Brown said.

Reed decided to change the direction of his questioning, and asked Brown about Ginger's family. Had he ever met them? How did he get along with them? He already knew how they felt about Brown, but sometimes it helped when the suspect was made to remember the victim as more than just an object of their hatred.

Brown surprised him with his answer. He didn't care for any of them. And further, he thought they all hated him. That was no help at all, so Reed told Brown a small lie.

"I talked to Lisa yesterday, Joe, and she said that you would help me. She seems to like you well enough."

Brown looked surprised. "Well, Lisa's okay, I guess. She's always been all right."

He told Reed that there was another daughter, named Misty, that really hated him. He claimed not to know where either girl lived. Reed asked Brown if he thought that Lisa was concerned about where her mother was. Brown admitted that the kids were probably concerned. He admitted also that they loved their mother, but once again stressed that the kids really didn't know what Ginger and Hobert were like.

Reed decided it was time to prod Brown's emotions. Lisa Thomson had provided the police records room with an eight-by-ten color photograph of her parents when she had made the missing person report. The photo had been taken professionally and depicted Ginger and Hobert Gasaway at a happier time in their lives. Reed brought the photo with him in a manila folder. He pulled it out of the folder just enough to expose only Ginger's image. Brown's eyes involuntarily went to the folder on the table, curious what Reed was doing.

When Brown saw the exposed portion of the photo,

his head tilted at an impossible angle, eyes darting to the ceiling. He moved back slightly, and his arms crossed his chest, almost hugging himself. His legs came together and pulled up sharply under his chair. He took a deep breath and didn't release it for a long time. When he finally did exhale, his eyes traveled slowly back to the table, then quickly back toward the ceiling again. The look of distress was unmistakable.

"Did she look like this photo the last time you saw her?" Reed asked.

Brown shot the investigator a startled look, like he was afraid the detective was able to read his mind.

"Why're you asking me?" he responded.

"I'm just trying to be sure that we have an accurate photo to pass around while we look for her," Reed explained. "And you were the last person to see her."

Brown gave the picture a furtive glance.

"How do you know I'm the last one to see her?"

"Well, you said you were with her at Caesar's. How long were you there, Joe?"

No answer. Just that look. Arms crossed, face turned away, Adam's apple bobbing nervously.

Reed pushed a little harder and asked how Ginger had been dressed or what she might be driving. Brown wasn't told that the detective had already located Ginger's green Ford Taurus.

Still, no response. The time had come to pull the photo of Ginger and her ex-husband into play. The eight-by-ten picture was laid on the table in front of Brown. His eyes widened at the sight, but he instantly averted them to the ceiling. His jaw clenched and he clutched his hands together until his knuckles turned white.

Reed interpreted Brown's body language to mean that he was becoming nervous and confused. The detective pointed at the photo and looked straight at Brown, hoping to regain eye contact with him.

"You tried to cash one of her checks on the thirty-first of August. I assume she gave it to you. Am I wrong?"

There was no way to answer the question without getting stuck. Of course, Brown could have remained quiet. But he didn't.

"Yeah, she gave me that check."

"And you told the Ohio state trooper who stopped you that you saw her on Friday at Caesar's Casino. Isn't that in Elizabeth?"

This time, Joe Brown didn't answer. He merely sat with his feet resting flat on the floor, arms tightly crossing his chest, hugging himself. This was the posture that Reed had called the "I ain't telling you shit and you can't make me" position. It's as though he was afraid that his own body was going to betray him, and he was trying desperately to hold something inside.

SEVENTEEN

The detective told Brown that he knew about the assault on Ginger in September 1999, and that afterward, Brown had gone to his sister Jennie's house in Terre Haute, where he told her children that he had "killed Ginger this time."

The story about the beating didn't seem to affect him, but his eyes widened at the mention of Jennie's name.

Brown admitted that he had choked and hit Ginger in that incident in the laundry room. He tried to excuse his actions by saying that she had kicked him out, and would not give him any money. This wasn't the first time they had fought and then gotten back together. Brown said Ginger was always kicking him out.

Brown and Ginger had gotten back together shortly after that incident, and the battery charge was the reason he was here now. He said that he had been sentenced to go to anger management classes, but failed to finish the program. Those classes were part of the Drug and Alcohol Intervention Program (DAIP) that Brown was required to attend. It was because he didn't attend those classes that the misdemeanor warrant was issued against him, and ultimately held him now as a suspect in a possible homicide.

Once again, Brown tried to turn the focus of the

discussion to past wrongs committed against him. The longer he could avoid talking about Ginger as a person, the longer he could avoid the truth about what had happened. Or at least he could avoid anyone else finding out the truth. So far in the discussion, Brown had never used Ginger's name. He referred to Ginger as "her," like in "you'd have to ask Hobert about her."

Somehow, Reed would have to make Ginger real again for Brown. Make him smell her scent, feel her flesh next to him, look into her eyes. But that was the trick, wasn't it? How do you make someone feel?

"Did you love Ginger, Joe?"

"Yeah, I guess I did."

Brown referred to Ginger in the past tense. That was not a good sign.

"I just want to see her come home," Reed assured Brown. "If you beat her up again, like the last time, maybe you just think she's hurt bad. Maybe she's lying somewhere hurt and needs help."

Brown just stared at the floor and shook his head. Did that mean that she was beyond help, or did it mean that he hadn't done anything to Ginger?

"Joe, you know that Ginger's been missing since Wednesday. The longer she goes without help, without some type of medical help . . ." Reed let the sentence trail off to see how Brown would respond, but there was no reaction. Reed hoped to explore the edges of Brown's memory to see if he would at least consider the possibility that Ginger was alive.

"Joe, if Ginger is dead, she doesn't deserve to be laying out in the elements, and possibly be eaten by animals and bugs."

Reed had set the stage by asking if Brown still loved Ginger. This was an appeal to that part of Brown that might still care.

But Brown wasn't taking the bait. He just sat stone-faced. At least now he seemed to be distracted, or in deep thought. It was as if a battle raged inside him, and he was close to panic.

After long moments, Brown looked up, and with a somber expression, he again denied knowing where Ginger was. His words sounded rehearsed. He said that the previous Tuesday was the last time he saw her.

Reed confidently assured Brown that he had seen the videotape footage of Brown's arrest by the Ohio police, and that on the tape Brown had told the trooper that he had been on the boat in New Albany with Ginger on Friday.

Brown adamantly denied saying this, and Reed again explained that it was on videotape.

"Joe, I know you loved Ginger. You would never mean to harm her, but sometimes things happen. We have to find her, even if she's gone, Joe. If she's dead, we have to find her and get her back with her family. She would have wanted that. You would want that for her, I know you would."

Silence.

"Joe, how is the family ever going to get over this? They will never believe she is gone, unless they can see the body, put her in the ground themselves. They should be able to visit their mother's grave, and not just an empty box in the ground, Joe. Ginger will never rest if she doesn't go home. Her daughters . . . Lisa will never stop expecting her mother to come home, Joe. That's not right."

Tears began to well up in Brown's eyes. He would not talk, but he was obviously stung by the remark. He looked at the floor for a moment, then faced Reed again. He stared straight into Reed's eyes, as if his line of sight could pierce through him like hot knives through butter.

"I told you that you're asking the wrong guy about her! These guys just come down on me and lock me up . . . ,"

Brown said, getting so angry that he couldn't finish his sentence.

Brown shut his mouth and turned his head sideways, face tilted up. This was Brown's angry pose. Brown had deflected the question of where Ginger was. It was like he changed channels to see what else might be playing.

"There is a warrant on you, Joe," Reed started to say. He wanted to resume the questioning about Ginger, but Brown wasn't ready for that yet.

Brown was caught in a bad spot now. If he admitted that Ginger was with him at Caesar's, the detectives could check the casino cameras to see if this was true. If he denied it, that would mean he had lied to the Ohio State Police sergeant. He used his angry act to stall for time to think up an excuse.

"I'm not talking to those bastards," Brown finally said, and shot an accusing look toward the two Ohio lawmen in the back of the room. "They bum-rushed me into this place, without any damn reason!"

Brown was getting louder. This was how he hoped to avoid talking about Caesar's anymore. It was an old trick that the detectives had seen thousands of times. His next trick would be to refuse to talk anymore because the detectives were just like the Ohio troopers. This was a good time to change tactics, so Reed went on the offensive.

"I told you, Joe, I'm not with the Ohio police, right?" Without giving Joe a chance to answer, he pressed on.

"You were Ginger's best friend in the whole world. You knew her better than her own kids. You treated her better than anyone." Reed let this last remark hang in the air for a moment to see if there was someone that Brown would want to rat out as an enemy of Ginger's.

Brown just looked back at the corner of the room. His face tilted slightly upward. The expression was more thoughtful now than angry. Something Reed said had turned a switch on in Brown's brain. The key points being Brown's relationship with Ginger, her relationship with her children, and the possibility that Ginger had been abused by someone in her past. These were avenues that needed visiting.

"Let me tell you something, Joe. I was at Ginger's apartment today. I sat on the front porch in one of those white plastic lawn chairs. I looked out over the tops of the apartment buildings and around the parking lots.

"It is such a peaceful place. I used to live in apartments like those, and I really miss the quiet times like that. I suppose you and Ginger must have had some good times sitting out there in the evening, drinking a good cup of coffee, having a smoke, just watching people mill around."

Brown sat cross-legged, hands trapped tightly in his lap, a stolid expression on his face.

"Joe, while I was sitting there, I tried to imagine where Ginger might have gone. But I just don't know her that well. I couldn't put myself in her mind. That's why I need your help."

Reed leaned close and spoke directly to Joe in a tone that said he was about to share something special.

"I have something to tell you, Joe. I used to work Homicide cases until a couple years ago. I had some cases that really got to me. This one guy, couldn't have been more than twenty years old, and he killed his brother's little baby boy. I couldn't help that child, Joe. He smashed its head on the floor. Stomped an eleven-month-old child to death."

"If you want to know where Ginger's at, you'll have to ask Hobert," Brown suddenly said.

Both Evansville detectives exchanged a glance that said, "It looks like we're back to square one." It appeared that Brown would never tell what he knew about the disappearance of his ex-lover.

"Joe, I have to find her," Reed said quietly, almost pleadingly. "I told you about why I quit working homicides. I need your help, Joe. You're probably the only one that will help me. I couldn't help that little baby, but I have another chance with Ginger. If I can find her before she's hurt . . ." Reed trailed off, looking at the floor.

Brown sat stone-faced, not looking at anyone. At this point, Detective Nelson, who had been sitting quietly taking everything in, now stood up.

"He's full of shit!" Nelson burst in. "He's not going to tell us a damned thing."

Reed knew this was a good cop/bad cop routine, but Nelson genuinely appeared angry, and probably as much with Reed as with Joe Brown. This wasn't Nelson's style of interviewing. He didn't believe in coddling suspects, and that was how this type of questioning looked to him.

"Why don't you go get a cup of coffee, Larry? I'd like to talk to Joe a little longer. He's trying the best he can to help," Reed said.

"Bullshit!" Nelson snarled. "He's just yanking us around."

"Go get some coffee," Reed said in a tone that was more stern than he had intended. After all, he and Nelson were the same rank, and, in fact, Nelson was the Homicide detective. Reed was just a Bunco-Fraud investigator. He was probably lucky to be here at all.

The two investigators glared at each other in a sort of standoff until a voice came quietly between them.

"You'll never find her, Rick."

A pin dropping would have been heard in the room. Nelson and Reed broke off their confrontational stare, and they both turned to face Brown.

"What did you say, Joe?" Reed asked.

"You'll never find her, Rick."

"What do you mean by that?"

Brown leaned close to Reed and looked directly into his eyes.

"Listen to me, Rick. You don't want to be the one to find her. Do you understand? You wouldn't be able to take it."

Reed did understand. Ginger was dead.

"What are you saying, Joe?" He knew the answer, but he had to hear Brown say the words. This would have to be very clear if there was to be a trial.

Brown took an exaggerated breath and said, "I killed her. I guess you'd say I murdered her."

"Tell me about it, Joe."

The story, when it came, was one that the men in the room were unprepared for. It was a story that could be told around campfires at night, or on hayrides during Halloween. In the eerie confines of the Warren County Corrections Facility, it was no less spooky.

Almost two hours had passed since the Evansville detectives had come to the Warren County facility to interview Joseph Brown, and the two men already had a long day before making the five-hour drive to Lebanon, Ohio.

Given Joe Brown's initial hostility and reticence, his sudden confession to the murder of Ginger Gasaway had been a complete surprise to the Evansville detectives and to the Ohio state troopers as well.

Now Brown was about to drop a bomb on the four lawmen listening to what can only be described as a bizarre twist of roles. It was as if Joe Brown were trying to protect Rick Reed from the emotional impact of finding that Ginger Gasaway had been murdered, or at least to keep him from being the one to find her remains.

Reed attempted to enlist Brown's aid in solving the disappearance of his fifty-three-year-old ex-girlfriend, and now Brown was warning Reed that the detective didn't want to be the one to find her.

Brown was looking at his feet, arms twisted together with his hands between his knees, like a small child. His posture conveyed the meaning "I'm sorry. I couldn't help it."

"What are you saying, Joe?" Reed asked.

Brown shook his head slightly, still staring at the floor. "I cut her up."

Four words. They came out so easily in the end. Four days of searching. Four days of questioning Ginger's friends and family members. It all led the detectives to this place and time, only to lead to more hours of questions, and an emotional roller-coaster ride that was the shared lives of Joe Brown and Ginger Gasaway. But in the end, it had come down to those four words.

"I cut her up."

EIGHTEEN

During the interview, Detective Reed asked Brown if Ginger still looked like she did in the photograph that he got from her daughter.

At the time, Brown said that he didn't know. But an hour later, he admitted that he had not only murdered Ginger, but he had also cut her up.

Brown seemed relieved to get this off his conscience. He had been carrying the tremendous weight of guilt with him and he wanted to put it down. At the same time, he was struggling for self-preservation. Reed had seen this scenario many times before in the faces of other homicide suspects. It was the internal struggle between good and evil.

Reed believed that inside every criminal there still beat the heart of a human being, and that even murderers desired the same things that we all desired: to be safe, to be able to sustain our physical needs, and to be accepted by the group. This was a simplification of Maslow's Hierarchy of Needs, but there's a basic truth in this theory that cannot be denied.

Maslow's theory basically stated that safety is our first need as a human being, and after that need is satisfied, the second need will become dominant, and then the third, and so on. In this particular case, Joe

Brown felt safe talking to the detectives because there was no immediate threat of violence to his person.

It can be argued that Brown still had the impending fear of life imprisonment, or perhaps even the death penalty as payment for his confession. But in Brown's mind, being in prison was more like being home than being on the outside, so there was no threat in imprisonment.

Following this theory further, it could be argued that Brown also knew that he would be fed and clothed in prison, and so there was no fear of losing his basic physical needs.

It was Detective Reed's belief, and hope, that the only thing Brown really feared, or desired, was something he had never known before, acceptance by society. By treating this fear, he would allow Brown to tell the truth. Joe Brown would have to feel that he could tell someone the truth, and that they would be accepting of that truth instead of judgmental.

Now that Brown was talking, the words rushed from him like air from a balloon with a hole in it. He gave the detectives details that sent involuntary shivers up their spines. This wasn't an ordinary murder, or a heat-of-passion type slaying. It was a premeditated and calculated destruction of another human being.

In killing Ginger, Brown savagely lashed out at every woman. She became the target of revenge for every person that he felt had wronged him in some way. He was destroying the thing that he could never have. And that thing was a life of acceptance, happiness, and comfort.

Ginger represented that kind of life to Joe, but in his mind, she had thrown him from the Garden of Eden, relegating him to a life of struggling for survival in a hostile world.

In his confession, Brown slowly put the pieces together for the detectives. However, he refused to sign a Miranda rights form, and he refused to allow his words to be recorded on tape. He had similarly refused to sign a Miranda form or allow recording when advised of his rights by the Ohio State Police. In fact, the Ohio state trooper's onboard video capture system was the only recording that law enforcement had at this point to prove that Brown's rights had not been violated.

Now that Brown was talking, he became much more relaxed. He almost appeared to be enjoying himself. Reed had read about such killers in criminal-behavior books written by active and retired FBI profilers. Some killers enjoyed injecting themselves into an investigation. The supposed reason for this was that the killer felt more in control of the investigation, and also it helped keep the fantasy alive that had originally brought the killing about.

Whatever Brown's reasons were, he was keeping them to himself, or perhaps he was unaware of them. In any case, he kept talking, and that was what the investigators wanted. They needed to prove their case.

Brown said he had spent part of the night on Tuesday, August 29, with Ginger at her apartment on Hatfield Drive. She had called and wanted to talk to him. He had gone there, thinking that they were going to reconcile, but she had told him that she had slept with Hobert. Brown said that was what caused her death.

Brown said that he killed Ginger early in the morning of August 30. He wasn't sure how he killed her. He wouldn't be more precise than that. Inside Brown's mind, a war was raging between doing what he knew was right for Ginger, and doing what was safe for himself. The idea of Ginger being eaten or carried away by predators won a small amount of compassion from Brown. He decided to tell where she was.

"I'm only doing this because I want to give her to her family . . . to be able to bury her. You know what I mean, Rick."

Reed told Brown that Ginger's family would be

grateful for what he was doing, and reminded him how horrible it would be for them to have had to put an empty casket in the ground.

Brown seemed pleased with this new role. He was in charge now and he knew it. He knew that without him, the detectives had little chance, if any, of recovering Ginger's remains. In return for his confession, Brown's only demand was that he would not be forced to sign anything, and that he would not be recorded.

With that being agreed to, Brown told the detectives that he would show them where the body parts were located and he continued his confession.

He stated that he went to Ginger's apartment sometime in the late evening of August 29, and that he had been "let in." Reed and Nelson didn't have any clue whether his being "let in" was voluntary on Ginger's part, but they didn't want to force the issue just yet.

The conversation with Brown jumped from subject to subject at that point. Brown stated that he had used a reciprocating saw to cut Ginger's body into pieces small enough to carry to the Mustang. He began explaining how they had made love, and then she was dead. He didn't know how she died. He just knew that he must have killed her somehow.

Brown told the detectives that he sat on the bed beside the unmoving body of his former girlfriend, and that his mind just went blank. He didn't know what to do, and was unsure of how long he sat like that.

According to Brown's story, an idea finally came to him. Ginger was much too heavy for him to carry her downstairs by himself, so he got the idea to cut her into pieces.

Neither detective believed this. For one thing, Brown was strong and could have easily moved Ginger out of the apartment. After all, he was a bricklayer, and that's a very strenuous occupation.

Reed believed that it was more likely that Brown had

decided that moving her body, by carrying her over his shoulder, presented too much risk of being seen by somebody.

The detectives believed that Brown might have heard stories while he was in prison about how to get rid of a body. This would be similar to the stories that kids tell each other around a campfire to try and outdo one another.

Brown swore that he came up with the idea of chopping Ginger into pieces on his own, and that he had never been told by someone in prison about this method of disposing of a body. His sister Jennie disagreed with that story.

According to Jennie, she spoke to Joe while he was incarcerated. She told Detectives Reed and Nelson that another prisoner told him that if you killed someone, the best way to avoid being caught was to cut the body into several pieces, and then to spread the pieces over several different counties where they wouldn't be found. Even if the parts were discovered, Joe told Jennie, the police would never be able to identify them. The real truth probably lay somewhere in between Joe's and Jennie's account.

At this point, Brown's confession had only been recorded in the minds and partial notes of the four lawmen. This may have been enough for a conviction in court, but more was always better. Hopefully, Brown would continue talking. Hopefully, the Crime Scene technicians in Evansville would find enough evidence to make their case airtight. But Reed wasn't satisfied. They hadn't found Ginger's body or body parts yet.

Brown did continue talking. He said that he brought the kitchen table extension into the bedroom and set it on the floor beside the bed. Then he laid her lifeless body on top of it. Brown made a trip to the local Home Depot and used one of Ginger's credit cards to purchase a reciprocating saw.

When he returned, Brown found that the saw was insufficient for cutting through flesh and muscle, so he found a kitchen knife that would do that job. He then used the saw to cut through the bones. But even this turned bad when Brown broke a blade while cutting through the large femur bone in Ginger's leg.

Undeterred, Brown drove back to Home Depot, where he spoke to an employee who would later recall that he thought Brown was cutting up a deer. Brown complained that the blade wouldn't cut through bone, and was promptly given one that would be more effective.

If Brown was telling the truth, it wouldn't be the detectives' responsibility to prove why he had disposed of Ginger in such a fashion. It was only their duty to prove that he was the one responsible, and that he did it intentionally. There was still much to do.

NINETEEN

Joe Brown's confession had made matters much easier for the two lawmen, in light of the fact that they had almost no solid evidence at the time they left Evansville to link Brown to Ginger's murder. The fact that they still didn't have a body would make it difficult to make Brown's confession stand up in a court of law.

Even if Brown gave up the location of Ginger's body, and further assuming that there was only one location, there still remained a multitude of legal obstacles ahead. The least of which was the fact that they were in Ohio, and the body was supposedly somewhere in Indiana.

While the detectives mulled over their options, Brown threw another wrench into the clockwork.

"I threw the pieces in three different counties," Brown said in his deadpan tone.

Reed's head must have jerked up at that one, because Brown immediately explained, "I told you that you wouldn't be able to find her."

Brown then made an offer that the detectives didn't know if they could accept.

"I'll show you where I put them. I'll take you to the parts, but I want to do it right now." The look on

Brown's face had gone dead serious. This point was not negotiable in his mind.

What Brown was referring to was his extradition back to Indiana. This is not as simple a matter as it is made to appear on television. Extradition is governed by several rules of local, state, and federal laws.

To bring Brown back to Indiana to face charges, Joe would have to appear in front of a judge in Warren County, Ohio, and sign a waiver of extradition to Indiana. Extradition can be voluntary, or it can be done by a governor's warrant.

If Brown decided that he didn't want to go to Indiana to face charges, a warrant would have to be signed by the governor of Indiana, requesting that Joe be released by Ohio and allowed to be transported to Indiana to face criminal charges. The judge in Ohio would then give Brown's attorneys ninety days to present a case stating why Joe Brown should not be extradited to Indiana.

Equally as bad, if Brown agreed to be extradited to Indiana, and signed the waiver form, he could still wait up to a month before the Vanderburgh County, Indiana, corrections people processed the paperwork to bring him back to Evansville.

Normally, things run a little smoother than that, and the suspect is brought back within a few days of being apprehended. But in this case, Brown was asking for something that had never been done before. He was asking to be transported across state lines prior to his extradition.

Brown wanted to be brought back to Evansville immediately, or he would not give the detectives the location of Ginger's remains. The detectives knew their case would be stronger with a body than without, but that wasn't the only concern that faced them in considering Brown's offer. The detectives were not aware of a law that stated that they couldn't take Brown out of the jail, as long as they had him back in front of the Ohio judicial system for his scheduled extradition hearing. On the other hand, the detectives had never heard of such a thing being done before, and to take Brown across two state lines made things even more complicated.

For the sake of Ginger's family, Reed hoped that it would be possible to achieve what Brown had proposed. He couldn't imagine what it would be like for them not to be able to bury their mother's remains. Without ever really knowing where she was, they might continue to harbor some hope that she was still alive. They would never be able to derive some comfort from closure.

Reed thought about his own parents. Both had been lost to a long battle with cancer, and not to some despicable crime, but he imagined what it would be like never to be able to visit their graves.

After a quick discussion, Nelson left the room to contact Stan Levco, the Vanderburgh County prosecutor for Indiana. Up to now, Lieutenant Charlie Hale, of the Ohio State Highway Patrol, sat silently as he watched Brown transform from a sullen, angry, and reticent suspect into a talkative and cooperative self-confessed murderer. He, too, left the room to contact the Warren County, Ohio, prosecutor.

Sergeant James Ertel, of the Ohio State Highway Patrol, acted as liaison with the Warren County facility. Meanwhile, Reed had persuaded one of the jailers to let him take Brown into the secured garage area of the corrections complex. Sergeant Kennard brought both men a hot cup of coffee and a pack of cigarettes, compliments of Warren County. Reed hadn't smoked for almost ten years, but under the circumstances, the habit came back easily. Brown was like a smoking machine, lighting one cigarette off another.

Through a large pane of bulletproof glass, a corrections

officer kept a watchful eye on the two men as they sat quietly on a long wooden bench. The coffee was good and strong. The cigarette smoke hung thick in the air as both men quietly pondered their own private thoughts.

Reed took advantage of the moment to decompress, and was barely aware of Brown taking a deep drag from his cigarette. Brown held the smoke in for what seemed like an eternity, and when he exhaled, a chill ran across Reed's upper arms. He sensed that Brown had made some kind of decision. He was almost afraid to ask what it was.

Brown put his cigarette in a Coke can, which one of the deputies had provided as a makeshift ashtray. He poured a little of his coffee into the can and stared at the tendril of smoke that was escaping.

"It's a good thing you caught me when you did, Rick. It wasn't over."

The remark caught the detective off-guard. He had been expecting Brown to say that he had changed his mind, and that he was now going to fight not only extradition, but that he had been pulling the detective's leg all along. Or that he was insane and he was now speaking with his attorney from the "other side"—and his attorney was Elvis. He was so surprised by the statement that all Reed could do was look at Brown.

"If you hadn't caught me . . . there was going to be a bloodbath."

Reed was stunned by the casual way Brown had made this revelation. While Brown sucked in another large lungful of smoke, Reed lit another cigarette himself, trying not to appear shocked.

"What do you mean?" Reed asked, hoping he sounded as relaxed as Brown appeared to be.

Brown just shook his head, not looking at the detective, enjoying his cigarette, enjoying being in charge of the direction of things for a change. Up to now, he had been hunted and on the run. Now that he was caught, he had to take comfort where he could find it. And right now, having the detective's complete attention, a smoke, and a cup of coffee was as good as it was going to get. Brown knew it was all he had.

"I was on a roll, you know what I mean? It wasn't over yet," Brown said.

Reed remained quiet. He thought that this was Brown's story and it would be wrong to interrupt with questions. Let him tell it his way and in his own time. He was close to some huge revelation, the detective was sure of that. But what could be worse than admitting to the murder and dismemberment of another human being?

Reed motioned for the guard to bring a fresh round of coffee. When it was delivered, Brown sat with his elbows propped on his knees. He sipped the steaming contents of his Styrofoam cup, with his head hanging low, as if it were too heavy for his neck to support. Reed felt sad when he looked at him. For some reason, he actually felt sorry for Joe Brown.

"I'll tell you the truth, Rick. I was going to see my brother in Zanesville. I was going to kill him and his family. Then I was going to Marietta, Georgia, to take care of that fucking no-good bitch sister of mine."

The words spewed like an angry stream of bile from Brown's mouth. After he said it, he appeared to be exhausted, like it had taken all of his strength to rid himself of the handful of words.

"Doesn't your sister live in Terre Haute?" Reed asked.

The thought of his sister Jennie seemed to give Brown some strength. He sat up straight and looked at the detective.

"That's my sister Jennie," he answered. "My oldest sister lives in Georgia."

He then told Reed that he hated his oldest sister, Sue, and that he "had nothing to lose now."

Reed asked who lived in Zanesville, and Brown responded that his brother lived there.

"None of them ever came to see me. The only one that ever had anything to do with me was my sister, Jennie," Joe said.

"Were you on your way to your brother's house?" Reed asked.

Brown didn't respond right away. Instead, he took another large draw on his cigarette, burning it down to ash. He muttered something under his breath as he crushed the cigarette out on the lid of the Coke can.

"What difference does it make now?" he asked.

"None that I can think of, Joe. I'm just interested to know if you planned on doing something."

"I was gonna cut the bitch's head off! She's the reason that my brother never had anything to do with me. But I wouldn't have hurt the kids. You know I wouldn't hurt no kids, Rick. I hate child molesters. Hell, I hate anyone that would hurt a kid," Brown said.

"Were you going to your brother's house to kill them, Joe?"

"I wouldn't have hurt the kids." He looked back at the ceiling again. "Hell, Rick, what did I have to lose?"

This was as close as Joe Brown would get to confessing that he had intended to kill his brother's family. That was until almost three years later, in September 2003, when Brown would again tell Reed the story of this trip to Ohio. In that recounting of the story, Brown would tell the entire tale of how he came to be in Ohio, and the grisly details of what he had done before he got there. And he was right about one thing. It was a good thing that he was caught. He really wasn't through yet. There really was going to be a bloodbath, and if Brown was telling the truth, there had already been one.

TWENTY

Sergeant Brian Kennard tapped on the window, and motioned that it was time for Reed and Brown to return to the interview area. Nelson and the Ohio troopers were already waiting for them.

Lieutenant Hale spoke to Brown for the first time since they had entered the interview room hours ago.

"Mr. Brown, I have to ask you if it is still your intention to go with these two detectives from Evansville?"

Brown merely nodded.

"You have to answer the question, Mr. Brown. A nod won't do it. I'll ask again. Do you still want to go with these two detectives to Evansville?"

"Yes, I do," Brown said in a strong voice. It wasn't because he was mad. He was just anxious to get out of the Warren County lockup.

Hale nodded at Sergeant Ertel, who, in turn, asked the corrections sergeant to take Brown back to his cell, and get him ready for a trip to Evansville. After Brown was out of sight, Nelson filled Reed in on what had transpired during his conversation with the Vanderburgh County prosecutor, Stan Levco.

"Levco spoke with the prosecutor here, and they agreed to let us take Joe with us," Nelson said.

Hale reiterated Nelson's news, advising that the

Warren County prosecutor had given his blessing as well. Both prosecutors also delivered a stern warning that Brown must be back in front of the Ohio judge in time for the extradition hearing, or there would be serious hell to pay.

The four lawmen looked at each other with various degrees of trepidation. They had all been deep into a case at one time or another, wondering where it would lead. They hoped for a successful conclusion, but at the same time, they braced themselves for failure.

One reason for their discomfort was the knowledge that all suspects were different. Brown might be cooperative one moment, and then do a one-eighty-degree turn and fight them every step of the way the next moment.

So far, nothing had been recorded, and Brown had refused to sign any paperwork. All the detectives had was their word for what had been said, if they had to prove or defend their actions before a jury.

That's not to say that the detectives didn't have options. They could keep Brown incarcerated in Warren County until his extradition hearing, which was scheduled for 11:00 A.M. the next day and just take their chances that he would be cooperative when they got back to Evansville. They also could have tried to prove that he murdered Ginger, based entirely on circumstantial evidence, without any help from Brown. But filing charges and getting a conviction were two different things. A conviction would be entirely up to a jury of Brown's peers, and juries could be unpredictable.

The last option was for one of them to return to Evansville, while the other waited for Brown's extradition hearing. Whoever returned to Evansville might be lucky enough to find some hard evidence, but Nelson and Reed both knew that the chance of finding the dismembered body parts on their own was unlikely.

Whatever they decided, they would only have about sixteen hours to get it done before Brown was expected to appear in front of the Warren County judge for a decision on his extradition.

As far as Reed was concerned, there never was a question. Finding Ginger's remains was his primary concern. If he got beat up in court for that decision, then so be it. The law was not always black and white, and he hoped that humanity would play some part in the decision-making process.

A unanimous decision was made to take Brown back to Evansville immediately. Now it was just a matter of getting him out of jail.

The Warren County corrections staff was an efficient lot. Brown was dressed, blessed (signed over to the Evansville detectives' custody), and loaded into the unmarked Evansville police car in less than thirty minutes. Reed commended Sergeant Kennard for expediting this, as well as for the use of their excellent facilities, not to mention the coffee and cigarettes.

Kennard laughed and explained that it wasn't efficiency—they just were grateful to be rid of Brown. He then added that they were glad to be of assistance. Apparently, Joe Brown had been giving the staff a hard time, and they never minded getting rid of a headache. Reed told the sergeant that he had once been a sheriff's deputy before becoming a city policeman, and having worked in the Vanderburgh County Jail for almost six years, he understood completely.

Hale followed the two detectives to their car while they situated their prisoner. He asked the men if there was anything else that the Ohio State Highway Patrol might offer them.

Reed asked if it would be possible to get an escort through Ohio so that they could expedite their trip. The clock was ticking. Nelson started the car and noticed that the fuel gauge read almost empty.

The detectives checked Brown's seat belt, handcuffs,

belly chain, and ankle cuffs. Everything appeared to be secure, so they left the parking lot of the corrections complex and followed the two OSHP supervisors back to the OSHP Post. Once there, they were to be given a free tank of gas and an official escort across the state to the Kentucky border.

Earlier, Nelson had driven during the five-hour trip from Evansville to Lebanon, Ohio, so Reed could make himself notes for the upcoming interview. Nelson was once again at the wheel, only this time Reed was seat-belted into the backseat next to their quarry.

The OSHP Post was set in the middle of nowhere. At night, in the darkness, it seemed even more remote, and may as well have been on the dark side of the moon. It only took a short time to get there, but as Reed sat in the back of the unmarked police car, next to his shackled prey, he began to wonder who the prey was, and who was the predator. Nelson accompanied Ertel and Hale inside the building and they seemed to be gone for a long time. Inside the car, small talk with Brown had grown stale.

Brown had grown quiet, almost morose, even turning down a cigarette. That was when Reed remembered that he didn't bring his department-issued Smith & Wesson nine-millimeter handgun on this trip.

"I'm not going to jail," Brown said, breaking the silence.

Those five words carried much more meaning in the pitch black of the car's interior than they would have in the sunlight. Since Reed's first murder case, he had recurring nightmares. In those nightmares, it was always dark, and he was searching for a light switch. When he did find one . . . *click* . . . nothing happened. It remained dark. And there was something in the darkness with him; something that wanted to harm him, maybe to rip him to shreds, and so he kept searching for the light.

Reed tried to make out the door of the station, but could only see a few feet across the gravel lot. There was no sound outside the car, and even the wind had died. He didn't know Brown well enough to know if he was serious about not going to jail. He tried to remember who had searched Brown before putting him in the car. Could he have a hidden handcuff key? Things like that had happened before. It was so completely dark that Reed couldn't even see the prisoner sitting beside him.

"Joe, you know you have to go back to jail until the trial," Reed said, trying to sound calm and unafraid.

"I'm not going to trial neither. What have I got to lose?" Brown responded just as calmly, but with a menacing edge to his voice.

Reed sat quietly, cursing himself for not bringing a weapon with which to defend himself. He had been so caught up in the mental exercise of the last several days that he had forgotten the golden rule: "He who has the gun makes the rules."

Instead, he sat in the blackened interior of a car, with a self-confessed murderer, who, only a few days ago, not only strangled his girlfriend, but then proceeded to commit unspeakable acts of violence on her body. And Reed's partner, the one that had remembered to bring a weapon, was somewhere inside a building that couldn't even be seen through the blackness of the night.

You can tell your children to go back to bed. Tell them there really is no bogeyman, and that the noise in the closet or under the bed is just the house settling in its foundation. You can try to convince them that pressure escaping from the water pipes is what caused the rattling sound inside the house. But here in this car, on this particular night, you would never convince Detective Rick Reed that he wasn't in the presence of the bogeyman.

And this wasn't even going to be the worst of it, not by a long shot. The real nightmare would begin in Warrick County, Indiana, as they began to search for and then find pieces of a dismembered body. In the dark. *Click . . .*

TWENTY-ONE

The moon emerged from behind the clouds and cast enough ambient light to see inside the back of the car. Brown's face was pale and drawn. Reed's concern for his own safety dissolved into a feeling of pity for his prisoner.

"What do you mean by 'you don't have anything to lose,' Joe?"

Brown didn't answer for several minutes, and when he did, his voice was so weak it was as if it took all of his strength to talk.

"I don't know, Rick. I don't know what I mean."

Brown looked out the window and, as he did, the clouds covered the moon, once again plunging the interior of the car into darkness.

In the darkness, he must have gathered some type of strength, because it wasn't long before he began to speak. His voice was stronger now, but his words were still of despair and bitterness. It seemed as if he drew his strength from hatred.

"I was out of money and desperate. I didn't have a clue where to go or what to do, you know what I mean."

"Joe, let me ask you something. Why did you confess to me?" Reed asked.

"You didn't bum-rush me, Rick. Like those troopers did, know what I mean?"

Reed nodded his understanding, but remained silent, wanting more information.

"If they would have been more polite . . . you know . . . like you was, then I would have talked to them. I was going to turn myself in anyway, you know what I mean, after . . ." He didn't finish the sentence.

"After you killed your brother?" Reed asked.

"I just wanted to talk to him. He never came to see me when I was locked up, you know what I mean? I wanted to let him make his peace."

Reed thought that was a strange remark, and he wondered what Brown meant by "make his peace." It wasn't long before Brown would use this same terminology to describe the circumstances of Ginger's death.

Before Brown could say anything else, a square of light appeared across the gravel lot. A door opened, and Nelson came out, accompanied by Hale and Ertel. They were carrying Styrofoam cups of something steaming. Reed hoped one of the cups was for him.

As the men approached the car, Brown became quiet once again. He leaned his head back and closed his eyes. There was no telling what thoughts were going through his mind, but Reed knew that he had made the connection to Brown that he needed. He was confident that Brown would keep his word and show them where he had disposed of Ginger's remains.

Brown jumped as Nelson tapped on his car window.

"I brought you some coffee," Nelson said as he opened Brown's door.

Brown reached out as far as his handcuffs and belt chain would allow, taking the cup.

"Thanks," he mumbled.

Ertel handed a cup to Reed, then told Nelson to drive the car to the back of the building, where it could be filled with gasoline.

As Nelson rounded the car to get in the driver's seat, Brown lowered the cup to his lap and his head slumped forward.

"I'll show you where I put her, Rick," he said. He didn't expect an answer.

Nelson began the long drive back to Evansville, with Reed and Brown in the backseat. On the way, Brown became more talkative.

"She knew she was going to die," Joe said.

"Who knew? Ginger?" Nelson asked from the front of the car.

Joe said that he went to Ginger's apartment on Tuesday night and that she let him in so they could talk. He went on to explain that it was very late in the evening, and she had expected him to drop her car by the next day. According to Joe, they talked for a while, then had sex. After they were finished, instead of pillow talk, Ginger told him that she had sex with Hobert, and that they were going to get back together again. She told Joe that she didn't want him to come around anymore.

After Ginger told him she had been intimate with Hobert again, Joe said, he held her for a while to let her "make her peace." She told him to kiss her. He did. And then he killed her.

"She knew that when she told me she'd slept with Hobert that she was gonna die, you know what I mean?" Joe said, as if it were a natural conclusion.

Nelson followed Ertel's car as it rocketed down I-70 West toward Louisville, Kentucky. Just on the other side of the Ohio state line, the Kentucky State Police would continue the escort until Nelson reached Indiana.

The handoff of the Evansville detectives from Sergeant Ertel to the Kentucky State Police went smoothly, and the new escort sped west from the Ohio state line. The gas tank was still full, but Brown was running on empty. They decided to make a stop.

Nelson followed the Kentucky trooper into an all-night gas station in Verona to let Brown use the restroom, and get something to eat and drink. The two customers inside followed Brown with suspicious eyes as he did the prison shuffle toward the men's room in the back of the little convenience store. Wearing a bright orange jump-suit and five pounds of chains, he must have been a sight for the residents of this little Kentucky town.

After getting Brown back to the car, Reed and Nelson pooled their cash, and Nelson went inside to buy Brown something to eat. Brown took advantage of the stop to smoke another cigarette. Reed lit him up and yelled at Nelson to get another pack inside the store. He figured Brown had better enjoy it while he could, because he'd be in a smoke-free facility when he was finally returned to Evansville.

While Nelson had been in the gas station, he had contacted Captain Clayton Grace in Evansville by cell phone. Captain Grace informed him that they— meaning nearly the entire EPD investigation unit, along with all of the Crime Scene officers—were put-ting "something" together at the abandoned Moto Mart station, located at US Highway 57 and I-64. Grace told Nelson that when the detectives got closer to Evansville, they should call him for further instructions.

"How did she die, Joe? I know you cut her up, but she was already dead when you did that, wasn't she?" Reed asked.

He hoped that she was, but Reed hadn't directly asked so far because the idea that Ginger might have been alive—when Brown started cutting—was almost too horrible to think about.

"I don't really know, Rick. I guess I must have stran-gled her," Brown said between long draws on his cigarette.

"She was dead when you cut her up?"

"Yeah. I left her on the bed while I went riding around and bought the saw. I told you that already."

The two men sat quietly for a moment before Detective Nelson returned with cold food for Brown, coffee all around, and a fresh pack of smokes. Hot coffee, cold food, and black lung—it didn't get better than that for the next forty hours.

Nelson pulled out of the gas station, and the Kentucky State Police escort led the procession westward toward Evansville.

While Brown threw some groceries down his neck, Reed continued to question him, but was careful not to sever the thread that kept him cooperative.

"Do you remember actually killing her, Joe?"

"I just killed her, Rick. I can't tell you more than that."

"Well, then, what did she die from, Joe? What caused her to die?" Reed hoped that Brown would have a better memory if he could put the death in different terms. He thought it might be easier for Brown to phrase it as "Ginger died from suffocation" instead of "I choked her to death." Telling the truth was usually a hard thing to do for someone who had run afoul of the law as often as Joe Brown had.

Brown thought a moment before answering.

"That, I really am not a hundred percent sure of. I spent the night with her on Tuesday night. She asked me to spend the night with her. We went to sleep because she had to get up early. She was working a lot of hours, ten to twelve hours every day, because, you know . . . she had a lot of bills to pay."

What Brown didn't say, but what the detectives had already guessed, was that most of the bills that Ginger had to pay were for things that Brown had wanted, things that he then took to sell for money with which to gamble.

"So I had the alarm set for three-thirty and we got

up," he continued. "Well, I actually got up about three o'clock. I always got up a little bit earlier. And we spent some private time together. And afterwards, she kind of went off, saying, 'I don't want you coming back around here no more' and all that," Brown said, mimicking Ginger's voice.

"And you know, 'Oh, by the way, me and Hobert slept together,' you know what I mean. And it just . . . it just . . . made me snap. I don't . . . I just remember looking down at her, and she was dead. I stayed there for a couple of hours, and kept looking out the window because I didn't know what to do."

Brown went on to explain that he knew he had to get rid of the body, so he drove around trying to think about what to do. He hadn't planned on cutting her up. The idea just came to him while he was driving around.

Up to now, Brown had refused to allow any of his statements to be recorded, and he still had not signed any paperwork. Despite that, he decided that he wanted to confess his crime publicly. Brown may have thought that a public statement now might help in his defense strategy later. It would be hard to find an unprejudiced jury if the news media already announced that Joe Brown was guilty. He announced that he wanted to call a television station, and he wanted to do it right then.

Desperate to get Brown to aid him in tracking down Ginger's body parts, Reed consented to his request.

Brown used Reed's cell phone to call CBS-WEVV Channel 44 news reporter Julie Knabel. He told her how he killed Ginger, dismembered her body, and then disbursed the pieces throughout three counties in southern Indiana. Brown told Knabel that he did it to get money to support his gambling habit. During the televised news report, Brown said that for three days after her slaying, he had gambled away all of Ginger's money.

When they reached the Indiana state border, the Kentucky state trooper turned around and headed back to his barracks. Once they were in their home state, Nelson, Reed, and Brown were on their own. The Indiana State Police had declined to give them an escort, saying, "We don't do that kind of thing."

Nelson just grinned and said, "Well, then, they had better stay out of the way."

For the remainder of the trip, Brown explained his relationships with Ginger, his family, her family, and his previous time in prison. Then he closed his eyes and tried to get some sleep.

The closer the men got to Evansville, the less Brown would attempt to doze. He seemed suddenly to be energized, more animated in his descriptions of the locations he would take them to.

He explained that he had worked as a bricklayer since he got out of prison in 1995, and that a lot of the jobs he'd done were out in the rural areas in the tri-state area. He also used to hunt and fish in some of these same areas, so it was easy for him to find the places where he had secreted the parts from Ginger's corpse.

Getting the apartment cleaned and cleared of incriminating evidence had proven to be painstaking and time-consuming. Brown said it had taken him most of a day to cut her up, bag all the body parts, and then start the cleaning up of blood and other items he thought might be evidence against him.

Nelson slowed as the car approached the exit ramp for US Highway 57. Brown sat straight in his seat, hands clamped in his lap, nose literally stuck to the car's window as he stared at the sight just to the north of the interstate.

He swallowed nervously and sat, white-knuckled, staring at the mix of SUVs, marked and unmarked police cars, and pickup trucks covering the weed-grown lot of the abandoned gas station.

"Is all that for me?" Brown asked nervously, but with a hint of pride in his voice.

Reed and Nelson looked at the mass of vehicles and people spread out across the huge truck stop parking lot. The "little something" that Captain Grace had put together amounted to nearly fifty police units from Vanderburgh, Gibson, Warrick, and Posey Counties. There were twenty-seven units on the scene from Evansville alone. This did not include the vehicles, people, and dogs that comprised the Emergency Management Agency (EMA) Search and Rescue Teams, which would assist in the search with their cadaver dogs.

"All these guys are here to help you find Ginger," Reed responded.

Brown nodded his understanding, never taking his nose from the window glass, as Nelson slid smoothly into the crowded parking lot in search of the Crime Scene commander, Captain Clayton Grace.

TWENTY-TWO

Warrick County

Crime Scene Unit technician Tony Walker began working on the scene at Hatfield at about 10:30 A.M. on September 4. It was now nearly 2:00 A.M. on September 5, and he found himself in the parking lot of the abandoned Moto Mart gas station, near I-64, waiting for the arrival of the prisoner from Ohio.

Deputy Chief Fehrenbacher and Captain Grace instructed several Crime Scene Unit officers to accompany Nelson and Reed to the locations that Brown had agreed to show them.

He didn't have long to wait before the detectives' unmarked vehicle appeared on I-64, and slowed down to turn onto the ramp that led to US Highway 57 North. As the car continued in the parking lot, a hush came over the crowd of law enforcement and rescue workers gathered there. This was what they had all waited for.

After a quick meeting between Fehrenbacher, Grace, and the arriving detectives, CSU officer Walker and Sergeant Kim Booker were called over to discuss the next move.

Booker had been at the scene at Hatfield for most of the day, as had several other CSU officers, but it had been her job to coordinate the activities and schedules of the officers that were assigned to this unit. Traditionally, Evansville had been a quiet town with one of the lowest homicide rates in the entire nation. With a population of more than 110,000 people in the city limits, the average of less than ten homicides a year was something to be proud of. But police budgets were based on assumptions, as were most large-company budgets. That meant that there were not enough supplies, manpower, or other resources to work a case of this magnitude without stretching the limits a little. The overtime pay for this "little something," which had been put together hastily, would undoubtedly eat up the overtime money for the rest of the year, and then some.

After surprisingly little discussion, it was decided that Booker and Walker would accompany the two detectives and Joe Brown into Warrick County, where they would attempt to locate and collect the first of Ginger Gasaway's remains. As these items were located, the CSU officers would be left behind with the remains to document and collect them.

Lieutenant Terry Brooks and the rest of the Crime Scene officers would remain at the abandoned gas station and wait for their turn to go on to the next counties that would need to be searched for missing body parts. Brown indicated that only the torso of the victim was in Warrick County, and that the other body parts were in Gibson and Posey Counties.

Several of the search-and-rescue teams would accompany the vehicle holding Joe Brown. Their cadaver-trained dogs would be needed to search in the pitch blackness along the farm fields and wooded areas, where Joe Brown would lead them.

The first caravan of men and dogs left the gas station at 2:30 A.M. and headed toward Warrick County. They drove east on I-64 to I-164, a tributary that connected I-64 with US Highway 41, south of Evansville. They drove south to Boonville-New Harmony Road, then east to Zoar Road. It wasn't long before the lights of the freeway were lost to the night, and the men were directed by Brown to turn north onto Gander Road.

Gander is a dead-end road that runs along the edge of the Ayrshire Mine stripper pits. This area had been mined for coal for countless years, had been reclaimed, and was now rolling hills and small lakes that made for great fishing. The area was about as secluded as you could get without leaving the planet.

The caravan stopped along the edge of the gravel road and waited for Brown to gain his bearings.

The detectives removed Brown from the vehicle and walked on either side of him as he shuffled along in his ankle chains and handcuffs. Brown veered off the gravel road into the high grass to the east. Peering into the dark, he motioned that what the men were looking for was just ahead.

"She's right over there," Brown said in an almost reverent tone. "About twenty feet out. She was in a hamper, and I pitched it as far as I could."

He was speaking of Ginger's headless and limbless torso. Brown had explained to Reed that he had put the torso in plastic bags, and put that down in the wicker clothes hamper from Ginger's bathroom.

The detectives waited in the dark, each holding on to one of Brown's arms, as Walker and Booker shone their powerful flashlights down the hillside of tall grass and brambles.

Walker spotted something white sticking up in the tall grass and made his way down the hill toward it.

"I have something here!" Walker yelled.

Everyone's attention focused in his direction.

Fehrenbacher and Grace joined the two detectives as Walker announced that he had found the wicker hamper, but the torso was missing. Booker almost reached Walker's position when he announced that he had found the torso.

Walker came back up the hill at a trot and headed for his vehicle to retrieve a camera, while Booker remained in the vicinity of the find.

"Her body must have come out of the hamper. It looks like it rolled down the hill a little ways, but it's still in the plastic bag," Walker said.

"Is there anything else down there, Joe?" Reed asked.

Brown's orange one-piece jail outfit fluoresced, backlit as it was by the vehicle's headlights. He swallowed hard, his gaze directed someplace in the night. His nervousness could be felt like a tangible thing through the darkness.

"Nothing, Rick. There's nothing else there, just the body, I mean her torso . . . or whatever . . . you know."

Walker asked Brown a few questions about clothing and other items that may be in the area, and he was told some rags might have also been in the hamper.

Brown was then led back to the detectives' vehicle.

Walker went to his car to retrieve camera equipment and bright orange flags to mark the two locations for later Global Positioning Satellite (GPS) readings. When it was daylight, aerial photos would be taken by using those readings. There was no other way to document the locations of the body parts because there was no permanent stationary item to measure the distance from, such as a telephone pole or a road intersection.

Detectives had to get Brown back to Lebanon, Ohio, by eleven o'clock in the morning, so time was of the essence. Only a small amount of time could be spent at the location searching Warrick County for other discarded items.

Booker and Walker remained behind with the Warrick County coroner to collect the torso of Ginger Gasaway. This would be taken to the Vanderburgh County

Coroner's Office, where the Evansville court would have legal jurisdiction over the murder case.

Lieutenant Brooks, of the Crime Scene Unit, arrived at the Warrick County scene and began taking GPS readings. While there, searchers located several other objects, including a black car mat, a washcloth, a towel, and a pillowcase that appeared to be bloodstained. Brown had used these in the hamper to attempt to soak up blood as he transported the torso in the front seat of the Mustang.

Under Brown's direction, the detectives worked their way through the twists and turns of the country roads, back to I-64, and headed toward the abandoned gas station once again. A second caravan of police and search-and-rescue workers were lined up on the entrance ramp to the interstate. They fell in behind the detectives' car en route to Posey County.

Posey County

The caravan picked up additional Posey County sheriff's units as it sped west on I-64. It was hard to mistake the satisfaction dripping from Brown's voice as he gave directions and filled the detectives in on more of his history with Ginger Gasaway, and his reasons for murdering her.

Brown looked out his window at the lights of a truck stop at the southwest corner of the intersection of I-64 and US Highway 65. The stretch of highway appeared deserted at this time of morning. There was no sign of other cars on the road or in the gas station lot.

"Ginger tried to have me arrested here, back in 1999," Brown said. He sounded almost nostalgic, as if he were reminiscing a good memory, and not remembering the aftereffects of his beating of Ginger a year earlier.

Brown had fled to Las Vegas after he had beaten Ginger unconscious. He thought that he had left her for dead on the floor of the laundry room at the Embassy Apartments. He was surprised to hear that she had survived. He was happy that she was alive and he then started a new campaign of terror with repeated calls from Las Vegas. First he would threaten her and then he would beg her to take him back. She finally told him that she would meet him to talk things over. Ginger immediately called the Vanderburgh County Sheriff Department and arranged for Brown to be arrested in the parking lot of the very same gas station that Joe now pointed out as they drove by.

Brown snorted with humor as he related to the detectives how the sheriff's "souped-up" pursuit vehicles were no match for his Mustang, regaling them with tales of how he had gotten away.

Reed and Nelson also looked at the gas station, but the memory for them was of a homicide and robbery in the mid-1990s. In that incident, two young men and a juvenile female had gone to the station late one night. While the young woman waited behind the wheel of the getaway car, the two men went in and robbed Charlie Simpson, the service station attendant, with a stolen pistol.

Simpson had cooperated fully, but one of the young men turned back at the doorway as they left, took the handgun from his friend, then ran back to the attendant and shot him until the pistol was empty.

"No witnesses," he had told his horrified friend.

Simpson was fifty-five years old. His assailant was nineteen, and the other two accomplices were eighteen and seventeen. A customer who witnessed the murder fled toward an outside pay phone to call the police. As he ran in horror, the teenage gunman pursued him and tried to shoot him with the now-empty weapon. This one man survived to help sheriff's deputies identify the robbers. All three of them were given hefty sentences, with the shortest sentence, of thirty years, given to the seventeen-year-old female.

Brown was so lost in thought that he forgot to tell the detectives to take the ramp that turned north onto US Highway 65. The caravan had to turn back to gain the exit. Once on the highway, Brown directed the men down a series of blacktop and gravel roads to an area about one thousand feet south of Poseyville Road.

This area was bordered with cornfields and a ten-foot-deep ditch on one side of the road. There was about two feet of water in the ditch, and it was to this area that Brown pointed. He told the detectives that there were some items in the water. Crime Scene and search-and-rescue workers found a cardboard box containing a bloodstained T-shirt and a quantity of newspapers lying in the ditch. They also found some unused black trash bags and an empty Hefty box.

About nine hundred feet south of Poseyville Road, along the wooded edge of a cornfield, searchers found two black plastic trash bags that held the discarded arms and legs of Ginger Gasaway.

As Brown hobbled along the dirt track between cornfields, he continued to answer questions posed to him by the detectives. He told Reed that he had been working all day to dismember Ginger's body and transfer the pieces from her apartment to the Mustang. He explained that he deposited her body parts into plastic trash bags, and then put the bags into boxes, which he then carried to the car.

This part of Brown's confession matched the observations of Crime Scene technician Ben Gentry, who accompanied the men that night in search of evidence. Gentry prepared a police supplement in which he wrote that officers found two plastic trash bags on the east side of the farm access road, and approximately nine hundred feet south of North Poseyville Road. The bags contained what appeared to be human remains.

The report also stated that searchers on the west side of the road found a cardboard box containing a stained T-shirt and a quantity of newspapers, some unused black trash bags, and an empty Hefty box, which were all collected as possible items of evidence.

Brown continued to explain that he put the body parts in the car, but had to make several trips from the apartment to the car to load them all. This took place at about 2:00 A.M., following the murder. Brown had spent most of the day severing Ginger's limbs, packaging them, and cleaning up. After he had everything in the car, he drove to Posey County.

It was in Posey County that Brown disposed of the arms, legs, boxes, other clothing, and bloody items. He was careful not to dump the body parts too close to any of the other items, in case they were found. He was confident that the body parts would never be discovered.

Brown said that he traveled to Gibson County to dispose of the head and other items, and then on to Warrick County, where he got rid of the torso last.

The remains found in Posey County were photographed, documented in detail, then collected and transported to the Vanderburgh County Morgue by John Werry, Posey County coroner.

The reason that all of the body parts that were found in Posey, Gibson, and Warrick Counties were taken to the Vanderburgh County Coroner's Office was not because the murder happened in Evansville, which is in Vanderburgh County.

In the late 1970s, these four counties' coroners had a meeting to discuss building a modern morgue. None of the counties had enough money to attempt such a venture independently. So, they pooled their resources, built the current Vanderburgh County Coroner's Office, in Evansville, for about $300,000, and hired a full-time forensic pathologist, Dr. John Heidingsfelder, to perform the autopsies. Autopsies for all four counties were performed in this facility as a result of that partnership.

Dr. Heidingsfelder had an excellent reputation as a forensic pathologist. He would have his work cut out for him when all of the body parts were found, collected, and transported to his morgue. It was his responsibility to prove that all of the parts came from the same body, and that the body could unquestionably be identified as Ginger Gasaway.

Gibson County

Joe Brown's uncanny sense of direction led detectives as they traveled north on US Highway 65, crossing from Posey into Gibson County. He advised the men that he knew these counties so well that he could travel them with his eyes closed.

Brown appeared to be in an almost jovial mood, feeling important. He had been instrumental in finding the torso, arms, and legs, and now he led the caravan of searchers to locate another precious piece of evidence: Ginger's head.

He confided to Reed that the next location they would travel to was close to where Ginger's daughter Misty lived. Reed wanted to ask if this was on purpose, but he didn't want to risk alienating Brown, and losing his cooperation.

"You didn't get along with Misty very well, did you, Joe?" Reed asked. This was a roundabout way of asking the question. If Brown didn't want to talk, he wouldn't push the issue.

"She hated me . . . you know," Brown said. He had earlier expressed hatred of Ginger's entire family, but now he seemed to have softened a little. Maybe he was beginning to realize what he had done to that family.

Brown told the detectives that he didn't have anything against Ginger's daughters. He said that he understood why they didn't accept him being a part of Ginger's life, because to them, it probably looked like he had come between Ginger and Hobert. He then answered the question that Reed wanted to ask. It wasn't his intention to leave Ginger's head near Misty's house. He wasn't quite sure why he went to that spot. He claimed to be in a panic while he was disposing of the remains, but he had been calm enough to try and clean the blood trail from the steps and walkway in front of the apartment before leaving.

Whatever his reason for placing the decapitated head where he did, it seemed odd to Reed that Brown would be the one to bring up the fact that Misty lived nearby the dump site.

Brown pointed to a cemetery at the top of a hill.

"Turn right there," he said, and the convoy of cars each followed in suit, heading east toward the small town of Fort Branch.

Local farmers primarily used the road. After only a hundred yards or so, it turned from blacktop to gravel. The car crunched along in the gravel for another hundred yards when Brown called for Nelson to slow down, and asked that his window be rolled down.

Nelson slowed and Brown kept a constant watch out his window looking toward the north. That side of the road was lined with tall brush and saplings, and a three-foot-deep ditch as well.

"You just passed it," he announced.

Detective Nelson backed up the car until an opening in the brush appeared on that side. A concrete culvert covered with dirt and gravel was lying in the ditch. Through the darkness, a dirt path, the width of a car, could just be made out.

"Pull in there," Brown directed.

Nelson had to keep one set of the car's tires on top of the deep ruts to keep the vehicle from bottoming out on the middle of the path. In the darkness, it appeared that both sides of this makeshift road were covered with chest-high weeds and grass, but in the daylight, it was found to be a pasture of wild wheat.

The car bumped and lurched along the path for about five hundred feet before Brown leaned forward and indicated that they should stop.

As Brown was taken from the car, Evansville Crime Scene officers, search-and-rescue members, and a Gibson County detective came forward to assist in the search.

Reed looked ahead in the direction that Brown led them. The high weeds diffused the bright headlights of the vehicles, so the men had to maneuver by moonlight and flashlights.

The men emerged out of the grass, just at the edge of what appeared to be a dense growth of shrubs and young trees. Brown came to an abrupt halt just at the edge of this wooded area. He seemed to be struggling to find his voice, and Reed realized that Brown was overcome with emotions.

"She's right over there," he said, motioning with a nod that what they were looking for was directly in front of them. He then collapsed to his knees and began to weep.

"I'm so sorry. . . . I'm so sorry," he repeated, over and over, in a hoarse, sobbing voice as searchers fanned out in front of the detectives and began to search in the dense foliage.

In less than a minute, one of the Evansville Crime Scene officers yelled, "I've got something here!"

More searchers called out, and the beams of their flashlights swept over more items of evidence. They found items in two separate areas on each side of the roadway.

It was in the wooded area to the west of the roadway that the first item was found. This was a black plastic bag that contained a large butcher knife. Its blade was encrusted with blood. There were also pieces of bloodstained carpet and padding, and a pair of scissors. A hill sloped downward to the west, where a small creek flowed. It was along this decline, approximately ten feet from the plastic bag and knife, that Ginger's head was located.

Although it had only been five days since her death, the head was little more than a bare skull. Typically, that degree of decomposition would not take place that soon. But warm weather, open exposure, and the number of animals and insects in that area sped up the process. Another large knife was found near the skull.

On the east side of the roadway, a large cardboard box was found to contain more carpet padding in a black plastic bag.

By the time it was verified that Ginger's head was located, Nelson and Reed had already loaded Brown back into the car and were heading to Warrick County.

Reed tried to draw Brown back into a conversation, but he was not in a mood to talk.

"We're going back to Warrick County again, Joe," Reed said at last. "I need you to show me where the reciprocating saw is. Okay, Joe?"

Without looking at the detective, Brown nodded and then stared out the window into the darkness.

TWENTY-THREE

Warrick County

As they drove down one gravel road after another, Brown would periodically tell them to stop, but then shake his head as if confused, and they would proceed. In the end, they did find the yellow metal box that the reciprocating saw had been purchased in, but the tool itself was never found.

During a final sweep of Warrick County, numerous other items were located, including bloody rags, sheets, boxes, and miscellaneous pieces of clothing. Some of these had been thrown off the roadside into fields of high grass and brush, and others were thrown in cornfields and stripper-pit lakes. None of these items would have raised any alarm or concern from innocent passersby.

Over the next several weeks, fire department divers searched four stripper-pit lakes and several smaller ponds, all with no success. It seemed odd to the detectives that Brown could be so exact in locating ten different body parts spread over three counties, but was unable to tell them where he had disposed of the power tool. Over the years following this case, detectives searched police databases of pawnshop transactions, but whatever Brown did with the reciprocating saw, he didn't dispose of it in any way that it could be tracked.

While Nelson and Reed drove Brown over a fifty-square-mile area to search for human remains and other bloody evidence of mayhem, other detectives diligently worked to take care of the things that are usually done behind the scenes. These are the jobs that don't make headline news, or bring praise and awards. The day-to-day tedium of real police work, of criminal investigations, is mostly paperwork, telephone calls, and typing endless reports.

Detectives made arrangements to bring the red 1993 Mustang back to Evansville from the Ohio State Police garage in Lebanon. Others were busy documenting the statements of potential witnesses that had been found in the neighborhood around Hatfield Drive, taking phone calls from other possible witnesses, and collecting bits and pieces of information that may or may not be important to the case at hand.

Grace and Fehrenbacher prepared for the next steps in the investigation, including the coordination of activities, and reporting protocol for four county sheriff departments, several city police departments, and fire and rescue K-9 teams and divers. It was a massive effort, and would end up costing the city of Evansville a small fortune in overtime pay alone. Whole yearly budgets for overtime and evidence-testing costs were eaten up by this single case.

They searched until the first rays of daylight peeked over the horizon. It was time to go. Joe Brown was due in court, in Ohio, in less than seven hours.

All things considered, the trip had been successful. The detectives should have been proud of their work, but the things they had seen and heard over the last fifteen hours—the things that nightmares were made of—would remain with them forever.

Nelson and Reed drove Joe Brown back to Evansville

to prepare for the return trip to Warren County, Ohio. Brown had napped in the car for most of the forty-five-minute drive to Evansville Police Headquarters. Once at the station house, the men offered to get Brown something to eat from the kitchen at the jail, but Brown declined. All he wanted was a cup of hot coffee and a cigarette.

Captain Grace advised Nelson and Reed that the Indiana State Police offered their lightplane to transport Brown back to Ohio, and that the detectives would have time to talk to him before they had to leave.

After a short smoke break and a cup of coffee on the back steps of the Detectives Office, Joe was taken back to one of the interview rooms, where he was asked to give a statement. Through clenched teeth, Brown reminded them that he had already told them several times that he wouldn't give a statement, or sign a Miranda rights form, until he was brought back to Evansville for good.

Reed was exhausted from the sheer mental stress of the last eighteen hours, and he looked forward to the short hop from Evansville to Cincinnati by airplane. That was when Captain Grace advised that the state police would not be able to fly them to Ohio, but two fresh detectives would make the drive back to Ohio with Reed and their prisoner. Reed would be needed in circuit court in Ohio to testify at the extradition proceedings.

Detective Corporals Mike Cook and Ray Schapker waited with the engine running as Reed escorted Brown to the car. Brown was obviously tired, but he would get to sleep the entire drive. Reed hoped to take advantage of some of that time as well. Nelson stayed behind.

At about 6:30 A.M., the men left for the return trip to Lebanon, Ohio. The goal was to get Joe Brown to the Warren County Correctional Facility before eleven o'clock. He would then be taken directly to court.

The detectives had come to the outskirts of Cincinnati, and were only ten miles from Lebanon, when Reed received a call on his cell phone. It was Captain Grace. He wanted to make sure that Brown had been read his Miranda warnings.

Reed assured the captain that Brown understood his rights, and reminded him that Brown had been read the rights statement on the videotape that the Ohio State Police had given them. Grace asked Reed to read them to Joe again before they went any farther.

As luck would have it, none of the detectives in the vehicle were in possession of a Miranda form. Reed had a Miranda rights pocket card to read the exact wording of these rights from, but didn't have any paperwork with him. The other detectives didn't bring any forms or their briefcases.

Reed explained their situation and restated that they were barely going to make it to the lockup on time if they hurried. Captain Grace asked if they had met with Sergeant Ertel yet, and Reed advised that they had pulled in behind him about five miles back. Grace ordered Reed to ask Sergeant Ertel for a Miranda form. Apparently, the Vanderburgh County prosecutor had called Captain Grace and strongly suggested that this be done.

Ertel was reached by cell phone, and he directed the Evansville detectives to pull off the highway at the next exit ramp. Once they pulled their cars over, Ertel provided Reed with an Ohio State Police Miranda form. Brown laughed as Reed brought the form back to the car and started to read it to him.

"I told you, I ain't signing anything until we get back to Evansville," he said.

"I know that, Joe, but I have to do this. You heard my part of the conversation. But if you refuse, I have to write 'refused' where your signature would normally go. You understand?"

Brown said he did, and leaned back again to nap.

Reed wrote the word "refused" for Brown's signature, and they were off again to the corrections facility. The entire delay had taken less than ten minutes. But those ten minutes had made them five minutes late for their appearance in front of the judge. The hearing was now postponed until one o'clock that afternoon, and Reed was worried about how the delay might affect the extradition.

The Warren County Government Center was bustling with activity. Brown was taken into the jail to get a meal before court, since it would be two hours before he would be taken in front of the judge.

Ertel offered to take the visiting Evansville detectives to a restaurant near the judicial center. The men finished their meal in time to get a tour of the Warren County Judicial Complex, and Ertel explained that the buildings were completed in 1979. They looked much newer.

There was an air of efficiency in the movements of the employees inside. It surprised the Evansville detectives when their case was called first. In Evansville courts, police were always the last cases called. It was nothing to arrive for court at eight in the morning and get finished at four in the afternoon.

Brown's extradition hearing was a matter of three or four questions directed by the judge, first to Brown, and then to Reed. The entire process took less than fifteen minutes. In another thirty minutes, the men were driving toward Evansville with Joe Brown in their custody.

Brown had surprisingly little personal property. Most of his things had been left in the red Mustang convertible, and that was loaded on the flatbed wrecker, which now traveled in front of them as they sped toward Evansville.

Reed felt like someone had sprinkled rock salt into his eyes, but he had to remain awake and try to get as much information from Brown while it was still possible. The drive home would take longer than their previous trips, partly because they no longer had a police escort, but also because there was no longer a need to rush.

Brown alternated staring out the window and resting his chin on his chest as he dozed. No one would ever know the thoughts that ran through his mind as he was taken to Evansville to answer charges for one of the most vicious murders that had ever been committed in southern Indiana.

The brutality of Brown's crime made him eligible for the death penalty, and could land him on death row at Michigan City, Indiana. At the time, there were twenty-five convicted murderers on Indiana's death row awaiting the enforcement of their sentence. There have been one hundred death sentences handed down in Indiana courts since 1977, with only eleven of those sentences carried out. Of those, two were executed by other states while they appealed their death sentences in Indiana.

Brown believed he would get the death penalty, and had mentioned this several times during the trip back to Evansville. But Reed believed differently. Even if a jury sentenced Brown to death, it still would be up to the judge to decide the prisoner's fate. The judge would have to weigh what were called extenuating and mitigating circumstances.

The mitigating factors were that Brown had led investigators to Ginger's remains. It was his cooperation that brought closure to the investigation and eventually to Ginger's family and friends.

On the other hand, in Brown's case, the extenuating circumstances were that Brown not only murdered Ginger, but he proceeded to dismember her body, and then tossed her away like human garbage. Added to the current murder charge was the fact that Brown stole money from Ginger's banking account after he murdered her. Also, Brown had spent much of his teen and postteen years in prison for various felonies—some violent, some not. This fact alone would enhance any sentence that he received, making it much harsher than someone with a minor past or none at all.

Reed had just been thinking these things when Brown turned toward him and said, "My life is over, Rick. Levco will kill me."

He was referring to the Vanderburgh County prosecutor, Stan Levco. For some reason, Brown had focused on Levco as his enemy. He had the mistaken idea that it was Stan Levco who had been the special judge in Princeton, Indiana, when he had received his first life sentence in 1977 for the robbery and kidnapping of Joe Bender.

In fact, at one point during the return trip to Evansville, Brown shook with rage, and he said that Levco wouldn't have the pleasure of having him found guilty in a trial because he was going to plead guilty right away.

He then asked if he had to be housed in the jail at Vanderburgh County. He explained that he had a problem in that jail before, and would like to be housed somewhere else. This was a small thing to ask under the circumstances, and Reed called the sheriff of Posey County, Melvin Buchanan, to see if he had an objection to housing Brown there until this was over. Sheriff Buchanan didn't hesitate to agree to put Brown up if Vanderburgh County had no objections.

Vanderburgh County sheriff Brad Ellsworth did not mind if Brown was taken somewhere other than his jail. In fact, given the amount of news attention the case had already received, he preferred that Brown be housed somewhere else.

After checking with Deputy Chief David Fehrenbacher

for final permission, an agreement was reached that either Vanderburgh County deputies or Evansville police detectives would be responsible for transporting Brown to and from court in Vanderburgh County. It was decided that Brown would be housed in the Posey County Correctional Facility.

When Reed told Brown that he would be able to stay in the jail at Posey County, he made special mention that this wasn't a favor or a condition for Brown to give a full statement. Brown could still remain quiet if he so chose. It is a requirement of law that for a statement to be given voluntarily and freely, it cannot be forced, threatened, or coerced.

TWENTY-FOUR

When they arrived back at Evansville Police Headquarters, Brown agreed to make a tape-recorded statement. Brown was read his Miranda rights once again and finally signed the form. Nelson was also present for the statement. Brown admitted to strangling and then dismembering Ginger's body. He confessed that he knew what he was doing, but he could not explain why he dismembered her. He said "he just did it." He said that he killed her because he snapped when he found out that she had been seeing her ex-husband again. He said that he had a bad gambling habit and probably spent about $50,000 of Ginger's money after her death on gambling. He also said that he had gone to the casino boats in Tunica, Mississippi, and also to the boat in New Albany.

Reed sat down with Brown and turned on the recorder. He announced the date of recording as September 5, 2000, and then began his questioning.

"When did you kill Ginger Gasaway?" Reed asked.

"I killed her Wednesday morning, about four o'clock."

"And then what did you do after that?"

"I got in the car . . . took off. I drove around trying to figure out what to do and . . . I knew . . . I had to get rid of her. I didn't know how . . . and it was done too late. I came back and I thought maybe . . . maybe it didn't happen. But it did happen. You know?"

"Do you know when you came back with the car?"

"It was about eight o'clock or eight-thirty. I went back up to the apartment and she was dead. I sat down there, and you might think it nuts, but . . . you know . . . I talked to her. She was dead . . . you know what I mean. I went to Home Depot, bought me a saw, and chopped her up. I just sat there. I sat in that apartment for three or four hours because I never hurt nobody in my whole life. It was like I was there, but yet I wasn't there. I just . . . I just hacked her up like a piece of meat. Just like . . . I don't know."

"The initial struggle, where did that occur? Was it in the bedroom?" Reed asked.

"There was no struggle to it," Brown replied.

He then said that Ginger weighed at least 150 pounds, and that he knew he couldn't carry her down the steps without being seen.

Brown continued to profess ignorance of how he killed Ginger, only stating that he must have strangled her. This would be his continuing story throughout the investigation, and all the way up until he was reinterviewed in September 2003. (In those interviews, he would tell Sergeant Reed that he had planned on killing Ginger after she kicked him out of their shared apartment in August. He had gotten wind that she planned on getting back together with her ex-husband, Hobert. In that statement, he claimed to have tortured Ginger Gasaway for hours before finally strangling her to death with his hands. Cutting her up had been an act of desperation. He knew that if Ginger was found strangled, the trail would lead to him first. He decided that he would have to dispose of her in a way that she would never be found.)

Brown changed the sequence of how he disposed of Ginger's body parts during his taped statement. Now he said that he disposed of the legs, arms, and head first, leaving the torso behind in the apartment. It wasn't until the next morning that he returned to the apartment for the torso.

After the interview, Reed contacted Posey County sheriff Mel Buchanan, and he agreed to house Brown. Evansville police detectives Fleck and Hailman transported Brown to the jail in Posey County. He would need to be picked up early in the morning for a nine-thirty arraignment hearing in Vanderburgh County.

The next morning, Nelson and Reed arrived at the Posey County facility at about six o'clock to pick up Brown and take him back to Evansville. Once again, he was manacled and the short chain between his ankles made him appear to be dancing a jig as he was led to the unmarked Ford Crown Vic.

It was still early as the men headed toward Evansville. Their intention was to turn Brown over to the Vanderburgh County Jail staff to be processed for court, but Brown had other plans. As they neared the city limits, he told the detectives that he could show them where more items were hidden.

Reed and Nelson exchanged an inquiring look. Brown hadn't actually been charged in court yet. He still didn't have an attorney, so technically they could still obtain information from him. They read Joe his Miranda rights again, as a precautionary measure, and proceeded on to Warrick County.

In Campbell Township, where Zoar Road dead-ends into Gander Road, Warrick County deputies and Evansville Crime Scene investigators met with Brown to narrow their search area. The stripper pits and reclaimed coal-mining land, which now was farm fields, covered many square miles, and for them to find anything of consequence would be a matter of luck without Brown's assistance.

Officer Shawn Clark, Sergeant Kim Booker, Lieutenant

Terry Brooks, and Officer Tony Walker had already searched much of the area without success. With Brown's guidance, the group was able to negotiate the maze of unimproved roads and go directly to the empty yellow metal box that once contained the reciprocating saw that Brown used to dismember Ginger's body. They also located several bags of clothing that belonged to both Joe and Ginger. Some of these items were still on hangers, covered in plastic, and bearing the tag from the dry cleaners.

Clark and Booker searched through a cornfield, where Brown said he had discarded more items, and located a woman's black leather handbag. One of the items inside the purse was a recent restraining order that Ginger had obtained against Joe Brown in Vanderburgh County Superior Court.

The search of the Warrick County area continued until the late evening, and again for several more days, but was performed by other investigators, because at nine-thirty that morning it was time to have Brown in court. The one item that investigators and Crime Scene officers had hoped to find—the reciprocating saw—was never discovered.

Arriving at the Vanderburgh County Jail, it was difficult for the detectives to turn Brown over to the waiting deputies. There was still so much they didn't know, so many questions they wanted to ask. But as officers of the legal system, their duty was to bring Joe Brown before a judge at the first available opportunity.

TWENTY-FIVE

September 6, 2000

This was Joe Brown's first appearance in an Indiana court for the murder charges, but it was only a preliminary hearing. The purpose of the hearing was to decide the appointment of defense counsel, present a formal reading of the charges, enter a preliminary plea of guilty or not guilty, and decide if bond would be set.

The preliminary plea in a case that could include the death penalty was almost always assumed to be not guilty. Bond would also be a moot point at this stage. Except in the rarest of situations, there's no bond for murder.

Brown would be appointed a public defender to expedite the hearing. If Brown, or his family, could afford their own attorney later, they would be encouraged to do so. In this case, that would never occur. Brown's family remained as invisible as they had been most of his life, and his sister Jennie would become a witness for the state's case against Joe.

Although the case was not routine, it's safe to say that almost everyone in the courtroom had an assumption that the day's proceedings would follow the normal pattern. The expectation was that Brown would sit

The house where Joe Brown was brought up in Cynthiana,
Indiana is now owned by another family and has been renovated.
(Photo by Steven Walker)

Joe Brown in
1969 as an
eighth-grade
student at North
Posey Middle
School.
(Yearbook photo)

Joseph Brown

In ninth grade, Joe Brown was on the North Posey High School basketball team. He is standing in the back row, third from the right. *(Yearbook photo)*

Hobert, Ginger, Lisa, and Misty Gasaway during happier times on Christmas, 1975. *(Photo courtesy of Dan Stewart)*

Carleen Brown's 1970 death was ruled accidental after she was found in her bathtub by her son, Joe Brown. *(Photo by Steven Walker)*

Beside Joe Brown's mother's grave are the graves of his brother, Michael, who died in 1974 while Joe was incarcerated for auto theft, and Joe's father, Gerald, who was found in his truck with a self-inflicted gunshot wound to the head. *(Photo by Steven Walker)*

Joe Brown was given his first life sentence for kidnapping and robbing Joe Bender at this house in Southern Indiana.
(Photo by Steven Walker)

Joe Brown lived with his aunt and uncle, Sharon and Roger Brown, in this trailer after he was released from prison in 1995.
(Photo by Rick Reed)

Joe Brown holds a dog owned by his second wife, Mary Lou Seitz.
(Photo courtesy of Mary Lou Seitz)

Joe Brown claimed that he picked up Andrea Hendrix-Steinert
in October 1997 in front of Bear Transmission.
(Photo by Rick Reed)

Joe Brown said he was living at the Alpine Motel in Evansville,
Indiana in 1997 when he claims to have killed Andrea Hendrix-
Steinert. *(Photo by Rick Reed)*

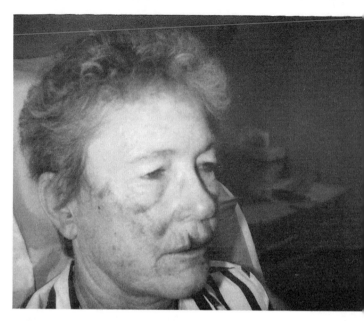

Ginger Gasaway was severely beaten by Joe Brown in September 1999 at the Embassy Apartments. *(Photo courtesy of Brad Evrard)*

Brenda Boyer, also known as "September," was an exotic dancer whom Joe Brown picked up for sex. He said that he felt sorry for her, and that she was "the one who got away." *(Photo by Rick Reed)*

The Exotic She Lounge is where Joe Brown picked up Brenda "September" Boyer in Evansville, Indiana. *(Photo by Steven Walker)*

The Casino Aztar riverboat in Evansville, Indiana, was one of the places where Joe Brown sometimes gambled. *(Photo by Rick Reed)*

A trail of blood was discovered leading from the second floor porch of Ginger Gasaway's apartment on Hatfield Drive. *(Photo courtesy of Evansville Police Department)*

Drops of blood left a trail from Ginger Gasaway's apartment to the parking lot below. *(Photo courtesy of Evansville Police Department)*

Notes from her daughter were left on Ginger Gasaway's apartment door stating that she would help Ginger move into a new apartment. *(Photo courtesy of Evansville Police Department)*

Ginger Gasaway had most of her belongings packed and ready to move when she was reported missing.
(Photo courtesy of Evansville Police Department)

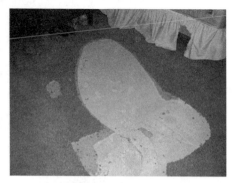

A piece of carpet was cut away and removed from Ginger Gasaway's bedroom. Police missed this clue during their first visit to the apartment. *(Photo courtesy of Evansville Police Department)*

Joe Brown passed several nonsufficient fund checks at financial institutions in and around Evansville, Indiana. This is the Fifth Third Bank in nearby Owensville. *(Photo by Steven Walker)*

Bank photo of Brown at Old National Bank shortly after Gasaway's murder. *(Courtesy of Old National Bank)*

This aerial photo shows the general location where Ginger Gasaway's head was found in Gibson County, Indiana.
(Photo courtesy of Evansville Police Department)

Crime Scene officer Shawn Clark collects Ginger Gasaway's purse from a cornfield in Warrick County.
(Photo courtesy of Evansville Police Department)

Ginger Gasaway at home with her daughter, Melissa, in Rockport, Indiana, in 1967. *(Photo courtesy of Hobert Gasaway)*

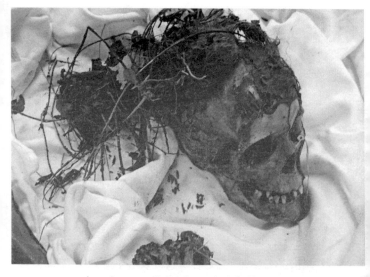

Police discovered the discarded skull and neck of Ginger Gasaway in Gibson County. *(Photo courtesy of Evansville Police Department)*

Vanderburgh County Prosecutor Stan Levco decided not to seek the death penalty against Joe Brown. *(Photo by Rick Reed)*

Evansville Detective Tony Mayhew was a lead investigator during Joe Brown's confessions in 2003. *(Photo by Rick Reed)*

Deputy Chief David Fehrenbacher, of the Evansville Police Department, looks over the case file during the investigation into Joe Brown's claims that he killed 13 women in addition to Ginger Gasaway. *(Photo by Rick Reed)*

Evansville Police Sergeant Rick Reed studies the Joe Brown case file. *(Photo courtesy of Jim Meyers, Evansville Police Department)*

Joe Brown is loaded into the back of a police van in preparation for his trip to show police where he claimed to have buried three of his victims. *(Photo by Rick Reed)*

Law enforcement officials stand by at the dig site in Posey County, looking for signs of human remains. *(Photo by Rick Reed)*

Joe Brown searches a field in Gibson County for the location where he claimed to have buried one of his victims. *(Photo by Rick Reed)*

Joe Brown is currently incarcerated in the Wabash Valley Correction Facility in Carlisle, Indiana, where he will spend the rest of his life. *(Photo by Rick Reed)*

quietly at his defense counsel's side as a plea of not guilty was entered, and a new hearing date would be set to discuss other related matters, such as the possibility of the death penalty's incorporation in the state's charges.

However, on that day, the gathered mass of news media and curious spectators were in for a treat.

Circuit Court judge Carl Heldt presided over the hearing. This case had drawn a lot of news interest, especially with the suspect calling a Channel 44 TV reporter and confessing on television. Added to that was the speculation by the news media as to why Joseph Weldon Brown was not being housed in Vanderburgh County.

Judge Heldt knew the answers to the media's questions. He was the judge that had been contacted at home to request that Brown be housed in Posey County. He also knew the reason for that request was because Posey County was Brown's home, and also because Brown had been cooperating in a murder investigation, and had expressed distaste for the Vanderburgh County Jail. Allowing him to be detained in Posey County was no problem.

The noise in the courtroom reached a crescendo and then fell silent as the bailiff stood and called, "All rise for the Honorable Judge Carl Heldt." After the judge was seated, the bailiff announced that court was in session and the courtroom took their seats.

Cameras are not allowed in Vanderburgh County courtrooms, but notepads were poised as Judge Heldt sat behind the massive oak desk and called for the first case.

Detectives Reed and Nelson sat at the prosecutor's table and watched as Joe Brown was led into the courtroom. His gait was less restricted now that the ankle chains were removed, but his movements were still jerky. He still wore handcuffs, but they were fixed in front of him without the encumbrance of the leather belt around his waist.

Prosecutor Stan Levco stood and stated, "Your Honor, the state would like to call the case of *State of Indiana* versus *Joseph Weldon Brown* on the charge of murder."

Attorney Barry Standley was seated at the defense table. He had been appointed as temporary defense counsel for this hearing just that morning, and had been given a short time before court to talk with Brown in a holding cell about his defense.

Standley leaned close and said something to Brown, who appeared to pay no attention to the attorney's words. Brown sat erect, facing the judge, his mouth set in a grim line.

When Judge Heldt asked Brown if he understood the charges that were brought against him, Brown put his hands firmly palm down on the defense table and looked the judge in the eyes.

"Your Honor, I'm guilty," he said matter-of-factly. "I killed her and I cut her up."

Standley turned in his seat and stared at his client as the courtroom filled with whispers. Judge Heldt interrupted Brown's confession, admonishing him to let his attorney speak on his behalf. But Brown would have none of that. He was guilty and he was going to have his say.

While Judge Heldt slammed his gavel down repeatedly, and called for order, Brown stood and continued his outburst.

"I'm guilty. I killed her. I don't need a trial. I killed her and cut her up," he repeated above the din.

Judge Heldt demanded that Brown be seated and remain quiet. Only after he threatened to clear the courtroom did it begin to quiet down.

Brown sat down, shook his head, and muttered, "This ain't right; this ain't right."

Standley had been in practice for more than thirty years and had defended numerous death penalty cases, but he admitted that he had never had a client quite like Joseph Brown before. It was as if Joe wanted to get the death penalty. He had sat helpless as his client committed legal suicide by declaring to a courtroom packed with media and spectators that he was guilty.

With the help of Judge Heldt, Brown had been contained for the moment. Standley entered the only plea that was possible in this case, and that was "not guilty." This plea was expected by the defense and prosecution because of a case in 1993, when the death penalty imposed on Vincent Prowell was overturned by the Indiana State Supreme Court because the suspect had been allowed to plead guilty without enough effort for a proper defense. It was because of the lingering effects of this case, which Reed was also involved in investigating, that the defense counsel and the court would not allow Joe Brown to plead guilty to the murder of Ginger Gasaway.

Then Judge Heldt appointed Standley to represent Brown for the remainder of the case. It was what he had expected.

There was no point in requesting bond in a capital-murder case. But the real question was whether the prosecutor, Stan Levco, would pursue the death penalty. If Brown continued this behavior, he would be very little help in his own defense.

Judge Heldt scheduled an omnibus date for November 21. This meant the court had set a deadline for the prosecutor to declare to the court if they are going to make any changes in the charges that were initially filed. In this case, this would be the latest date that the prosecutor could file the death penalty.

Judge Heldt also scheduled a holding date for November 10. In some counties, this was called a "readiness conference" and was an opportunity for the defense and prosecutor to get together and discuss the direction the case would take. In some cases, a plea negotiation could be worked out during the readiness conference.

The end of the hearing was anticlimactic as Judge Heldt ordered Brown to be held over without bond, and to continue his incarceration at the jail in Posey County.

At the back of the courtroom Standley approached Levco and the two detectives. He asked Reed and Nelson if they would take Brown back to the Posey County lockup. He rolled his eyes as he advised that Brown had requested them, but he also admonished them not to ask his client any questions without his presence.

The hearing itself was short, but the impact on the audience in the courtroom was obvious. This would be an interesting and newsworthy case. There have been numerous defendants in this courtroom that have caused quite a stir in the public eye, but none demanding to be sent to prison without the benefit of a trial.

The *Evansville Courier & Press* reported the next day that "a tearful Joseph W. Brown entered a Vanderburgh County courtroom Wednesday to face a murder charge, and begged a judge to let him plead guilty to 'get this all over with.' As Circuit Court Judge Carl Heldt repeatedly advised him to keep quiet, the 45-year-old Brown, who could face a death sentence for the slaying and dismemberment of 53-year-old Ginger Gasaway, rested his head on the defense table and wept."

In a superior court courtroom, at almost the exact same time as Joe Brown made his appearance in circuit court, deputy prosecutor Martha Posey made a motion on the state's behalf. The original charge that Brown was detained on by the Ohio State Police was a misdemeanor warrant for "failure to appear" on the September 1999 battery of Ginger Gasaway.

In that case, on September 9, 1999, a bench warrant was issued for Joe Brown and an alert was issued, which meant that a protective order was entered into the computer system on behalf of Ginger Gasaway and against Joseph Weldon Brown, ordering him to stay away from her or be in contempt of court. On September 28, 1999, Brown was apprehended on this warrant and pleaded guilty on October 27, 1999.

At the sentencing hearing on this battery charge, Brown formally pleaded guilty to battery and invasion of privacy, both misdemeanor charges. He was sentenced to a $50 fine and 180 days in the Vanderburgh County Jail for each count. The jail portion of the sentence was suspended on two conditions. The first condition was that Joe Brown would attend anger-management-counseling sessions with the Drug and Alcohol Intervention Program, which administered several other programs besides just treating alcohol abuse. The second condition was that Brown had to stay away from Ginger Gasaway permanently. It was noted that a protective order against him was already in place. There would be a review of his progress in this sentencing on November 24, 1999.

On November 24, 1999, Brown appeared in court, but he asked for more time to pay the fine and to attend the anger management classes. His request was granted and the matter was set for review on January 5, 2000. On that date, Brown again asked for a continuance and it was further deferred until March 8, 2000. On that date, it was again deferred at Brown's request until May 10, 2000, and yet again until July 26, 2000.

Apparently, by July 26, 2000, Joe Brown didn't believe there would be any forthcoming punishment if he failed to appear at his hearing because he never even bothered to show up on that day. A bench warrant was immediately issued.

The very next day, after learning that the court had issued a bench warrant, Brown turned himself in. The court withdrew the warrant and rescheduled the matter for August 1, 2000.

On August 1, 2000, Brown appeared in court and asked that the matter be rescheduled. The court gave him until August 9, 2000, to pay the fine and start attending the anger management sessions.

When he failed to appear on August 9, 2000, the court issued a bench warrant for the third time.

When Brown was finally arrested on September 4, 2000, and admitted to killing Ginger, the need to complete the anger management classes became a moot point. Now, being in custody for the murder and dismemberment of the woman he had originally been charged with savagely beating, prosecutor Posey asked that the matter be deferred again, until the court decided Brown's fate on the murder charges.

Ultimately, it would take until October 3, 2001, before the court dismissed the battery sentence. The actual court docket read: "Court finds the defendant to be indigent and waives fine and costs; court further waives the counseling (DAIP) requirement."

If the criminal justice system had acted on the 1999 battery charges against Joe Brown with greater vigor, Ginger Gasaway could still be alive today.

TWENTY-SIX

After returning Brown to the custody of Posey County's jail, Reed and Nelson drove to the Vanderburgh County Prosecutor's Office. They needed to obtain a search warrant to give the Ford Taurus and Mustang a thorough going-over for evidence. The search warrant was prepared, signed, and delivered to the Crime Scene Unit by 3:00 P.M.

Crime Scene detective Ben Gentry started with the Taurus. He documented a detailed description of the car and photographed it. Then he vacuumed it fully and collected the samples to be held in evidence.

During his search, Gentry found a copy of another protective order filed by Ginger against Brown in August 2000 inside the vehicle's glove compartment. He also found a small cardboard box that contained bank transaction records from the Fifth Third Bank account of Ginger Gasaway.

Gentry noted that there was a three-foot by six-foot piece of beige-colored carpet inside the trunk of the vehicle. This piece was the same color as the carpeting in Ginger Gasaway's apartment at Hatfield.

Reed thought that Brown might have picked up this piece of carpet to try and patch the spot where he had cut the carpeting out after murdering Ginger. Gentry completed his report with a note that there was no blood discovered in the vehicle, and no latent fingerprints were found.

After finishing the search of the Ford Taurus, Gentry drove that vehicle to a storage area at Mike's Towing, where the EPD keeps vehicles in a separate impoundment. It would later be released to Ginger's family.

Gentry then returned to the Crime Scene garage and began to search the Mustang. This vehicle had been wrapped in a tarp as it was transported from Lebanon, Ohio, to Evansville, Indiana, in order to preserve it in the condition that it was found.

Gentry went through the procedure of documenting and detailing the condition of this vehicle, and then photographed it from every angle. He then collected items of evidence, processed it for blood and fingerprints, and ended with a thorough vacuuming for evidence such as hairs and fibers.

Inside this car, he found a motel room key #19 in the area between the driver's seat and the console. This key was checked with area motels and was found not to belong to any in Evansville. Gentry also recovered from the front passenger floorboard an empty bottle that had once contained Prozac. This bottle was apparently a free sample from a doctor's office. Lisa mentioned that her mother took Prozac. Brown also told the detectives that Ginger took Prozac and that he would take Ginger's medicine without a prescription. The discovery of this empty bottle appeared to back up that portion of Brown's story.

In his report, Gentry noted that he discovered a substance that was consistent with the appearance of blood, between the passenger-side ground effects, directly beside the seat. Using a piece of equipment called a Hema-Stix, he performed a test to confirm his suspicions. He then cut out a small piece of carpet adjacent to the stained area. The Mustang would remain in the Crime Scene garage for the present time.

While Gentry was collecting evidence and documenting the condition of the vehicles, Reed and Nelson drove to Terre Haute, Indiana, to meet Joe's sister Jennie. They tape-recorded her statement. She said that she hadn't seen Joe since he beat Ginger in the laundry room a year earlier. She said that Joe had encouraged Ginger to stay away from her own family because he didn't like them, and he knew that they didn't like him either.

Jennie confirmed some other things—such as the fact that their mother died when Joe was young and their father later killed himself. She said Joe had a daughter named Jamie, who was born in 1977, right before Joe went to prison. Jennie said that Jamie lived somewhere in Marietta, Georgia.

Jennie was the only member of the Brown family who kept in touch with Joe while he was in prison at Michigan City, Indiana. She said that she felt sorry for him because of the way he grew up, and that she tried to help him out several times after he got out of prison in 1995. She said that she even bought him a car so he could get a job, but he sold it for gambling money.

Jennie said that while Joe was in prison, he would sometimes call her. On one occasion, he wanted her to give some money to a woman. He told her that he owed this woman's husband money in prison, and he needed her to pay it for him. She didn't want to do that, and Joe became hostile. She said that he told her that he had been told how to kill someone without getting caught. He told her that by dismembering a victim and dumping their pieces all over the place, you would never be caught or charged for the crime. She said that he told her this story several times when he was mad at her about different things, but usually about money. She added that Joe had not talked like that since he got out of prison, and that he never made any threats to Ginger in her presence.

Jennie said the last recollection she had of Joe was in January or February 2000 when he had gone to her son's apartment on the east side of Evansville. Joe banged on his door and wanted to borrow money. She said her son wasn't as much afraid of Joe as he was aware that if he let him in and loaned him money, he would never get rid of him again.

Jennie called the police from Terre Haute and they went to her son's apartment and found Joe outside. The officer called her back and said that Joe wanted cigarettes and coffee, and that he looked too frail to be a threat to anyone. The police got Joe some cigarettes and coffee, and then they took him to a shelter.

Jennie said that Joe called her the next day and wanted to know why she had called the police on him. She told him, "Joey, I love you, you're my brother. But I can't let you hurt my kids, and you're scaring them. I don't want you to call anymore."

Jennie said that Joe honored her request and she never heard from him again.

As soon as they returned to Evansville, Reed received a call from Jennie. She told him that Joe had just called her from prison. She said that she asked Joe how he killed Ginger, and he told her that he just snapped her neck like a chicken. He told her he used to work at Tysons, and that it wasn't any different from cutting up a chicken. He didn't even think about it. She said that she would be willing to testify against Joe in court if she was subpoenaed.

Another call came into the Detectives Office that day. It was from Indiana state trooper Joe Towns, who was in charge of security at Caesar's Casino. He had been called by the Ohio State Police to verify Brown's story that he had been with Ginger at the casino and that he left her there.

Towns said that the casino logs showed that Brown had been on the boat several times in August. He also checked the casino's video system and found that Brown had come on the boat alone and left alone on September 1, 2000—the day that Brown claimed to have been on the boat with Ginger. Towns also talked to one of the blackjack dealers that he had observed on the video talking to Brown. The dealer confirmed that Brown was alone that day. Towns made a copy of the videotape and mailed it to the Evansville Police Department. It would be put into court records evidence during the subsequent hearings.

A subpoena was also obtained to collect all videotapes from Channel 44 that contained interviews with Brown since the first of September.

Prosecutor Stan Levco requested that a hearing be set to discuss the case with Brown's defense counsel on September 18 and Brown would need to be present. It was at this hearing that Brown would learn if he would face the death penalty.

On that date, Joe Brown was transported to Vanderburgh Circuit Court and sat before Magistrate David Kiely. Barry Standley filed a motion for discovery, which meant that the prosecutor's office would have to supply the defense with any evidence and names of witnesses that they planned to use in the trial. Kiely appointed attorney Barbara Williams to assist Standley in Brown's defense.

Levco advised the court that he would be filing for a sentence of life without parole, and would not pursue the death penalty. This was in part due to the wishes expressed by Ginger's daughters and her ex-husband, Hobert.

"We don't hate Joe. We just hate what he did. He's a sick man. You can't hate someone because they have cancer. Joe's mind is sick like that. Killing him would make us no better than he is," Hobert said.

Brown sat quietly and showed no reaction to hearing that he would not have to face the death penalty. The case was set for trial by jury to take place February 12, 2001, at 8:00 A.M.

Brown had been held in the Vanderburgh County Jail overnight. Apparently, after the court hearing on September 18, it had been discovered that the trial date set by the court of February 12, 2001, was a holiday and a new trial date had to be set.

On September 19, in the early hours, Brown was led into court once again and seated beside his attorneys. The hearing was short and the trial date was reset to February 26.

TWENTY-SEVEN

A series of hearings took place in which Joe Brown had waived his right to be present. On September 28, 2000, Levco filed a motion to obtain blood samples from Brown, and the court approved it. The next day, Detectives Rick Reed and Loren Martin transported Brown from Posey County to the Vanderburgh County Health Department, where blood samples were drawn in accordance with the court order. The samples were processed at the Indiana State police laboratory and compared to blood found inside the Mustang and at Ginger's apartment on Hatfield Drive. There was no match. The blood trail at the apartment and in the car had all belonged to Ginger.

At the public's expense, Brown's defense team grew to include attorney John Goodridge and private investigator Mark Mabrey. Goodridge was an excellent legal researcher and would be responsible for much of the defense's objection to Brown's extradition. Mabrey was a retired chief deputy of the Vanderburgh County Sheriff Department, and he was very familiar with how police worked and thought.

Utilizing Standley, Williams, Goodridge, and Mabrey, the defense planned a two-pronged attack. Their first point would be that Brown's Miranda rights had been violated by the Evansville detectives when they first interrogated him, and that his rights were repeatedly violated as they continued to interrogate him as they brought him to Indiana and elicited information from him.

They pointed to the fact that the Evansville detectives had not read Joe his Miranda rights when they first interrogated him at the Warren County Detention Center in Ohio. Their plan was to prove that Brown had not been advised properly of his Miranda rights during any of the subsequent trips to and from Indiana over the next forty hours. They also insinuated that Brown was in emotional and physical distress brought on by the fact that he was not given food or allowed to rest during this period.

The defense team would also question the validity of the Indiana warrant with which Ohio State Trooper Randall Adams initially arrested Brown. The defense's contention was that this warrant was for such a minor offense that it did not justify the arrest and detention of Joe Brown for the almost nine hours that he spent in custody awaiting the arrival of the two Evansville detectives. They would point out that this was a misdemeanor warrant, and that the courts do not typically allow out-of-state arrests on such minor warrants.

The second prong of the defense attack brought into question the extradition procedures of the Evansville and Ohio State Police. Brown had been brought to Indiana on the night of September 4 without benefit of a court-sanctified extradition. The defense argument would be that Brown had agreed to accompany Reed and Nelson to Indiana without the benefit of defense counsel. The defense would claim that such action was outside accepted law enforcement procedure and was a violation of Brown's constitutional rights.

They would argue that the police had violated Brown's constitutionally guaranteed civil rights; therefore, all of the evidence collected by the police as a result of that violation was inadmissible in court.

This was important to the prosecutor because if the defense won its argument, all of the evidence discovered as a result of Brown's trip to Warrick, Gibson, and Posey Counties would be inadmissible. The fact that they had found Ginger Gasaway's remains would be withheld from a jury. Brown's confession would also be withheld from the jury, and the investigators would not be allowed to mention any of this during a trial. In essence, there would be no evidence against Joe Brown at all.

Reed was able to get CSU to release some of the items that had been collected from Ginger's apartment. He sat in front of two large cardboard boxes that contained paper grocery bags and plastic evidence bags full of hundreds of pieces of paper that he hoped, in some way, would connect Ginger to Brown. The bags were full of paid and unpaid bills, notes, greeting cards, letters, and other material. Reed spent the entire day taking one bag at a time and reading each piece of paper inside it.

He had not expected to find anything of importance to the case, but while going through a paper sack marked "#123: top drawer of bedroom chest of drawers," he found what appeared to be a receipt.

The handwritten receipt read, "I Joseph W. Brown promise to return said 1993 Mustang GT (Indiana license plate) #82L3658 back to the owner Ginger R. Gasaway on Sept 25, 1999 in the same condition as I received it on Monday Aug 9, 1999." This was signed Joseph W. Brown and dated August 9, 1999. There was also a signature of a witness: Ginger R. Gasaway. This was the top half of a piece of yellow legal pad. The bottom half was torn away, indicating that Joe most likely had the other half of the receipt. That half was probably identical to this one.

The discovery of this piece of evidence was not

crucial, since Ginger had not been killed in 1999, but it was indicative of a possible motive for the murder. Reed continued digging.

In the last paper sack, marked "#92: top of living room coffee table," Reed found something of interest. This was a single sheet of lined yellow legal pad in a handwriting that closely resembled the receipt he had found earlier. It read, "You said I can have the car till the 30th, Wednesday night. I will call you and let you know where it's at! I can't stay right here, and come Wednesday, I will not only be homeless but without transportation and a way to work, which is all my fault too." This letter was signed "Love always, Smokey." Smokey was Ginger's pet nickname for Joe. Ginger was killed on Wednesday, August 30.

After reading the letter, Reed called Ginger's daughter Lisa. It was late, but she answered on the first ring. Reed had asked Lisa previously about the agreement between her mother and Brown for the return of the Mustang, but she had not been certain of the conditions. Early in the initial investigation, she had told Reed that her mother had threatened to charge Brown with auto theft if he didn't bring the car back.

Ginger was a meticulous housekeeper and the fact that this letter was found on her coffee table indicated that it was fairly recent. Further, the fact that Brown had an outstanding warrant for his arrest for the original battery charge from 1999 would mean that he couldn't afford to have the police called on him. The final piece was the information from Lisa that her mother had given Brown an ultimatum: "Bring the car back by Wednesday or I'll have you arrested."

The two pieces of paper Reed had found in this haystack gave Brown the motive for murder. Add to that the fact that Brown thought Ginger was getting back together with her ex-husband, Hobert, and the picture was complete. Reed would pass this evidence along to the prosecutor.

At an October 10 hearing, the court denied the defense's ex parte motion and proclaimed that the prosecution would be allowed to be part of the process of picking expert witnesses for the defense.

To the defense counsel, the ex parte motion was an important item to have granted by the judge. The prosecutor had control over his own finances, so he could decide for himself whom he wanted to hire as an expert witness. The defense counsel was limited in funds. They had to rely on court orders from the judge for money to pay expert witnesses. To get this money, they couldn't just have a secret meeting with the court. They must request hearings that the prosecutor had the right to attend, and then could ask the court for the money. The prosecutor generally didn't object to whom the defense counsel wanted to hire as an expert witness, but they had that right. And now that they would be aware of whom the defense was going to ask for an expert opinion, the prosecutor could contact that expert and ask questions or prepare to impeach that expert's credibility.

Brown's defense lawyers didn't feel this was fair, since the prosecutor could interview whomever they wanted, and only provide a list of the witnesses they planned to use in court. The defense, due to this denial of the ex parte motion, would now risk having witnesses that they didn't want called to testify.

On January 3, 2001, Standley made a motion in court to once again allow defense experts access to Brown at the Vanderburgh County Jail. This would mean that Brown would be brought from Posey County and held by Vanderburgh County while the experts worked with him.

The defense hired Dr. Eric Engum, from Tennessee, to evaluate Brown. They wanted to determine if an insanity defense might be appropriate, and they had concerns that Brown's illegal use of the prescription drug Prozac might have clouded his ability to think clearly at the time that he allegedly committed his crimes and during his subsequent interviews with detectives.

Engum performed a battery of psychological tests on Brown for several days. The results of Engum's evaluation did not prove to be helpful to the defense's case. Engum wrote: "He has a history of recurrent major depressive disorder, an obsessive-compulsive disorder, pathological gambling addiction, and a mixed personality disorder along with a variety of psychosocial, interpersonal, and vocational stressors.

"However, both review of pertinent records and the results of the present clinical assessment failed to evidence the presence of psychosis or other severe mental disease or defect which might support the inference that Mr. Brown meets the criteria for the defense of insanity at the time of the alleged commission of the charged offenses.

"Absent any type of psychotic condition which might impair reality testing, it is this examiner's opinion that the defense of insanity is not supportable in the present case."

On January 23, all parties were ordered into court for a readiness conference, where the defense advised they would make a motion to postpone the trial, again, from the February 26 trial date already set to April 23, 2001.

Between January 23, 2001, and the final determination of the case, the trial by jury date was moved back five more times, ultimately being set for August 20, 2001. The reasons for the resetting of the trial date were various and were requested by both the defense and the prosecutor.

TWENTY-EIGHT

Standley filed a notice on March 16 that his office would take depositions from several state witnesses. The first subpoena was issued by the court to Detective Reed.

Reed's deposition was taken on March 27 in the offices of the public defender by Barry Standley and Mark Mabrey. Present for the state was deputy prosecutor Martha Posey.

Standley asked Reed when he first found out that Ginger Gasaway was missing.

"It all started on September 1, 2000. I was working the white-collar-crime unit, and I had received a call from Old National Bank . . . ," Reed began.

From there, the questioning would get into the past history of Joe Brown and Ginger Gasaway and the history of violence that had marked their relationship. It would cover the search for Joe Brown and the trail of apartments that the couple had sometimes shared. Also brought out would be the fraudulent checks Brown had been kiting and the theft and forgery of Ginger's checks by Brown.

For the next thirty-four pages of questions, Reed would detail how the investigation had unfolded, exposing Ginger's pattern of unusual absences from work, as well as her not keeping an important appointment to pick up the keys to her new apartment. It would detail how Ginger's car was found under suspicious circumstances and how a missing person report was finally entered into NCIC.

But the focus of Standley's questions at this point seemed to be whether Ohio state trooper Adams ever received notice of a felony warrant for Brown prior to his apprehension. Standley wanted to clarify that Brown had been arrested on the basis of the misdemeanor warrant that had been issued for him in regard to "failure to appear" on the old battery charge from September 1999. He also wanted to show that it was clear to the Ohio authorities that it was a misdemeanor warrant that they were arresting Brown on.

Reed explained that although the warrant from Indiana was a misdemeanor, once it was entered into NCIC and a subject was apprehended outside of Indiana, that a charge of fugitive from justice, or unlawful flight to avoid prosecution, was often added by the outside arresting agency. This would be Ohio's state charges and not charges placed on the arrested person by Indiana.

Reed further advised that he had requested a felony warrant for fraud on a financial institution be filed on Brown prior to his arrest, but the Vanderburgh County Prosecutor's Office had determined that it was not needed. This was their area of expertise, and it wasn't up to a police detective to question their legal knowledge.

Then the questioning turned toward Miranda rights. Reed was asked if he had read the Miranda rights form to Brown and the answer to the question was no. The fact of the matter was that Brown had been read the Miranda rights warning that morning by the Ohio State Police at the time of his arrest. Reed had seen this on the video from Trooper Adams's car.

Reed tried to explain to the defense attorney that Brown would not listen to his rights again. In fact,

Brown said something to the effect that they (the Ohio officers) had already read him his rights, and he knew what they were. Reed added that he asked Brown if he still understood his rights, to which Brown answered yes.

Another question was whether the Evansville detectives had tried to get Brown to sign a Miranda rights waiver form. Reed's response was that neither of the detectives had brought a form with him, but even if they had, Brown had refused to sign anything, or allow anything he said to be taped.

Standley pointed to a segment of one of the supplements that Reed had prepared for the case file. Standley directed Reed's attention to a section of one report and asked him to read that section into the deposition record.

"'I asked Joe if he had been read his rights by the Ohio troopers and he said that he had. I asked him if he still understood his right not to talk and to have an attorney present, and he stated he did,'" Reed read.

"Is that an accurate reflection of your supplemental report?" Standley asked.

"Yes, it is."

"And nowhere in there do you allude to the fact that you Mirandized him?"

"No, sir."

"Or that he waived his rights? Is that correct?" Standley persisted.

Reed explained again that he hadn't read the Miranda rights warning from a form, but that Brown had indicated that he knew he didn't have to talk and that he could get an attorney before answering questions. Reed told the attorney that Brown had stated that he understood his rights.

What Standley was getting at was that Reed had not asked Brown the direct question "Are you waiving your rights?" Reed had to admit that he had never worded a question exactly that way.

The last thing that was pointed out was that Reed had been inside Ginger Gasaway's apartment twice: once without a warrant, and the second time with a search warrant. Standley asked Reed if he had seen any evidence of foul play. Reed had to admit that he had missed the evidence on his first entry. The missing piece of carpeting wasn't obvious to him until the second entry.

The tape-recorded deposition would be typed, and Reed would later be given a chance to read and sign it.

For the next several months, both the prosecution and defense counsels requested hearings to make motions for one thing or another. In July, the prosecutor's office issued subpoenas to Carol Blair, the manager of Embassy East Apartments, Tonya Gaddis, who was the manager of Village Green Apartments, Susan Laine, who was a DNA expert working for the Indiana State Police, and Sergeant Greg Oeth, who worked in the lab at the Indiana State Police Department.

Subpoenas were also issued for Steven Sparks, Nancy Kleczka, Richard Wentzel, Donald Angel, David Jones, and Phillip Britton, who were all neighbors of Ginger's or who had worked with Joe Brown, or both. One other subpoena that was issued was to Carol Courtney, who worked in personnel at T.J. Maxx, where Ginger had been employed.

Judge Heldt issued a "certificate to summon a witness to testify at a criminal proceeding in the State of Indiana" on July 16 at the request of Brown's defense counsel. Standley wanted to be able to take depositions from the law enforcement witnesses from Ohio.

This was the beginning of the second prong of attack the defense had planned. They would question the legality of Brown's arrest in Ohio and his subsequent transportation to Indiana by Evansville detectives.

Their claim was that this was all unconstitutional. At a hearing on July 18, the defense verified their motion to suppress and notified the court of their intention to take depositions via telephone from Lieutenant Kelly Hale, Sergeant James Ertel, Trooper Randall Adams, and Geraldine Redfern.

Redfern was the Ohio State Police dispatcher who handled the radio and computer traffic for Trooper Randall Adams on the day that Brown was found sleeping in Ginger's Mustang at the rest stop area along I-70.

Defense attorney Barbara Williams took the telephonic deposition of Ohio State Police trooper Randall Adams. In that deposition, Trooper Adams disclosed that he regularly worked the 6:00 A.M. to 2:00 P.M. shift and that part of his assigned patrol area took in the rest area on I-71 that runs through Lebanon, Ohio.

Trooper Adams said that on September 4, 2000, he picked up his paperwork as usual at headquarters and went on patrol. He explained to attorney Williams that part of his duties while on patrol was to check the rest areas in his assigned area.

In the rest areas, he made sure that there were no problems that required police assistance, and he also routinely checked registration of the cars in the rest area to check for people wanted on outstanding warrants.

When Trooper Adams came to the red Mustang, he called the license plate in to Geraldine Redfern at dispatch. Adams said that Redfern checked the vehicle registration through NCIC and also through the Ohio State Police version of IDACS called Law Enforcement Automated Data System (LEADS). He said that Redfern advised him that the vehicle's registered owner was Ginger Gasaway, from Evansville, Indiana, and that Ms. Gasaway was reported as "involuntarily missing."

Adams said that he called for assistance prior to approaching the vehicle. When his backup arrived, they approached the Mustang. The Mustang had fairly dark-tinted windows, but when they got up close, he could see the outline of a person who appeared to be sleeping.

Trooper Adams knocked on the window of the Mustang and Joe Brown sat up and put his face close to the window. The troopers ordered him out of the vehicle.

Attorney Williams asked Adams if his police vehicle was equipped with video equipment, and if so, was it operating at the time this occurred? Trooper Adams explained that on the Ohio State Police vehicles, the camera came on anytime they switch on their overhead emergency lights. The camera was mounted on the windshield of the police vehicle and could be positioned to record whatever the trooper desired. He said that he had turned his emergency lights on before approaching the Mustang, and had the camera pointed at the suspect's car.

Williams was interested in whether the trooper could turn off the video or audio while the emergency lights were activated, and he assured her that it was possible. But he explained that on the video it would show if he had turned his microphone off during the car stop because of indicators that showed on the tape itself.

According to Trooper Adams, it was Trooper Hall who did most of the talking with Brown. He explained that once they had Brown out of the vehicle, they patted him down for weapons. After that, Trooper Hall asked Brown where Ms. Gasaway was, and he said he "had no idea." Hall then asked when Brown had last seen Ms. Gasaway, and Brown responded that it had been a couple of days ago, over the weekend, on a gambling boat in Indiana.

Trooper Hall continued questioning Brown about the whereabouts of Ms. Gasaway and Brown finally stated that he and Ginger had gotten into a fight and that he had left her at the gambling boat. That was why he didn't know exactly where she was.

Adams said that Trooper Hall then asked Brown why he was driving Ms. Gasaway's car and that Brown claimed ownership of the car. Brown said he had been making the payments on the car for the last two years and that made it his.

The point of Williams's questioning was to ascertain what Brown believed was the reason he was being questioned by the Ohio troopers. Trooper Adams explained that during the previous questioning the only thing they had told Brown was that there was a "hit" on the Mustang, meaning that it was entered into their computer system, claiming Ms. Gasaway was involuntarily missing. They had pointed out to Brown that he was the one driving the vehicle registered to Ms. Gasaway and she was not present.

Adams said that he again called Geraldine Redfern on the radio and she told him she had contacted Evansville, Indiana, and they had advised they were looking for Brown in the disappearance of Ms. Gasaway under suspicious circumstances. The person she had talked to in Evansville also mentioned something about Brown using Gasaway's checkbook and writing a couple of checks.

It was Adams's understanding from talking to Redfern that Evansville was going to enter some warrants into NCIC for forgery, but they hadn't done so yet. He was given the go-ahead by Redfern to arrest Brown based on her communications with the Evansville Police Department. Trooper Adams then read Brown his Miranda rights and placed him under arrest.

Attorney Williams asked upon what charges had Trooper Adams arrested Brown. At the time of this deposition, his best recollection was that he had told Brown he was under arrest for writing bad checks and that he was the number one suspect for the murder of Ms. Gasaway, and that Evansville police wanted to talk to him about this.

It was partly because of the questions asked of Trooper Adams that another defense issue would arise. Adams had stated on his deposition that in his understanding Brown was going to be charged with forgery. It was further his understanding that a warrant was being issued for this charge. This was part of his reason for placing Brown under arrest. Attorney Barbara Williams knew that no such warrant was ever issued or served on her client.

Williams pressed Trooper Adams on the point of the warrant, asking what steps he had taken to insure that such a warrant actually was issued. He answered that verifying the warrant was actually the job of the dispatcher, and that Geraldine Redfern would have performed that function. It was his understanding that Redfern had confirmed the warrant or she would not have advised him to arrest Brown. In any case, he said that he never got to see the warrant itself; only the NCIC "hit" was necessary. The warrant was handled by dispatch and the jail.

Williams also attempted to find out if the trooper believed the warrant was a felony or a misdemeanor. He said that he didn't know.

Williams pressed Adams further. She wanted to know what it was about talking with Brown that made him believe he was engaged in the commission of a crime.

Trooper Adams answered that they had talked with Brown about Ms. Gasaway being missing, and that he was the prime suspect in her disappearance.

"Joe Brown was calm, cool, and collected. No emotion whatsoever. I think a normal person, if you told them, 'I think you killed somebody and the authorities from another state are going to come and talk to you about it,' I think that most normal people would be upset at that. But he wasn't upset the whole time."

TWENTY-NINE

A telephone conference call was made to Sergeant James Ertel on July 26 by defense attorneys Barry Standley, Barbara Williams, and John Goodridge, and by Martha Posey for the VCPO. The questions were asked by Barbara Williams.

When his deposition was taped, Sergeant James Ertel had been with the Ohio State Troopers for twenty-three years. He was assigned as a supervisor with the Investigations Division of the Cincinnati area. He actually worked out of Post 31, which is the Cincinnati Post but is located in Blue Ash, Ohio.

Sergeant Ertel said Lieutenant Kelly Hale received a phone call from their district headquarters in Wilmington, Ohio, on September 4, 2000, and had passed the information on to him regarding the arrest of Joe Brown at a rest area on I-71.

Lieutenant Hale had advised him that troopers from the Lebanon Post had arrested Joseph Brown, and that the Indiana authorities were interested in talking to him. Ertel was asked to go to the Lebanon Post 83, and to provide assistance to the Evansville detectives when they arrived.

Ertel stated that he went to the Lebanon Post and viewed a videotape of the arrest of Joe Brown that was made by the camera in Trooper Adams's car. Brown was not present at that time, and had already been taken to the Warren County Detention Center in Lebanon, Ohio, where he was being housed on the charges from Evansville.

After viewing the videotape of the arrest, Sergeant Ertel waited for the Evansville detectives to arrive. He said that he believed it was around six o'clock that evening when Reed and Nelson arrived and that Lieutenant Hale also arrived around that time.

Ertel told the attorneys that Sergeant Adams came in to brief the men on the arrest and that he allowed Reed and Nelson to view the videotapes. Afterward, Ertel said, he and Lieutenant Hale led Reed and Nelson to the Warren County Government Center, where the detention center is housed.

Sergeant Ertel explained that he and Lieutenant Hale were present in the room while Brown was questioned. He added that neither of them had any direct conversation or interaction with Brown.

Williams asked Ertel if he had made any notes or prepared any reports in connection with his involvement in the case. He told the defense attorney that he did not take notes, and that his only involvement was to assist the Evansville detectives. This was not an Ohio case. He also explained that he was not involved with the court proceedings for extradition, nor had he checked to see if Brown was charged under any kind of warrant.

Williams then asked what other assistance Ertel had given Nelson and Reed after they interviewed Brown. Ertel told her that the two detectives wanted to take Brown to Indiana with them to locate body parts of the victim, so he called the Warren County, Ohio, prosecutor, Tim Oliver, and laid out the scenario as he understood it. He explained to Oliver that Brown had agreed to go with the detectives and show them where he had disposed of the remains of Ginger Gasaway, whom he had confessed to murdering.

Williams asked Sergeant Ertel if he had initiated that conversation with Tim Oliver, and what his purpose was in doing so. Ertel said that he had called Oliver on the telephone from the detention center. His purpose was to obtain permission for the jail to release Brown to the Evansville detectives.

"Did he just tell you to let him go?" Williams asked.

"He said that if the Indiana authorities approved of it, that he basically did not have a problem with them taking Brown, as long as they brought him directly back to the Warren County Jail after he showed them what they needed to see," Ertel answered.

Williams then asked a question that would be supportive of their motion to suppress evidence. She asked Sergeant Ertel if he had seen any paperwork from a judge in Ohio, or any paperwork from the state of Indiana, giving authorization to transport Brown from the state of Ohio, back to the state of Indiana.

Ertel stated that he had not seen any such papers.

She then asked if either of the Evansville detectives had ever spoken directly with the Ohio prosecutor, Tim Oliver, to which Ertel answered, "To my knowledge, they did not."

Sergeant Ertel also told Williams that Tim Oliver did not come to the Warren County Detention Center and did not ask about any arrest warrant or authority for the Evansville officers to take custody of Brown.

Williams also pointed out the fact that Sergeant Ertel did not speak directly to the Evansville prosecutor, but had instead relied on the word of the two Evansville detectives that their prosecutor had given permission to take Brown out of Ohio. She also made a point that permission had been granted by the Ohio prosecutor, Tim Oliver, to transport Brown out of the state of Ohio prior to his extradition hearing, without first contacting a judge or magistrate in Ohio.

The questioning from that point went to whether Brown had been allowed to eat anything or to get any sleep. Sergeant Ertel said that he personally never saw Brown eat or sleep, and advised that he only knew that one of the detectives from Evansville had taken Brown into the secured garage area and allowed him to smoke.

Ertel was asked whether or not Brown had been read his Miranda rights warning in his presence. Ertel remembered that one of the Evansville detectives asked Brown if he had been read his rights and if he still understood his rights, and that Brown responded that he had been read them and did understand them.

She then wanted to know if Sergeant Ertel had read the Miranda rights warning to Joe Brown personally, and how he knew if Brown had ever been read his rights. Ertel responded that he had seen the video from the trooper's car and that on the video, the trooper read Brown the Miranda warning, and Brown said he understood.

He was asked to explain how and why he had escorted the Evansville detectives with their prisoner to the Ohio state line. Sergeant Ertel simply answered that he had been asked to do so by the two detectives. Williams seemed to have some question as to whether it was because Brown was technically still in the custody of the Ohio State Police and Ertel answered that was not the case. He was merely assisting the two detectives.

The last question was directed to Sergeant Ertel's involvement in Brown's extradition proceedings the next day, September 5, 2000. Ertel told Williams that he met up with the Evansville detectives on the interstate

near Cincinnati, and he escorted them back to the
Warren County Detention Center so that Joe could
be taken to court for the extradition hearing. He said
that he showed the Evansville detectives how to get to
the court building and then he left them there.

THIRTY

On July 26, 2001, at 2:45 P.M., defense attorney Barbara Williams took the taped deposition of OSHP lieutenant Charles Hale over the telephone. Also present during this deposition were the defense team, Barry Standley and John Goodridge, and Martha Posey for the VCPO.

Lieutenant Hale stated that he had been with the Ohio State Troopers for twenty-three years, and that he was in charge of the Investigative Office in the Cincinnati district. His recollection of the events on the day in question was that it was a holiday and that he was called in to work because of the arrest of Joe Brown.

Lieutenant Hale said Sergeant Adams, from the Lebanon Post, had contacted him at home. He explained that neither he nor Sergeant Ertel prepared any paperwork to document this incident because the arresting officer, Trooper Randall Adams, would have generated all of the paperwork that was needed.

Hale said he was told that two EPD detectives would arrive at the Lebanon Post at about 6:00 P.M. that day, and he contacted Sergeant Ertel to meet with them. He requested that Sergeant Ertel assist the two Evansville detectives in whatever they needed to interview Joseph

Brown, who was held at that time in the Warren County Detention Center.

Hale was asked if he knew why the Evansville police were coming to interview Brown, and if he had ever seen a warrant for Brown's arrest. He told the attorneys that he had been advised that Trooper Adams had found Brown inside a vehicle at a rest area and that there was an NCIC entry on the vehicle that showed it belonged to Ginger Gasaway, who was entered into the computer as a "critical missing." Hale said that Trooper Adams had ascertained that Evansville police were sending a Teletype detainer to hold Brown in the Ohio prison until they could arrive to interview him.

Williams wanted to know if Lieutenant Hale had ever seen an actual warrant for Brown, to which Lieutenant Hale responded that in that type of situation, all that Indiana was required to do was to send the Teletype to hold Brown until they got a warrant. He explained that all of that was taken care of prior to his or Sergeant Ertel's involvement.

Williams asked Lieutenant Hale if the Evansville detectives had presented him with any paperwork when they all met at the Lebanon Post. Lieutenant Hale said he was sure he had not been given any papers. He explained that he would not be the one that would receive any paperwork, and that all of that would have been worked out between Evansville's dispatch and the Warren County Detention Center where Joe was being held.

He was then asked what took place at the Lebanon Post among himself, Sergeant Ertel, and the two Evansville detectives. Lieutenant Hale said there was a short meeting in which they took a quick look at the videotape from Trooper Adams's car showing Trooper Adams reading Brown his Miranda rights warning.

From there, the men went to the detention center, which is about five minutes away from the Lebanon

Post. They spoke to the deputies at the jail and were given an interview room to use.

Hale told Williams that he and Sergeant Ertel were present while Brown was being interviewed by Detective Reed, but neither of them spoke to Brown or advised him of his rights.

Williams asked if either of the Evansville police officers had advised Brown of his rights. Hale explained that Reed had asked Brown if he had been read his Miranda rights by an Ohio trooper, and if he still understood those rights. He said that Brown acknowledged that he did understand and had already been read his rights. Lieutenant Hale further stated that Reed had asked Brown if he knew that he had the right to have an attorney present and that Brown said he knew that.

Hale was asked to give an account of the interview with Joe Brown.

"Brown admitted in my presence to the Evansville detectives that he was responsible for the death of Mrs. Gasaway and that he had used a reciprocating saw to dismember the body. He said that he dumped it in more than one location in Indiana," Hale said.

He went on to explain that he was not familiar with Indiana geography, but the dump sites were supposed to be somewhere near Evansville. He told the attorneys that Brown had offered to show the two detectives the location of the body parts, but there was a stipulation—they had to do it immediately.

He further explained that Brown had told the detectives that he wouldn't tell them where the body parts were, but he would show them. That was when Sergeant Ertel contacted Warren County prosecutor Tim Oliver.

Hale was asked many of the same questions that were asked of Sergeant Ertel. How was the Ohio prosecutor advised of the facts? Was there an actual warrant for Joe Brown? Hale's answers were basically the same as Ertel's had been.

Additionally, Hale remembered Detective Nelson speaking on the telephone to someone in the Vanderburgh County Prosecutor's Office while Sergeant Ertel was speaking to Tim Oliver. Both prosecutors agreed that the detectives could take Brown back to Indiana to locate the body parts, and then they had to bring him back to Ohio in time for his extradition hearing the next day. Hale said that the Warren County sheriff also approved this, and Brown was released to the custody of the two Evansville detectives.

Lieutenant Hale told Williams that he asked Sergeant Ertel to escort the Evansville officers to the state line. Ertel agreed and they left. Hale said that was the extent of his involvement.

Geraldine Redfern gave the next telephonic deposition that afternoon. During the questioning by attorney Barbara Williams, she disclosed that she had worked as a dispatcher for the Ohio State Highway Patrol for almost twenty-two years. Her work duties at Post 83, located in Lebanon, Ohio, included answering the telephone, handling all the radio traffic, and operating the computer that accessed LEADS and NCIC when troopers asked for information.

On September 4, at about 7:00 A.M., she was working dispatch alone when Trooper Randall Adams's voice came over the radio advising that he was en route to the northbound rest area on I-71.

Redfern said the routine for the troopers working the interstates was to travel through the rest areas on the northbound and southbound sides, and to read off the license plate numbers of suspicious vehicles to the dispatcher.

Williams wanted to know if it was typical for the troopers to read off every single license plate in the parking areas, and Redfern explained that if the trooper knew who the vehicle belonged to, such as a rest area worker or caretaker, he would probably not worry about that one.

Redfern continued with her story and said that when Trooper Adams gave her the license plate number of the Mustang, she ran it through NCIC and the registration came back to Ginger Gasaway, with a message stating that she was reported "missing-endangered." This meant that the person was reported missing by the agency that entered the information, and that agency had reason to believe this missing person was in some type of danger. The entering agency was the Evansville Police Department. She printed this information out and held it for Trooper Adams.

Redfern said that Trooper Adams arrived at the post at around 8:40 A.M. with his supervisor, Sergeant Adams. She explained to Williams that the troopers had to pass by her radio console when they came into the station, and that Sergeant Adams came up to her console to ask her for the paperwork on the Mustang and Joe Brown.

Williams questioned her for more detail about the actual conversation between her and Trooper Adams while he was still at the rest area. Redfern said that when she gave Trooper Adams the information from the license plate inquiry on the Mustang, she asked him if he was "signal 58," which is a code known to the troopers that meant, "Can someone else hear what I'm saying to you?" This was their way of ensuring that the information they were giving the troopers would be given privately and not in the presence of a suspect. If a suspect did hear some of the radio traffic, they could present a possible danger to the trooper.

Redfern said that Trooper Adams assured her he was alone, so she told him about the NCIC information on the vehicle, advising him that the vehicle was involved with a missing and endangered person.

She then asked if he had a red Mustang and the

trooper answered in the affirmative. She asked if there was a white male in the vehicle and he again answered yes. Redfern said that upon hearing that, she alerted Sergeant Adams and Trooper Hall to go and back up Trooper Adams at the rest area.

When asked if there was any warrant information included in the computer printout she had received from Evansville Police Department's computer, she answered that there was not. But she added that there was information that Joseph Brown might be in possession of the Mustang and he was possibly connected with some foul play involving Ginger Gasaway. The computer information requested that they contact the Evansville Police Department immediately if anyone contacted this vehicle.

Redfern told Williams that she was on the telephone with the EPD at the same time she was in radio contact the with Trooper Adams at the rest area. She passed on the information she was given by the EPD to the troopers at the scene. While she was doing this, she also wrote everything down and gave the information and the NCIC paperwork to Sergeant Adams when he arrived at the Lebanon Post with Joe Brown.

Williams wanted to know if the NCIC entry had directed them to arrest Brown. Redfern stated that all the NCIC advised was that Ginger was a missing person and Brown was a suspect in her disappearance. There was no mention of making an arrest if he was found. The information to arrest Brown had come from her telephone conversation with the Evansville Police Department. She did not recall there being any type of arrest warrant from Indiana.

Williams asked how Brown came to be charged with fugitive from justice, and Redfern explained that Sergeant Adams had advised her on the radio that he was "signal 42" with Brown on a fugitive from justice charge from Evansville Police Department. Signal 42 meant that Sergeant Adams had arrived at the Lebanon, Ohio, Post with Brown.

Williams also questioned Redfern about any knowledge she might have concerning charges of fraud on a financial institution being brought against Brown. Redfern had no knowledge of any other charges.

THIRTY-ONE

Attorney John Goodridge filed a motion on July 26 to compel disclosure and production of NCIC reports. He specifically was interested in the NCIC entries that had resulted in Joe Brown's arrest by the Ohio authorities. The motion was withdrawn by the defense on July 27 when they realized this already had been anticipated and given to them by the prosecutor.

Over the next week, subpoenas were sent to all of the Evansville police officers involved in this matter. Attorney John Goodridge appeared in court to file a notice of intent to request the court to take judicial notice of the statutes and common law of the state of Ohio. This would be an integral part of their intent to prove that a constitutional violation had occurred when the two Evansville detectives took custody of Brown and then transported him over state lines. Their contention was that because Brown was never read an arrest warrant, the Evansville detectives had no legal authority to take custody of him.

The defense theory was developed almost immediately upon their interview with Brown. He advised his attorneys that he had been sleeping in the rest area when the Ohio state troopers took him from his car, arrested him without a warrant, and took him to a holding facility until the Evansville detectives arrived. He had been read his Miranda rights, but had never been read a warrant, or shown anything that allowed them to detain him. He didn't think the Ohio troopers had the right to arrest him, and his defense attorneys agreed with his assessment.

Their strategy had some validity because Brown was not arrested on a printed warrant. Instead, he had been detained by the Ohio troopers on an NCIC hit that reported Brown as a suspect in an involuntary missing person and that the vehicle he might be driving would belong to the victim. Upon receiving that information, Redfern called the Evansville police and was told that Brown had a misdemeanor warrant for failure to appear, and that other charges were being prepared. Redfern felt that was enough to allow the Ohio State Police to detain and arrest Brown, as well as ask some preliminary questions in regard to the disappearance of Ginger Gasaway.

The prosecution argued that a Teletype was sent to the Warren County Detention Center by Detective Reed before the detectives left Indiana. Its contents confirmed that there was an arrest warrant in Indiana for failure to appear and directed them to hold Brown on that warrant, so it was not outside the law to arrest Brown without showing him a written warrant.

Reed asked Detective Loren Martin to prepare a case file on the fraud on financial institution charges that were eventually going to be criminal charges against Brown. Martin prepared the file listing the felony charges against Brown and took it to the prosecutor's office. The deputy prosecutor he spoke to decided that the misdemeanor warrant for failure to appear was sufficient to arrest and hold Brown until the state of Indiana decided what charges it would file on him. This turned out to be a serious mistake in procedure, but was not to the case.

The defense attorneys' theory was that because the state of Indiana did not have a felony warrant or an order from a judge to arrest Brown, his detention had been illegal and unconstitutional. Further, they proclaimed that the two Evansville detectives who interviewed Brown did so as private citizens, because they had no arrest powers in the state of Ohio, and, therefore, could not take legal custody of Brown to transport him outside Ohio. Additionally, they planned to argue that the police escorts that were provided by the Ohio State Troopers and the Kentucky State Police were an attempt to legitimize their illegal trip. Defense attorney Barbara Williams said that the actions of the two detectives were tantamount to kidnapping.

Judge Heldt ordered the Vanderburgh County Sheriff Department to bring Brown to court on August 6 for a suppression hearing. The defense team wanted to prove that Brown was arrested illegally and that any evidence after his detainment should be inadmissible in a court of law. Even though Brown had not been present for much of the matters that had been attended to by his attorneys, he would be included at this hearing.

Testimony was heard from all the people who were questioned in the defense's preliminary investigation. Reed, Redfern, Adams, Ertel, Hale, and everyone else gave the same account of what happened as they had before. Their testimonies would be heard in court for two days and each person called to the stand would be questioned by the defense and then cross-examined by the prosecutor.

At the end of the second day of testimony in the motion to suppress, the defense and state rested. All of this testimony had been given in front of a judge and not to a jury. The determination would be Judge Heldt's alone. If Judge Heldt found for the defense, then the state's case would be in serious trouble. All of the statements from Brown, verbal and taped, would be inadmissible in a trial. All of the evidence found as a result of Brown's initial arrest would be inadmissible—the remains of Ginger Gasaway, the blood found inside the Mustang, the fact that Joe was found in Ohio, would all be as if it never existed.

However, if the judge found in favor of the state, and all of the evidence was admitted for trial purposes, the defense case would be dealt a drastic blow. If a jury found Brown guilty of the murder, they would also decide his sentence.

At the end of the hearing, Judge Heldt advised that he would take the matter of suppression under advisement, and asked both sides to file briefs within two days. These briefs would contain any legal precedence that supported either the defense or state position why the evidence should be suppressed or not suppressed.

When Reed left the courthouse with his wife, he confided to her that he was worried that things might not go well. Brown had told Reed and Nelson during one of the trips from Posey County on his way to court that his attorneys were going to file kidnapping charges against Reed and Nelson. Reed didn't think that the attorneys meant actual kidnapping charges. He thought they might possibly try to file a violation of constitutional rights against them, and that was a serious matter.

Now it would all come down to the decision of Judge Heldt.

After almost a year of legal wrangling, hearings, motions, and depositions, on August 10, Judge Heldt denied the defense team's motion to suppress evidence. All of the evidence gathered in this case would be admissible to a jury at trial. Barry Standley and Stan Levco were notified by telephone. They then notified the appropriate involved parties, including Joe Brown.

The court set a pretrial date for August 17, 2001, at 9:00 A.M. This would allow the defense and state to discuss the possibility of some type of agreement between them in lieu of a full-blown trial.

The stage was set and the players were ready to go. But according to attorney Barbara Williams, their client was not willing to go through a trial. Brown had enough of the judicial system and wanted to "get this over with"—as he had said during his first appearance in court almost a year earlier. After being notified by Barry Standley that the motion to suppress had been denied, Brown requested that his attorneys let him plead guilty.

This case was not comparable at this point to the Vincent Prowell case, where there was an inadequate defense. Brown's attorneys had fought on his behalf for almost a year. Brown had been evaluated on two occasions by a psychiatrist selected by his attorneys and paid for by the court. The results of that psychiatric evaluation would do nothing to help him in court. In fact, those results might even hurt him at his sentencing because they did not raise any issues that would be considered mitigating factors, or reasons that the court should be lenient in sentencing.

Although his attorneys pleaded with Brown to reconsider, he would not back down. They were willing to wage war for him at a trial, but his mind was made up. Brown had wanted to plead guilty a year before, but the court had made a decision to spend taxpayer's money and time to ensure that he received a proper defense.

Joe Brown appeared before Judge Heldt on August 16, once again. With deputy prosecutor Martha Posey present for the state, and Barry Standley and Barbara Williams present for the defendant, Brown withdrew his plea of not guilty and entered a plea of guilty as charged, without the benefit of a plea agreement. Without a plea agreement, Brown gave up any rights to an appeal. Whatever sentence he was given by Judge Heldt would be final.

Heldt advised Brown of his constitutional rights and the defendent signed and filed an acknowledgment of rights with the court. With that document, the court then found a factual basis for the plea and that he had entered it voluntarily. With this done, all that was left was the penalty phase.

The sentencing was set for August 23 at 9:00 A.M. On that date, Joe would appear in court with his attorneys to hear what his fate would be. Although the state was requesting a sentence of life without possibility of parole, it was still up to the judge to make the final determination.

The defense asked for a sentence of fifty-four years, that is less than the sixty-year maximum sentence for murder in the state of Indiana. Their reasoning was that Brown was forty-six years old at the time of sentencing, and that with a sentence of fifty-four years, he would be in his seventies before he would be eligible for parole.

Part of the process in the penalty phase was to allow the state and defense to call witnesses to support their request of sentence. Reed was once again called to the stand to testify for the state in their bid to sentence Brown to life without parole. Brown had no one to testify on his behalf.

At the end of the testimony, Judge Heldt ordered that a presentence investigation be prepared by the Circuit Court Probation Department, and final disposition of the case was set for September 4, 2001.

A presentence investigation was a standard order at the end of a case where a defendant was convicted or had pleaded guilty, and was expected to be sentenced to either probation or to prison time. This investigation was done by teams that work for circuit court and not by law enforcement. The investigation encompassed things that would not normally be found in a criminal investigation, such as the defendant's home life, if parents were alive, alcohol and/or drug abuse, and prior criminal activity, among other things. Even members of the defendant's family could be interviewed during this procedure.

On September 4, 2001, exactly a year from the day he was captured in the state of Ohio, Joe Brown was brought into court one last time to sit in front of Judge Heldt and be sentenced. There would be no trial by jury.

The entire defense and prosecutorial teams were present, as well as Detectives Rick Reed and Larry Nelson. As Judge Carl Heldt entered the courtroom in his intimidating black robes, a hush came over the room. The outcome could go either way, but one thing was sure: Joseph Weldon Brown would be put away for what would probably be the rest of his natural life.

Another procedure also can take place during the sentencing phase. That procedure was the allowance of the victim's family, or a representative of the family, to make a last statement. The suspect would be allowed then to make a last statement before he was sentenced. Judge Heldt asked if any of the family would like to make a statement to the court.

Hobert Gasaway described Ginger as a loving and caring wife, mother, and grandmother. He said that she was the type of person who would give everything she had to help someone else, even when she needed help herself. She liked quiet times and would crochet afghans. She liked camping and fishing. Most of all, she loved her family.

Ginger's daughter Lisa was able to make a statement before the judge handed down Brown's sentence. She bravely stood to face the man who brutally murdered her mother.

"There are only a handful of people that could possibly understand the pain and torment that you have caused me and my family. No words could ever begin to describe the bad things that I have thought about doing to you, putting you through the same kind of hurt as my mother and my family went through. But that would make me no better than you, and I do not wish to lower myself to your level.

"I can only hope that someday you will understand that emptiness and the hole that you left in our souls by taking away the compassion and a life of loving memories and companionship shared with my mother. That will be something that I no longer have a chance to share with her.

"No longer will I get to call her when I'm having a bad day or when I just want to talk. My kids will not be able to know their grandmother and enjoy the many things she could have taught them. She won't be there at their graduation or wedding day. She was robbed of her hopes and dreams, and so were all of us dear and close to her. We will be the ones to keep her memories going.

"My only prayer is that you are charged with life without parole so that you will always be in prison and never get out to have a chance to hurt anyone again," Lisa said.

Brown, who had been looking directly at Lisa during the reading of this letter, now looked down at his shackled hands with tears in his eyes. He was given a chance to speak and what he said was not a plea for leniency, but rather a plea to be put away for the rest of his life.

He admitted his guilt in the gruesome death of his ex-girlfriend and apologized to her family for what he had done to them. He then turned to Judge Heldt and said that he had wanted to plead guilty all along. He said that he didn't ever want to get out of prison because he didn't know what he might do. He wanted to think he wouldn't kill again, but he wasn't sure that he wouldn't. After all, he said, he never thought he would have done what he did.

Brown held his head high while the judge ordered him to a sentence of "life without the possibility of parole." His attorneys showed more emotion than Brown did. He had known the outcome from the beginning.

There was no one there in the end for Joe Brown. The closest friends he had in the courtroom were Detectives Reed and Nelson. He looked glumly at them as he was led from the courtroom by the two sheriff's deputies. Then he mouthed at Reed, "I need to see you." Reed nodded agreement.

After court, a call came in to the Detectives Office from the Vanderburgh County Jail. Brown wanted to see Reed and Nelson before he was taken to Posey County for the last time. Brown didn't know it, but he wouldn't be going back to Posey County. His things would be sent to the Vanderburgh County Jail, since they would be responsible for carrying out the judge's orders and transporting him to the Indiana Diagnostic Center, near Indianapolis.

The diagnostic center would prepare a file on Joe Brown, issue his Department of Corrections (DOC) inmate number, and make the arrangements for housing at the Wabash Valley Correctional Facility.

Nelson and Reed went to the jail and brought Brown down in handcuffs and belly chains. The men took him to a small concrete porch area just outside the back door of the Detectives Office, where Brown would get his last cigarette.

"I did the right thing, Rick," Brown said glumly.

Reed agreed that Brown had done a very good thing.

Nelson brought Brown a cup of coffee and lit another cigarette for him. Brown shuffled around and looked at his feet. It was apparent he had something to say.

"I want to ask you guys for a favor," he finally said.

"I want you two to take me to prison when I go. Can you do that?"

Nelson and Reed looked at each other. They knew this probably wouldn't be allowed, but they agreed to try anyway. Brown nodded his satisfaction.

When Nelson went for another cup of coffee, Brown leaned close to Reed and asked another favor.

"You need to come and see me when I get to where I'm going." Lowering his voice even more, Brown added, "I got something to tell you. Something big, but not yet."

Reed agreed that he would try to visit, and he had every intention of making good on that promise. But it wasn't until "something big" was revealed that the detective was brought into the nightmare of Joe Brown one more time.

PART III

A KILLER'S CONFESSION

THIRTY-TWO

Detective Reed once described Joe Brown as a "news whore." He got his first glimpse of that when he transported Brown from Ohio to Indiana. It was at that time that Brown demanded to be allowed to call a television news reporter.

Maureen Hayden, a reporter for the *Evansville Courier & Press*, didn't cover the story at that time, and she wrote off the incident as another tragic love story about a man who wanted a woman who didn't want him.

About two years later, she received a letter dated August 27, 2003, from an unfamiliar inmate in the Indiana Department of Corrections. After working the religious beat for five years at the newspaper, Hayden assumed that it was just another letter from a criminal who found God in a jail cell, and she opened it with a callous reserve.

The envelope was stamped with a warning that an offender at a correctional facility had mailed the correspondence. It also contained a disclaimer noting that the facility was not responsible for its contents. Inside was a handwritten letter, scrawled in black ink, on college-rule notebook paper. Its contents took Hayden's breath away.

The letter began, "This is no prank or joke. Contact

Detective Rick Reed of the Evansville Police Department. He will tell you I don't play. I have information on thirteen murdered women between the years 1995–2000."

Brown went on to write, "I am never getting out of prison. When the time is right, I will do the right thing in turning over all the ID's I have of these murdered women, and I'll confess to all 13 murders."

Brown wrote of how he desperately wanted to find his daughter and stated, "I'm wanting to finally empty my closet of all skeletons."

Hayden tracked down Reed's phone number, grabbed a telephone, and called him at his home. She said that she read him the letter that she received from Brown all the way through to the end.

Reed, on the other hand, said that Hayden didn't call him until September 5, 2003, and that she initially only asked him if he remembered Joe Brown, and if he was a credible person.

Reed told Hayden that as far as he knew, Brown never lied to him, and he asked her why she wanted to know. She finally told him that she had received a letter from Joe Brown, and that he claimed to have knowledge about murders of thirteen women.

"Getting more than that out of her was like pulling teeth. I could see visions of headlines and awards dancing in her head. I could also see the possibility of a screwed-up investigation looming on the horizon if there would be interference by the newspaper," Reed said.

The race to be first to get Joe Brown's confession had begun between the newspaper and the police department.

Hayden soon discovered that Brown had sent nearly "carbon copies" of the letter that she had received to two other reporters at the newspaper where she worked. One of the reporters lived at the same apartment complex as Ginger Gasaway during the time that she was murdered. That reporter told Hayden that she still remembered walking past the trail of blood on the outside stairway, and that she didn't want to have anything to do with Joe Brown.

Leigh Ann Tipton was the other reporter. She was a young woman who wrote a weekly sports column, and she was anxious to pursue something more exciting.

Hayden and Tipton convinced their editor to allow them to work together on the story. They sent a response letter to Brown, which stated that they were eager to talk with him. They also filed a request to visit with Brown at the Wabash Valley Correctional Facility.

Their hopes were dashed, however, because Brown was already isolated in the Segregated Housing Unit (SHU), under maximum security, for stabbing a fellow inmate in the neck. Brown's victim was labeled as a "Chester," meaning he was a child molester, and Brown's only regret was that he had failed to puncture the man's carotid artery deep enough.

Visits from members of the media were strictly off-limits while a prisoner was in the SHU, so Hayden and Tipton had to rely on corresponding with Brown through the mail.

In the meantime, Reed called the Wabash Valley Correctional Facility in Carlisle, Indiana, and spoke with Internal Affairs investigator Carl Lemmons, who arranged for Reed to interrogate Brown. He also contacted Evansville deputy chief Fehrenbacher to request that he be allowed to take Detective Tony Mayhew with him.

On September 17, Reed and Mayhew made the hour-long drive north to the Wabash Valley Correctional Facility. The prison has a national reputation for housing some of the country's more notorious criminals.

Just three months earlier, Joseph Trueblood became the eighth Indiana death row inmate to be executed by lethal injection since 1995. He was executed for the crime of murder after being found guilty of killing his former girlfriend and her two children on August 15, 1988.

When Reed and Mayhew arrived at the prison, Internal Affairs investigators Don Tyler and Carl Lemmons met them. Tyler gave Reed a letter that Brown had written. In it, Brown asked if Reed would be allowed to visit. Joe Brown's question was about to be answered.

THIRTY-THREE

September 17, 2003

Two large corrections officers led Joe Brown down a long green-concrete-and-gunmetal corridor that led to the interrogation room at the Wabash Valley Correctional Facility. Like a chameleon, Brown's skin seemed to take on the gray ash color of the concrete under one overhead light, and then the pea green color of the painted metal walls under the next.

Reed was a bit nervous as he watched him approach. He thought that Brown probably blamed him for making this prison his home. Brown knew that he was never going to get out, and to Reed, he looked like a dead man walking.

Brown entered the interrogation room, and a crooked smile spread across his face when he saw Reed there. Then his expression turned to stone.

It had been two years since Reed had to look into Joe Brown's face, but the image never faded from his memories or his nightmares. It was Reed's job to plunge back into the mind of a sociopath and a murderer. It was his job to visit once again the darkness that had taken him the last two years to push aside.

"Hi, Joe."

Reed reached out his right hand, and Brown took it firmly in both of his without answering. Brown's hands were locked in stainless-steel handcuffs that were attached to the front of a three-inch-wide leather belt that wrapped around his waist. To walk, Brown had to shuffle his feet, which were connected by a short chain and metal ankle cuffs. He wore a one-piece orange jumpsuit. His dark brown hair was cut short and uneven, and was now showing signs of gray.

The tall, slinky man that Reed remembered was now filled out to over two hundred pounds, and he looked healthier than ever before.

Attached to the chain between Brown's handcuffs was an eight-foot-long tether that was looped under the chain connecting Joe's ankles, and was held by a guard who stood behind him. The idea was to be able to dump the prisoner on his face if he decided to get frisky. All the guard had to do was to yank on the tether to lift the prisoner literally off his feet and cause him to fall on his face. Reed would become familiar with that eight-foot length of leather. For the next two months, he would spend hours holding it while he interviewed Brown.

Reed wasn't sure if he would be able to find out the truth about Brown's claims to have killed thirteen other women. Brown either did commit the murders or didn't. Either he would tell the truth or he wouldn't. In the end, Joe Brown was really the only one who knew what the truth was.

Reed Mirandized Brown and asked him to sign a waiver stating that he understood his rights, and was willing to be interviewed voluntarily.

Brown said that he had been released from Michigan City Prison on June 19, 1995, after serving twenty-five years of a life sentence for robbery. In truth, he actually only served eighteen years of his sentence, which included an additional five-year sentence that he had picked up in 1980 for battery on another inmate while he was inside.

Court records show that Judge Walter H. Palmer, of Gibson County Circuit Court, committed Brown to the Indiana Department of Corrections on October 11, 1977. He was sentenced to a life term for the offense of kidnapping Joseph Bender.

He was also sentenced to serve ten years for the offense of committing a felony while armed, which was filed under case number CR-77-52.

On February 11, 1980, Brown was sentenced to five years by Judge Carl T. Smith, of Madison County Circuit Court, in Anderson, Indiana, for the offense of a battery Class C felony for attacking another inmate while he was incarcerated. This sentence was to be served consecutively to the sentences from Gibson County.

On December 19, 1992, Brown was discharged from the life sentence from Gibson County, and began serving his consecutive commitment from Madison County.

On June 19, 1995, Joe Brown, considered to have been rehabilitated, was released from the Indiana Reformatory. He was to be released from parole no later than December 18, 1997. He was given $75 when he was released from prison and free transportation to Evansville, Indiana. During his eighteen-year stay in Indiana correctional facilities, Brown had saved a total of $1.15 in his inmate trust fund, which was also refunded to him at his release.

Reed began his questions.

"Did you do anything before you went to prison? In 1973, had you done any murders?" Reed asked.

"I never . . . I never harmed no one. No. I was pretty much a loner. All I done was gamble. That's all I done."

"Oh? You gambled when you were younger too?"

"Oh yeah. Started about when I was thirteen. I used to leave the house at midnight to play pinball, shoot pool, or play cards, you know? That was my way of dealing with being molested when I was a kid. Back in the '50s and '60s people just swept it underneath the rug. They didn't want to talk about it. I didn't have no one to talk to. I didn't know what was bothering me. As long as I gambled, it didn't bother me or nothing, you know? I didn't wake up crying or nothing."

During the ensuing investigation, Reed discovered that in 1970, when Joe was fifteen, his mother was found dead in the bathtub at their home. Her drowning was ruled an accident, attributed to her dependence on prescription drugs. Those who knew the family whispered that it might have been suicide, brought on because of the ever-present physical and mental abuse at the hands of her husband.

After spending countless hours interviewing him, Reed felt that Joe had more than a witness's role in the death of his mother, but he had no way to substantiate those feelings without a confession from Brown.

After his mother died, Joe moved in with his aunt and uncle, Roger and Sharon Brown, in a trailer court in Evansville. It didn't take long before he stole several of their checks, made them out to cash, and forged their signatures. Roger and Sharon pressed charges against Joe, and he spent the rest of his youth in and out of juvenile facilities known as the Boy's School and the State Farm.

Reed continued his questioning and focused on Joe's past. Brown told him that he joined the U.S. Army in 1972 when he turned eighteen years old. He said that he took his basic training at Fort Ord, California, and then went to Fort Hood, Texas. Reed was at both of those locations during his term in the army between 1971 and 1974, so that gave them something in common to chat about. Brown became a little bit more comfortable.

The U.S. Army charged Brown with being absent without leave, and he was dishonorably discharged from service. Brown could have avoided that, as well as jail time for auto theft, if he would have just returned to his company. Brown preferred to face a jail cell rather than the possibility of being shipped to Vietnam.

Reed decided that he would change his line of questioning to more recent events. He asked Brown what he had planned to do in Ohio, in 2000, if the police hadn't picked him up after he killed Ginger Gasaway. Brown replied that he was going to get even with some members of his family.

"It was pretty much downhill after that, Rick. You guys caught me at the right time in Cincinnati, because I knew what I was getting ready to do and all that, you know. You saved me. This saved me, you know what I mean? I would have went on and killed my family. That's where I was going—to kill my brother."

Joe was referring to his younger brother, David, who disassociated himself from the family, moved to Ohio, and started a family of his own.

"I wouldn't have hurt the kids. I hate child molesters anyway," Brown added without being prompted.

"What about the wife?" Reed asked.

"Yeah, I would've killed her too. Oh yeah, and I was going to go down to see my oldest sister, Sue. I might have done something real nasty to her."

Reed picked up on a pattern where Brown had inadvertently blamed his mother for his killing instincts. In other conversations with Reed, Brown had related stories about a neighbor boy who had molested him when he was about eight or nine years old. He blamed his mother for this also. When questioned directly about his relationship with his mother, Brown would become defensive of her, and say that he would never hurt her.

Regardless of whether or not his mother was responsible for molding Joe's psyche, she did play a role in his relationships with women, even if Joe wouldn't admit it. Brown compared her to Ginger Gasaway because Ginger's husband had an alcohol problem, and according to Brown, he was abusive to her. This mirrored the relationship of Joe's parents.

Brown also talked about another woman, Wanda Hedge, whom he met prior to Ginger. She worked at the Quality Quick in Owensboro, Kentucky. Brown thought the name of this little convenience store was the Quick Pick. He said that he went there often to buy coffee, and that he began asking Wanda out.

"She was an . . . uh . . . older woman. She's probably seven years older than me, just like Ginger was, and I started seeing her. She was an old country girl, you know what I mean, uh . . . had a hard life. Her husband abused her all the time, you know what I mean, uh. . . . She was trying to finish raising her girls, and, I guess, in some ways, she was like the mother to me that I never had. I treated her the best I ever treated anyone, besides Ginger.

"I gave her flowers all the time. I sent her bouquets at her workplace, took her to big-time restaurants, and stuff like that, you know what I mean. She liked to play bingo and I took her there every Wednesday night. I took her there, you know what I mean."

Brown talked about his obsession with Wanda, although he denied ever having a sexual relationship with her. He talked about how he spent all of his money to entertain her and keep her in his company, and in the same sentence, he talked about how she "drove him nuts" and how he felt obsessed to know where she was and what she was doing all the time.

"I guess we became girlfriend and boyfriend. I never had sex with her, though. I treated her with respect. I did spend the night with her, but I never took advantage of her, you know what I mean. But she drove me nuts . . . drove me fuckin' nuts, man. I should have known right then that something was wrong because I kept thinking, 'I'll stop that bitch,' you know.

"I couldn't wait to get off work to go back home, find out where the fuck she was at and what she was doing. She was never doing nothing except helping her daughter clean her house inside and stuff, you know what I mean. But I always seen it a different way. I'd think she was going out with somebody else or whatever, but that wasn't the case. That's just the way I perceived it, and every day it got worse.

"I started missing work because I had to go see her first thing in the morning. She worked the morning shift at Quick Pick, like four-thirty in the morning until two-thirty in the afternoon. I started driving by her apartment three or four times a night. I'd get up at midnight and drive by to see if she was there. I guess in a lot of ways, I was stalking her.

"It got to one point where we were supposed to go out on a date in the middle of the week, but I guess she forgot about it. She marked it on her calendar, but I guess she forgot because she was at her daughter's house helping out, you know. . . . She had a little grandson . . . helping with him; she just plumb forgot.

"It drove me mad that she wasn't home. I was expecting her to be there, you know, 'cause she said she would be there. Her daughter worked at Quick Pick too, so I went by there to ask her where her mother was. She told me to go back to the house and that her mother would be there. This went on for a couple of hours. Then I saw that she was home, but she wouldn't answer the fucking door. She was taking a shower because she was painting, but I didn't know that. I thought she was ignoring me, so I beat the hell out of the bedroom window, and she came out of that shower and just had a bath towel on her.

"I said, 'What the hell's wrong with you? We were supposed to go out tonight,' and she paddled back in the apartment to look at the calendar. She said, 'I'm sorry, I forgot,' and it just drove me nuts. She saw that something was wrong with me, and she said, 'I think it's better that me and you just quit.'"

Brown later admitted that he figured that he had scared Wanda with his behavior, and that he might have killed her if their relationship had kept going. He described her as "lucky."

When Reed later interviewed Wanda, it was clear that she remembered things differently. She described Joe Brown as "weird" and "strange," and didn't remember ever receiving any flowers from him. She worked at the Quality Quick convenience store when Brown started to come in regularly for coffee. She said that he kept asking her out on a date and she finally agreed.

Wanda said that Brown admitted to her that he had spent time in prison, but told her that he had been with someone else who committed a robbery. Brown told her that he was arrested and convicted as an accomplice, not as the main perpetrator.

Wanda also acknowledged that she and Brown had gone out for dinner on several occasions. She said that Brown told her he was a foreman of a construction company, and he would go on and on about how much money he had. She said that she doubted his story because she had seen where he was living, at Whitey's Motel.

She said that one day Brown took her gambling at the Casino Aztar, in Evansville. She said that they were sitting outside and Brown tried to kiss her.

"I told him that I didn't want to do that, and that I would never sleep with him. That made him really angry and he said, 'Oh yes you will!'" Wanda said.

She began to fear Brown. She said that the evening ended abruptly and Brown drove her back to Owensboro, Kentucky, traveling dangerously fast the entire way. Wanda said that her ex-husband had abused her, and she could see the same look in Brown's eyes. She knew then that he had an uncontrollable anger problem.

Wanda said she remembered the time that Brown spoke of, when he came over and beat on her door and bedroom window. She said that she wasn't taking a shower. She was inside hiding from him, hoping he would go away. After that, she decided not to see him again.

THIRTY-FOUR

Reed's conversation with Brown began to flow smoothly, and Joe appeared to be coherent in his recollections. Reed thought it would be a good time to delve deeper into Brown's past. Even though he knew that they would stray from the topic at hand—the murders of thirteen women—Reed believed that by listening to Brown talk about his past, he might better ascertain the truthfulness of his recollections of the more recent events. He was able to get Brown to talk a little bit more about the time that he spent in prison from 1977 until 1995.

Brown said that the entire time that he was in prison, not one of his family members came to visit him. His sister Jennie Egli occasionally corresponded by mail or telephone, but that was the extent of his communication with the outside world.

Brown said that he never read newspapers or watched the television news while he was locked up, and that he actively disassociated himself from society. He said it was the only way that he was able to maintain his sanity during the extended sentence that used up the bulk of his life.

He then digressed to his childhood. Brown said that a family member and a neighbor boy had molested him. He also said that his mother molested him, but then changed his story, saying that it was someone else, but his mother knew about it and did nothing to stop it.

Reed wasn't sure what to believe. It could have been any of the scenarios or none, but whatever the case, Brown seemed to believe that he had been molested. He refused to answer any questions directly related to his mother, but Brown referred to her as a "bitch" and said that she didn't care about him.

Reed pressed a little harder to get Brown to talk about his mother, but he refused to talk about her any further, except to say that she had died early in his life. It was time to move the conversation ahead to the time that Brown was given his freedom.

Records show that Joe Brown was released from prison on June 19, 1995, and went to live with his uncle and aunt, Roger and Sharon Brown, on Carolina Avenue in Evansville. They told Reed that Joe came into town on a Greyhound Bus. He called them from the Evansville Rescue Mission and asked them to pick him up.

The parole office initially tried to place him with his sister Jennie, but she refused to take him. Joe had harbored a grudge toward her ever since. The parole office also tried to place Brown with Harold Geiselman in Somerville, Indiana. Harold and his wife told the parole office that they were retired and traveled a lot. They did not want Joe to move in with them.

Roger and Sharon were the last resort, and they agreed to let Joe move in with them. Bryan Brown, their son, even gave Joe a job at his masonry business, Artistic Design. Bryan lived nearby on Mill Road between Kratzville Road and St. Joseph Avenue.

Joe Brown met Mary Lou Seitz while he stayed with Roger and Sharon. She worked at a convenience store located at Kratzville Road and Allen Lane. She was living with her uncle in the same trailer court, just two lots away from Roger and Sharon. Even though they had just met and hardly knew each other, they decided to get married in December 1995.

Joe described their relationship:

"At the time, you got to realize I was just getting out of prison and had been locked up for a couple of decades. I didn't have the slightest idea what to do out there, you know what I mean. I was so used to corrections taking care of me.

"My aunt and uncle had a friend, and he had a niece named Mary Lou. They set me up with her. I mean, I needed somebody. I needed somebody, and she needed someone to take care of her, you know what I mean. There wasn't no love, no feelings, no nothing."

Mary Lou later told Reed that Roger and Sharon Brown didn't let Joe live with them for very long, and they helped him get an apartment on West Iowa Street in Evansville. Brown and Mary Lou lived there together for a brief period of time. Mary Lou said that Brown had been acting strange and became suicidal. She took him to her doctor, and he was given lithium. She said that Brown started thinking clearly for the first time in his life and it really scared him, so he refused to continue taking his medicine. Instead, Mary Lou said that Brown began to take up to eighty Sudafed tablets a day.

Two months after they were joined together in marriage, Mary Lou filed for divorce in February 1996. Brown attempted to reconcile with her for several months, and in May, Mary Lou phoned in a request to postpone the marriage dissolution because they were attempting to reconcile. She finally had enough and kicked him out of the apartment in June. She said that Brown scared her. The court granted a dissolution of the marriage in July.

Brown blamed their marital problems on his gambling addiction. Mary Lou said that it was because of his "perverted sexual demands" and his obsession with wanting to always have anal sex with her.

Brown was so desperate for money that before he left, he stole the refrigerator and some copper plumbing valves, presumably to sell. He even left a note behind apologizing to his landlord for stealing the items, saying that he would try to get him some money back in return. Then he got into his yellow 1979 Chevy Scottsdale pickup truck and headed to Tunica, Mississippi, to do some gambling. That was where, Brown said, he committed his first murder.

Without hesitation, and with clear detail, Joe Brown was able to answer all of Reed's questions to re-create the first of many grisly scenes to come.

"The Sheridan Casino and Hotel. They got an old parking lot in the back. I met her at the Horseshoe Casino, and killed her in the parking lot at the Sheridan next door. I murdered her in my truck, strangled her."

"How did you meet her?" Reed asked.

"She was a prostitute. It was right after Mary Lou kicked me out that I went on a killing spree. I went to Tunica to gamble. It was just the same old thing I used to do before when things didn't work out. I went and gambled.

"I just tried to think about beating the big wheel, you understand what I'm saying. That made me feel like somebody. And hell, that's where I learned how to pick up prostitutes—at the casinos, because it's easy there. They come looking for you. You don't have to look. Well, she came looking, and wanted to go back to my motel room. I wasn't renting a motel room, so I said, 'Hell, I've got a truck right here, so why pay for a room?' It was just a blow job. It wasn't like she was going to have to clean up or anything afterward."

Brown said that the woman had grayish brown hair, was about five feet four inches tall, and weighed around 145 pounds.

"We got in an argument on how much she wanted. She said she wanted a hundred dollars for a blow job. I told her she was out of her fucking mind, you know what I mean, and I strangled her. It was dark, and there wasn't nobody back there. She was the first, and I buried her."

"Where is she buried at?"

"Right there in Tunica, about a mile and a half away from the casino. Be easy to find. She ain't but four feet down in the ground. There's only one way to come into the Horseshoe, and one way to go out. You go down and there is a gas station on the right. It's out in the fuckin' desert, you know what I mean. They bought up all that land, and they built eleven casinos out there. There are no houses or nothing out there, just a gas station on the right. You make a right, go down about a mile and a half, and she's buried on the side of the road."

"Do you know her name?"

"Candy."

In a letter that Brown wrote to the *Evansville Courier & Press,* he described Candy as a thin young woman with shoulder-length brown hair. He also wrote that he buried her in a soybean field in Robinson, Mississippi. Brown's description of the woman and the location of her burial place did not match. Reed noted the discrepancies in Brown's statement.

THIRTY-FIVE

After killing Candy in Tunica, Mississippi, Brown said that he returned to Evansville to check in at his place of employment, but he didn't stay. He traveled north to Terre Haute, Indiana, and spent the night at a rescue mission. Then he said he traveled west on I-70 and stopped in Cincinnati, Ohio, where he worked at a bakery for a couple of days to get some money for gas.

Brown said that he was on his way to Zanesville, Ohio, to search for his brother David, whom he had seen only once in the last thirty years. During his initial interview, Joe said that he was unable to find his brother. Later, he said that he did visit with his brother in Zanesville, and that David even invited him back to Ohio for Christmas. Regardless of which version is true, Joe wouldn't make it back to his brother's house, because he would end up behind bars before the holiday season.

According to Brown's statement, it didn't take long for him to find his second victim. He said that he picked up a hitchhiker at a rest area just a couple of hours after he left Cincinnati. In his statement, Brown said that he wasn't sure if he met her in Ohio or in West Virginia, but in a letter that he wrote previously, he named the location as Lebanon, Ohio. He may have been thinking of Lebanon, because that was the location of the barracks for the Ohio State Police.

Brown said that this girl was not a prostitute. He thought she might have been a college student on her way to Pittsburgh, Pennsylvania.

"She was on her way home. She was pretty young, like twenty maybe."

"White girl?" Reed asked.

"Oh yeah. I don't go out with niggers."

"How did you meet this girl?"

"She just walked up to me. I guess she saw my out-of-state license plate. She asked me where I was going and I told her Pennsylvania. She said that's where she was going—to Pittsburgh. She got in. I never had trouble picking up people. I always kept clean-cut, you know what I mean."

In a letter confessing his crimes, Brown wrote that he took the hitchhiker to a motel just outside of Columbus. He wrote that they drove to a Red Roof Inn next to I-71, had sex, and then he strangled her to death with a shoestring afterward. He claimed to have put her body in a garbage Dumpster behind the motel.

"And what did she look like? Do you remember?"

"She's about five foot three inches tall, and a hundred and twenty pounds. She had short reddish-brown hair. It's like my mom used to have. The same kind of hair color. It wasn't long. It was like a—you know—a DA haircut. Did you ever hear of a DA haircut?"

"What did you talk about?"

"Not much really. She said she was going to Pittsburgh. She had family there. She might have been a college student. This is the time college was getting out, you know what I mean.

"I would think that the manager of BFI (Browning Ferris Incorporated) would keep track of the years and locations where they dump stuff at. You'd find a lot of bodies in there, you know what I mean."

Brown didn't have anything else useful to offer about the second girl that he claimed to have killed, so he continued to talk about his journey east.

"I felt like I was losing it. I just wanted to run away. I just got off parole and I took off. I was going to the East Coast, you know. I'd never been there, so that's where I was going. That's the main reason why I left. I just wanted to get away from everything, you know what I mean."

Brown said that he traveled through part of West Virginia and then stayed a couple of nights at a halfway house in Pennsylvania. He said that he got $240 worth of food stamps while he was there, and then sold them for $120 in cash.

Reed and his partner, Tony Mayhew, continued to interrogate Brown, but their line of questioning jumped from one victim to another, and from incidents that took place in 1996 and then 2000 and then back to 1997. Brown was becoming confused and his answers were unproductive. The confusion began to spread on both sides of the interrogation table as the three men tried to plot Brown's course using a United States atlas.

"So you picked up one girl in Ohio, around Cincinnati? I remember you said you picked her up at a rest area."

"What am I looking at, Ohio?"

"But it could have been Ohio, Pennsylvania, or West Virginia?"

"I know it wasn't in Pennsylvania," Brown said.

"But it's prior to when you went east toward West Virginia. It's prior to getting to the mountains?"

"Yeah, I thought I took 70 all the way, but obviously I didn't. I know I stayed in Cincinnati a couple of days when I worked at the bakery place. I know I didn't go through Columbus. I didn't go through no big cities. Look! There's Zanesville right there! There is Zanesville, Ohio. I must have went through there and cut over to I-70."

"Then you went onto 71, I think. You said you were near Lebanon, which is near Columbus. I don't see it on the map. Is that it?"

"Yeah."

"Wait a minute. Where is Cincinnati?"

"Right there," Brown said as he pointed to the map.

"You were up in here someplace?"

"Yeah, that's Lebanon right there. I was right outside of Cincinnati. I must've took 71 and then cut back over to 70. Where's Pennsylvania at?"

"It will be north of West Virginia. It's on the north . . . I'm sorry, on the east side of Ohio, kind of north would be Pennsylvania."

"I wasn't near that way. Oh wait, that's South Dakota."

They decided to take a much needed break for lunch, and to get some better maps so they could pinpoint Brown's path with more detail.

Some fresh air and some food did wonders to clear the detectives' heads, but they were not able to locate a map with greater detail. Reed and Mayhew decided to push on with the interview anyway and returned to the interrogation room.

In a letter confessing his third murder, Brown wrote that he headed back to Louisville, Kentucky, and two days after leaving Pennsylvania, he turned back toward West Virginia on I-64, where he picked up a hitchhiker.

During the interview, Brown described her as a pretty girl, in her early twenties. He said that she had streaked blond or brownish hair, was about five feet five inches tall, and weighed approximately 130 pounds.

According to Brown, this girl was also on her way to Pittsburgh, Pennsylvania, and he was more than willing to give her a ride. He said that they stopped at a rest area just before reaching Wheeling, West Virginia, and decided to spend the night. She didn't see the rising sun of the next morning.

Brown said that he beat this girl up pretty bad, but he never mentioned having sexual intercourse with her. Straying from his normal modus operandi, Brown said, he killed her by strangling her with his bare hands instead of using shoelaces. He claimed to have deposited her body in a garbage Dumpster, then headed back to Indiana.

Brown returned to his apartment on West Iowa Street in Evansville, and he made an attempt to reconcile with wife Mary Lou Seitz. She wanted nothing more to do with him and threw him out again. On July 11, 1996, their marriage was legally dissolved.

Brown continued to work construction for his cousin, Bryan, and he found himself a new apartment on South New York Avenue, in Evansville. It was in August, Brown said, that he first procured the services of a crack-addicted prostitute named Andrea Hendrix-Steinert. He just called her "Slick."

Brown said that she was the only prostitute with whom he could really talk honestly. He liked Andrea because she listened to him, with what he perceived to be genuine interest. He began to see her somewhat regularly, and said that he actually began to trust her. Brown said that she also talked to him about her life, her addiction to cocaine, and her desire to make a better life for herself. He said that he liked Slick too much to want to kill her.

A year later, his opinion changed.

For several months after he killed his third victim, Brown said, he managed to stay out of trouble and keep to himself. Then in October, he claimed to be driving in the area of Diamond Avenue and US Highway 41 North, in his yellow 1979 Chevy pickup truck. He said that a prostitute flagged him down, but he only had $17 with him.

Brown said that he told her he had more money at his new apartment at South New York Avenue, and he took the prostitute there with him. He described her as twenty-five to thirty years old, shoulder-length brown hair, about five feet one inch tall, and weighed around 115 pounds. Brown said that she had a sunken face and looked almost anorexic, having very little or almost no breasts.

Brown thought the girl lived on Chestnut or Cherry Street in Evansville, but he couldn't remember how or why he remembered that.

In a letter of confession, Brown simply wrote, "I had sex with her, then strangled her with a shoestring. Then I dumped her body in a garbage dumpster at the Lincoln Projects."

Reed said that Brown told him he beat her until she was unconscious, and then he strangled her with his bare hands.

On October 30, 1996, Brown was arrested in Henderson, Kentucky, on a warrant for theft that was issued in Warrick County, Indiana. Bryan Brown filed the charges against Joe for stealing most of the tools that he had let him work with at a construction site in Boonville, Indiana.

Reed asked Brown what he did with his 1979 Chevy pickup truck after he was arrested for the theft. Brown told him that it was repossessed while he was in jail. On December 12, 1996, the Department of Corrections once again let Joe Brown enter freely into society.

The interrogation continued.

"Do they let you have writing materials and stuff in here?" Reed asked Brown.

"Yeah."

"We're going to be leaving soon. I know that you're probably tired too. We have to go back and talk to our boss, and then write something up about what we talked about and try to put it in some kind of order.

"To help us tomorrow, we'll get better maps so we

can be more detailed about where everything is. If you would tonight, sit down and try to remember where and when everything happened."

"I can do that," Brown said.

"Try to figure out who, what, a description of them, where you picked them up, where you murdered them, and where you dumped them at. Whatever you can remember."

"I'll help you with that. Like I said, if you had a trucker's map with all the rest areas and stuff like that. You know, that would help a lot."

"We'll have one tomorrow Joe."

"How do you know there are thirteen of them?" Reed asked.

"Because I know."

"You never really have forgotten this or how—"

"No, I never forgot. I know there's thirteen."

"Is that counting Ginger?"

"No, that's not counting Ginger."

"So there was four in Indiana?"

"Four in Indiana, two in Mississippi, and one in Clarksville, Tennessee. There was two in Denver—well, one in Denver and one in Mesquite, New Mexico. There's two in St. Louis. One in, I think I was out on, I might have been in Ohio when I killed her. I'm not—"

"Not in West Virginia, then?"

"Yeah, but I killed two. I thought one was in West Virginia, and the other one was in Maryland, but maybe one was in Ohio and the other one was in West Virginia, you know."

"I think we probably ought to go ahead and end this. We have to get back up here again at eight in the morning. Let's go ahead and show the end of this statement is going to be at fifteen hundred hours."

THIRTY-SIX

September 18, 2003

The paper in front of him read, "Knowing that I may have an attorney in my behalf present and that I do not have to make any statement nor incriminate myself in any manner. I make this statement voluntary, of my own free will, knowing that such statement could later be used against me in any court of law, and I declare that this statement is made without any threat, coercion, offer of benefit, favor or offer of favor, leniency or offer of leniency by any person or persons whomsoever."

Joe Brown signed it.

EPD sergeant Rick Reed spoke into the microphone.

"We're starting a new tape here. We just resumed our interview with Joe Brown in the counselor's office here at Wabash Valley. The time is seventeen-ten on September 18, 2003. Show present, Detective Mayhew, Sergeant Reed, and Joseph Brown. We're also video-taping this at this time.

"Joe, do you remember all the rights I read to you?"

"Yes, sir."

"Okay, and you still are wanting to talk to us?"

"Yes."

"When we left off, you talked about your fourth

victim, a girl from Evansville. Let's go ahead now and begin with victim number five. Do you know who it was, and where you were at?"

"Well, I murdered the fourth one on New York Avenue and I dumped her over by the projects. It was a couple of weeks later that I got arrested for stealing my cousin's scaffolding and brakesaw, and I was locked up in Warrick County Jail. I'd like to think I got out the first week of December. It was colder than hell.

"I had to walk all the way back to Evansville. I walked all the way, couldn't get a fuckin' ride from nobody. It was colder than hell and all I had on was a long-sleeve shirt, you know what I mean. I spent a couple of weeks in the rescue mission, and then I finally got me another car at Greg Goebel's Auto Care on Riverside Road.

"I bought me a black 1991 Nissan Stanza XE and I was working for Kenny Spahn at the time. I was in the union, and I was going to get my journeyman's license.

"I picked up this prostitute on Fares Avenue. I guess it was sometime in the spring of '97. It was probably in April or May. I think I picked her up down by the Old National Bank. It was either there or at the intersection of Morgan Avenue and Fares Avenue.

"I rented motels. I know I stayed at St. Mary's Motel, but I never killed nobody there. I think I took her to the Royal Motel."

From Columbia Street to Diamond Avenue, there's a strip of run-down, Indian-owned motels. The Royal Inn Motel was one of the better establishments along this route, but that wasn't saying much. Reed later said that he would give it a $3\frac{1}{2}$ roach rating.

"It was the Royal Inn Motel. I, uh . . . had sex with her. I didn't rough her up or nothing like that, but I killed her afterwards. I, uh . . . strangled her with a shoestring. Some of these murders, especially the first six . . . it's like I couldn't stop. It's like when I killed Ginger. I just couldn't stop myself. That's the way it was.

I wanted to stop and I couldn't. It was like I was going through the motions, and I felt remorse after most of them . . . uh, a couple of them.

"Like Slick, it was like there was a little bond between her and me. I didn't let myself get close to prostitutes, but she was the only one that I talked to. And she talked to me a little bit, you know what I mean. When she tried to steal twenty dollars from me, it's like she just broke whatever trust I had. I don't know why I trusted her. I guess 'cause she was in the same situation, like she needed somebody to talk to. When she stole my money just like that, I guess I, uh . . ."

"Do you remember the room number you had at the Royal Inn?" Mayhew asked, trying to get Brown to focus back on the fifth murder victim.

"I ain't gonna sit here and lie to you, Tony, I can't. But I know what she looked like. She was about five foot five inches tall, with shoulder-length brown hair that was black underneath. She was probably in her mid-twenties, but with some of these prostitutes, it's hard to judge their age, you know what I mean. She weighed about one hundred twenty-five pounds. I always picked them up where I know I could throw them in the Dumpster somewhere.

"I just had basic sex with her and I got dressed. Then I strangled her with shoestrings. I had shoestrings with me at the time. She was awake, putting her clothes on, with her back turned toward me, you know. I can't understand why she didn't fight back. The only one that really fought me was a San Diego State college student. She put up a fight, but the rest . . . they just . . . and Ginger was the same fucking way, you know. She knew what I was going to do. She had to know, but she just gave in."

Brown then said that he got rid of his fifth victim by putting her in a Dumpster at the Diamond Valley Apartments, about two miles west of the motel on

Diamond Avenue. He said that he also threw her purse in a Dumpster, but that he always threw his victims' property in different Dumpsters from where he threw their bodies.

"The ones you killed on the interstate, did you have to drive a good distance to find another Dumpster to throw their stuff away?" Reed asked.

"No. I'd just go to the next exit until I found a Dumpster, you know what I mean. That's where I tossed the shit at. Some of them might have had money, I don't know. I wasn't interested in that. I just wanted their IDs."

"Was that because you were afraid that if somebody found a body, they might be able to identify it?"

"That sounds good. It's possible, you know what I mean."

"When you killed the fifth one, were you still in your black Nissan Stanza?"

Brown became animated and laughed out loud.

"Yeah. You're gonna like this one. I only made one payment on that car. It was a piece of junk, you know what I mean. I was coming off Diamond Expressway onto 41 and I was trying to get over in the far end lane. All of a sudden, there's this pickup truck right in front of me and I couldn't stop. *Bam!*"

"So you had a wreck on 41?"

"Took the whole front off."

"Was it reported to the police?"

"Probably, but the guy I ran into, the S10 pickup, he didn't have no driver's license, so he wasn't gonna sit there and hang around. He's out on Highway 41 with a beer bottle in his hand, stuck on stupid, you know what I mean.

"The police didn't come while I was there, so I took the car and kept it for a couple of months. I took the brand-new battery out of it, and then I dumped it out in Greg Goebel's Auto Care. I let them deal with the bank while I got mine," Brown said; then he laughed out loud again.

"Are you ready to do number six?"

"Yeah."

In June 1997, Joe Brown stayed in room number four, at Whitey's Motel, on Highway 60 West, in Owensboro, Kentucky. During a later interview with Brown's next-door neighbor Christie Beaven, she said that Brown showed up at Whitey's one day and was covered in blood. When she asked him about it, Brown told her that he had been on a trip to Tennessee and that he had cut his finger.

"If that was true, he must have bled a couple of pints," Beaven said.

The next day, she said, Joe told her that an escort service girl had cheated him, and that he had gotten even. Beaven's statement gave some credibility to Brown's account of his sixth victim.

"Number six was, um . . . things started happening real fast then. I planned this one. She was from Savage Entertainment. I set this one up myself, you know what I mean. She came there in a taxi and asked for money up front. They charge you seventy-five dollars just to show up. I guess that goes to the company, but then you got to deal with them. It's a big fuckin' rip-off," Brown said during the interrogation.

"This was at the Schmidt Motel?"

"I'm pretty sure. I only killed one at the Royal. Yeah, it was the Schmidt. It was night, but it wasn't that late, probably around seven or eight o'clock. It was dark outside. I wanted a petite woman. I like petite women, you know what I mean. She was about five foot three inches and one hundred twenty pounds. She had shoulder-length brownish hair, a real pretty face, and nice legs. She might have been a dancer because what they wanna do, most of them that worked for that company, is just to get naked and dance around, you know what I mean.

"Fuck that. I could look at a *Playboy*, you know what I mean," Brown said with a hearty laugh.

"I planned this one all the way out. I had duct tape and everything. I had a bad experience with one of them fuckin' exotic dancers out of the same company in, uh . . . February of 1996. She charged me two hundred dollars for nothing. I might have done her in, but a friend of mine came over, plus she had an escort. I guess they were scared back then.

"This one wasn't, though. It was pretty wild. She just wanted the money, and didn't give a fuck what I did to her. I'm not Chuck Berry but I let all my frustrations out on her, you know what I mean. I tied her hands behind her back, and rode her as hard as I could. I didn't hit her or nothing like that, but I tied her up and strangled her, though."

"What did you do with the duct tape?"

"Taped her mouth."

"Why? Did she try to scream?"

"No. I just taped her mouth, like I done to Ginger. I just did."

"Did she struggle with you at all?"

"No."

"She just thought you were playing games?"

"Yeah. Ginger thought I was playing a game too. Even them two prostitutes in St. Louis, you know. If you pay them money, they will pretty much do anything you want, you know what I mean."

"Were her hands tied with shoestrings?"

"Shoestrings, yeah."

Brown said that the girl came to his door and asked if he was calling for the escort service. He told her that he was and gave her $75. After that, she told him how much she charged for the different services that she provided. When Brown explained what he wanted, she told him that it would cost him an additional $125.

"That was for herself?"

"Yeah, I gave her the money. Oh yeah, 'cause I knew that I was gonna get it back anyway. It really didn't matter to me. I was going through the rigmarole, you know. I knew the money was coming back to me."

"After you gave her the money, what happened then?"

"We had sex. I tied her hands behind her back and, uh . . . Ginger's the one that . . . I gotta slow down now."

"Okay, let's just concentrate on this one for right now," Mayhew said.

"Joe, I know it's hard, but you're doing a lot of good here. You may be preventing this from happening ever again. There might be an innocent person that lives because of this," Reed added.

"I just couldn't stop what I was doing. I mean, I knew what I was doing, but I just couldn't stop myself. Just like with Ginger. I didn't want to kill her, but I just couldn't stop myself. It's been hard the last couple of years, dealing with this. It shouldn't have been like this.

"It seems the last couple of years that it's like I've been dead on the inside. I wake up at night with cold sweats and stuff, you know what I mean. I've been having violent nightmares. I've been having dreams about Ginger. I always dream about her taking the car away from me, you know what I mean."

Brown didn't mention remorse for killing Ginger and chopping her body up into little pieces. Instead, his nightmares seemed to be focused on Ginger taking her car away from him.

"I've been having nightmares about walking city block to city block, trying to find the car 'cause that's what she done. When she wanted to get back at me, she just took my car away."

Maybe Ginger's ghost was coming back to haunt Brown, and to get back at him one last time for killing her the way he did. Maybe the sociopath was finally developing a conscience, and the only way he could feel guilt was by imagining that Ginger was taking the car away from him, and he manifested his guilt through his dreams. Maybe he was simply making the whole thing up to gain sympathy. Whatever the case, Reed believed that Brown was acting sincere.

"I told Carl Heldt that I don't hold no animosity toward you guys," Brown said.

Heldt was the judge who presided over Joe Brown's sentencing hearing.

"Heldt, Levco or none of you . . . you guys done your job. I knew I'd get the maximum. That's what the public wanted. I don't have no animosity towards people like that. That's why I wrote Heldt . . . to tell him I was having a real hard time dealing with what I did, and the main thing was, I wanted to try to bring some closure to the victim's family. I'm hoping that when it's all said and done, that maybe I can have closure with myself, you know."

Brown also said that he was worried about how people would perceive him.

"My therapist said that the news media would be all over my family. I told her that I don't have no family. It ain't about that no more. I'm tired of worrying about what they do. I mean, I'm sick of it. I'm doing something for myself."

It was time to change work shifts at the prison, which meant that Brown's cuffs and shackles also needed to be changed.

"Okay, I'm going to stop the tape. It's five forty-five P.M. We're going to resume the tape. It's five forty-seven P.M. We stopped long enough to have the handcuffs changed by the guards that are going off-duty."

"Where'd we leave off at?" Brown asked.

Reed reassured Brown that his confession of the crimes he claimed to have committed were going to bring good consequences for generations to come, and hopefully prevent similar crimes from being committed in the future.

"You know I never got to read the newspapers. I didn't get to see the television much, although I had one of my own over in the county jail. I didn't get to watch the news stations and stuff like that. The only time I got to watch was on Fox News, when they was taking a public vote on whether I should receive the death penalty or not, you know."

"I don't remember them doing that," Reed said.

"Yeah, eighty-three percent said kill him."

Reed and Mayhew found it impossible to stifle a laugh.

"I want to get more of the FBI Behavioral people to work with you, and they may talk to you over the next couple of years. The things you're talking about, and what you've done, can add so much to their collective knowledge of how to combat this, and how to find it and stop it. If I hadn't stopped you when I did, you would have kept going," Reed said.

"Stop the killing."

"And how do we do that? We can't stop somebody from doing that unless we can talk to the people that are doing it and figure out how to stop it."

"Looking back, I can say that it was so easy. A couple of times, I should've been caught, but I wasn't."

"Getting back to number six, did anyone from Savage ever come by and check on her or anything?"

"No."

"Did the taxi wait for her? What taxi service was it?"

"River City."

"You said that you planned this one because you had tape and shoestrings and all that stuff. You taped her mouth. Did you tape her anyplace else? Did you have sex first and then tie her up?"

"No, no. I tied her up first. She said she wasn't into anal. She didn't want to do no anal, but I ain't into that shit anyway, you know what I mean. She took her clothes off, and I took my clothes off, and I had the tape and shoestrings underneath the bed. Like I said, I had this all planned. I tied her hands behind her back and I started, uh . . . I call it rodeoing, you know what I mean.

"I felt like I was in power. I don't know if you can understand that or not. I taped her mouth and that made it more . . . that made it more, uh . . . uh . . . made it more . . ."

"Is this the first time you taped someone's mouth shut?"

"Yeah, and I was taping her and I just had to . . . It was like . . . that's just the difference, you know what I mean. That extra excitement, I guess. I got some sexual gratification out of it, by tying them up, even hitting them. I ain't gonna sit here and pretend it wasn't, because it was. By tying them up and making them look defenseless, it just added that more excitement to it."

"So then after you tied her hands together behind her back and you taped her mouth shut, you had sex with her then?"

"I probably had sex with her . . . uh . . . I got myself excited, you know what I mean. I was having a hard time getting off. I don't know why."

"Were you thinking that you were going to kill her while you were having sex with her?"

"Yeah, a couple of times, but I never had trouble with that before in my life. Somehow I just couldn't . . . uh . . . you know what I mean."

"Ejaculate?"

"I just couldn't. It didn't make no difference how I done it. I turned her which way or another. I just couldn't, and that made it frustrating for me that I didn't. I thought I was gonna have an ultimate show, so to speak, a rodeo show, but I just, uh . . . I don't know why. I just couldn't ejaculate, you know what I mean."

"By rodeo, do you mean doggy style?"

"Yeah. That's the first one that I tied her hands behind her back."

"Okay."

Brown began to ramble on almost incoherently.

"That one I picked up in Lebanon, we had a really good time, know what I mean. She said, 'I'll give you the thrill of a lifetime,' right? I said, 'Well, okay.' She was . . . out of all the prostitutes that just fake it, like a dead fuck, so to speak. It wasn't there, you know what I mean. A couple of them was dead fucks, so to speak, and that made me more frustrated 'cause here they wanted money, you know what I mean. Forget it. It's like duh. That's why it kind of pissed me off . . . that one I picked up off the Diamond Expressway going through my apartment and uh . . . she was just a dead fuck, man. So I just tried to . . . uh . . . you can't hurt them. I hear people say, 'I'm gonna fuck the shit out of them.' Well, you can't hurt them. I don't care who they are, you ain't gonna hurt them, you know what I mean. So I don't even get that idea, you know. You can't, you can't. . . . If they can have a baby, it ain't gonna hurt that much, you know what I mean. Believe me, it kinda pissed me off, like I said.

"And like I said, sometimes I wonder if I wasn't just looking for an excuse just to justify myself and then strangle them, you know what I mean. Especially the first couple, you know what I mean. But the further I got along, it just didn't matter.

"Just like when I killed Ginger. It just didn't fuckin' matter, you know what I mean. Choppin' her up like I did. It didn't faze me at all—"

Mayhew interrupted Brown and tried to get him to refocus on the questions at hand.

"You say you couldn't ejaculate and got frustrated. What did you do then?"

"I strangled her," Brown answered without a second's hesitation.

"You strangled her right there?"

"I strangled her right then and there."

"Did you use your hands?"

"Yes."

"No shoestring?" Reed asked.

"I used a shoestring and . . . uh . . . she, uh . . . she put up a little struggle, but there wasn't a fuckin' thing she could do. Her mouth was taped. Her hands were tied behind her back, you know what I mean. That probably gave me more gratification than trying to rodeo her, if that makes any sense. I mean, I was fucking her and I couldn't get off, yet strangling her like that . . . I felt more, um . . . gratification out of it. Does that make sense?"

"Were you still screwing her when you were strangling her?" Mayhew asked.

"No."

"You quit?"

"I quit. You know, like I said, this went on for a couple of hours. Most of them, after five or ten minutes, they just are like hurry up. That pissed the shit out of me, you know what I mean. But I paid her whatever she wanted. She was willing to do whatever I wanted to do, but like I said, some of them, especially toward the first one . . . when I was strangling them, I knew I was doing wrong, but I just couldn't stop. I couldn't stop. I couldn't stop. . . ." Brown's voice trailed off with almost a whimper.

"So after you strangled this girl, what did you do?"

Brown explained how he dumped the body in a garbage Dumpster at the Village Green Apartments off Greenriver Road, and then he gave the police directions on how to get there. Brown said that he had worked for a contractor at the apartment complex in 1996, and that was why he was familiar with it.

"Was she dressed or naked when you threw her in there?"

"All of them was dressed, except for Slick."

"But you killed her while she was still tied up and naked right?"

"Oh yeah."

"So did you have to dress her?"

"Yeah."

"Did you leave the binding on her, the shoelaces and the duct tape?"

"No. I always threw them away. I never left it on them. It's just like the best thing I can describe. It's like you use a pair of latex gloves. When you get done, you shuck them things. That's what I done with the shoestrings, you know what I mean. I was getting rid of something dirty, you know what I mean."

Brown said that he went through the woman's purse and took back the money that he had given her, along with her ID, which was most likely a driver's license. He said that he probably threw the rest of her things in a different Dumpster from the one he disposed of her body in.

"I never threw the purse, the backpack, or this one had a suitcase . . . I never threw them in the same Dumpster. I always went to a different Dumpster and threw the shit away."

Further questioning about this murder revealed little more and Brown said that by this time, he was getting way out of hand. But he wasn't finished yet. He was only halfway through describing the number of murders to which he had laid claim.

THIRTY-SEVEN

The interrogation of Joe Brown continued for twelve hours a day. He claimed to have killed his sixth victim in 1997 at the Schmidt Motel. She allegedly was a prostitute, sent to the motel by a company called Savage Entertainment.

Having developed an insatiable appetite for dominating women and then murdering them, Brown decided to call the escort service again in January 1998. He received no retribution for his actions against his sixth victim, so he decided that he would try again. He even rented a room at the same place, the Schmidt Motel.

According to Brown, the girl that was sent over to him was called "September."

Once again, Brown's statement was full of broken sentences and he had difficulty focusing, but in general, no matter how many times he was asked the same questions, and no matter how much time elapsed between interrogation sessions, his stories remained relatively constant, except for this one account, where he changed his story.

"I didn't have no car, no nothing, but I just had that . . . uh . . . I don't know, compulsion seems like the right word. I had it just like the same thing I had when I wanted to gamble.

"I don't know, I'm pretty sure I went back to Schmidt's motel and . . . uh . . . I rented a room and called the escort service. I had them send somebody out. She drove herself there, right, and she had a pager and all that, and they called her to make sure that she was there, you know what I mean. They wanted to know if she was all right, and that she would receive the seventy-five dollars, and, uh . . . I mean, if that wouldn't have happened, I would have killed her, ain't no doubt.

"I would've killed her, but I probably would've been busted by her having to answer the phone. Well, I had to answer it, but they wanted to talk to her, right, to see if she was all right and all that, you know what I mean. And that kind of made me scared, so to speak. . . . I went back to Michigan, you know what I mean."

"Did you have sex with that girl?" Reed asked.

Brown said that he didn't, and that he just gave her $75 and she went on her way.

"What did she look like?" Reed asked.

"She's a pretty one. She's probably in her early thirties. She's about five foot nine inches tall, medium build, maybe one hundred thirty pounds. She had a nice build to her, you know what I mean. She was pretty, you know what I mean. So . . . uh . . . that was one that got away."

Christie Beaven said that she remembered Brown bringing a girl over to his place around this time and that "they made a god-awful racket."

She said that she saw Brown leave early the next morning and that she never saw the girl again. The Evansville police were able to track that girl down. She was a stripper who worked at the Exotic She Lounge on Diamond Avenue in Evansville.

Her name was Brenda Boyer, but she went by the name of September because that was the month in which she was born. Brown's mother was also born in September. According to Brown, September's boyfriend abused her, and she was a regular drug user—just like Brown's mother had been.

In a statement taken by Detective Mayhew on October 10, 2003, Boyer said that she was working at the dance club when Joe Brown came in and offered to pay her to have sex with him.

She said that she wanted $100, but Joe only had $50. She agreed to have sex with him anyway. Boyer said that Brown did have a car, and that he drove her to Whitey's Motel, just outside of Owensboro, not the Schmidt Motel.

She said that they spent about two hours together, had sex, and then talked for a while. Then he drove her back to Evansville and dropped her off at the Exotic She Lounge, where she picked up her car.

Boyer said that they just had normal sex, and that Brown did not try to tie her up or do anything unusual to her.

"He was really nice. You know, he seemed like a caring person," Boyer said.

During another questioning period, Brown described September as a very petite girl, standing only five foot one inch tall, and weighing about 110 pounds. He said that she was still very pretty, even though she wore rings on her pierced nipples.

"She was spending the night with me for a hundred bucks, you know what I mean. That wasn't a bad deal. I was gonna kill her. I had it all set up, tape, shoestrings, everything, but something, I mean, after we had sex and stuff, she turned the tide on me. She, uh . . . started talking about her husband abusing her. She hated working at the strip club, but she had to get on her own feet. She didn't have nobody to turn to, you know what I mean.

"She was in her early thirties, probably about the

same age as Slick was, but it just . . . I don't know if it's the right word, but I felt pity for her. I felt sorry for her because she was someone I could relate to," Brown said.

"She was like you," Mayhew said.

"Yeah, so, uh . . . she got away. She got away," Brown mumbled on the brink of tears.

In July 2004, Sergeant Reed found Brenda Boyer, alias September, living in Princeton, Indiana. She agreed to show Reed the location of the motel that Brown had taken her to.

During the drive to the motel near Owensboro, Kentucky, Boyer told Reed the story of how Brown picked her up while she was dancing at the club in Evansville. She said that Brown had been a perfect gentleman, unlike most of the men she had met at the strip club. She said that at first, she felt safe and comfortable in his company.

Boyer told Reed that her feeling of safety and comfort vanished when they had arrived at the motel. Everything inside was a complete mess, except for one part of the floor that appeared to have been cleared off recently. She felt even more uneasy when she saw what was on the only table in the room: a roll of duct tape and a new bundle of clothesline.

Boyer admitted that Brown had paid her $100 to have sex with him, and that she had agreed, but she told him that she was not into bondage.

Her fears were soon dispelled, when, after talking to Brown, and telling him about her father molesting her, he seemed to change. She told him about an abusive childhood that continued on into her adult years, and how she had to perform at the strip club just to survive. She also told Brown about her abusive boyfriend and how she had learned to fear men.

Boyer said that Brown seemed to lose interest in having sex. They did have sex, which she described as "not very good," but he seemed in a hurry to get rid of her. She said that he dropped her off near the Exotic She Lounge, and she walked to her car. She never saw Brown again.

Brown was asked to go through his list of victims on several different occasions. He was able to repeat many of the details of the grisly murders with relative consistency, but he sometimes mixed up the order in which he claimed to have killed the women. This was especially true about his claim of killing Andrea Hendrix-Steinert. One time, he would say that she was his sixth victim; other times, he would mix her up with his alleged ninth victim.

Regardless of what number she was, Andrea—whom Brown referred to as Slick—had left an indelible impression in his mind. He brought her name up almost as often as Ginger's, and he said that Slick was the only woman with whom he really felt comfortable.

Andrea was a prostitute and a drug addict. Brown said that he first met her in the summer of 1996, and that they met occasionally for sex. He said that he liked her because she listened to him, and that he never thought about killing her because he trusted her and felt sorry for her.

Andrea Hendrix-Steinert was reported missing on October 27, 1997, and her nude body was found two days later on County Road 350, near Francisco, Indiana. This was the same road that Brown's father killed himself on, but in a completely different location. Brown could have read about Andrea in a newspaper or heard about the incident in prison, but he was able to describe the location and position of the body. After being given time to think about the order of his victims, he decided that Andrea must have been his sixth victim.

Brown said that he talked with Andrea on the street

by the courthouse in Evansville in early October 1997. Reed later verified that she, in fact, had gone to court on a prostitution charge at that time. Brown said that he picked her up on Fares Avenue about two weeks later. He was still driving his black Nissan Stanza at the time.

He said that they drove to the Schmidt Motel and had sex. After they were finished, Brown said, he got up and went to use the bathroom. He added that he wouldn't normally leave a prostitute alone with his clothes or money, but he trusted her. While he was in the bathroom, Brown said, he saw Andrea messing around with his pants. When he came out of the bathroom, he pretended that he hadn't noticed, but when he checked his pockets, he found that she had taken money.

Brown said that he grabbed her around the neck from behind, squeezed hard, and shoved her to her knees. Then he struck her in the side of the head and knocked her unconscious. According to Brown, he left her lying on the floor of the motel room, and he walked outside to his car. He got a shoestring, then came back inside and strangled her to death with it. Brown said that she urinated on herself after she died.

Because she had already dressed, he stripped off her clothes and sat beside her naked body for about an hour. He was angry with her, but he was also disappointed that he had to kill her because he felt that they had connected emotionally.

"I could have thrown her in a Dumpster like the rest, but I wanted to humiliate her because she didn't have to steal no money from me. I would have given her money if she would have asked. To me, she just stabbed me in the back," Brown said.

Brown claimed that he put Andrea's purse and clothes in his car; then he carried her naked body outside and set her in the passenger seat. He said that he seat-belted her upright and drove around town, hoping to humiliate her.

After about an hour, Brown said, he drove on Highway 41 until he reached the Dream Motel, near Patoka.
He said that he turned the car around there, then
turned onto a side road. He didn't travel far down this
road because, he said, he could still see Highway 41
when he dumped her body on the side of the road.
Brown said that there was snow on the ground, and he
didn't attempt to hide the body because he felt that if
she was found lying there naked on the side of the road,
it would humiliate her further.

There were several reasons that Reed believed Brown
had told the truth about killing Andrea. He accurately
described her location, the position of her body, and
her physical condition, including her tattoos. Brown also
told Reed that her stomach felt "funny . . . like she just
had a baby." Reed later discovered that Andrea, in
fact, did give birth several months before she was killed.
According to Sharon and Harold Matthews, her aunt
and uncle, Andrea told them that the father was a
black police officer in Evansville with whom they had
seen her on several occasions. They did not know his
name. They did say that the baby was given up for
adoption through the Van Husen Church. None of
these allegations regarding the black police officer
could be verified. In fact, the aunt and uncle could not
describe this person except for his being black and wearing dark clothes. They assumed he was a policeman.

THIRTY-EIGHT

It was around the time that Brown spent his evening with September that he also spent some time living at the Evansville Rescue Mission.

"I talked to Steve Perry. He was the chaplain there, but he also was the head administrator," Brown said in a voice that had become more pronounced as his vocabulary and grammar suddenly showed signs of some intelligence. Brown often seemed to be two different people. At times, his language was barely intelligible, and his handwriting barely legible, while at other times, he hinted at a spark of intellect, attention to detail, and neatness in his script. Then suddenly he would revert back to reveal his lack of education and sophistication.

"He helped me turn my life over. I took Jesus as my Savior. Steve was really kind toward me. He knew I was in trouble. He knew that something was tormenting me. He just wanted to try to help me. They had a Disciples Program there, but I wouldn't do that. I minded my own business, went to Gamblers Anonymous meetings, worked every day, and then that's fuckin' when I met Ginger.

"I didn't have no fuckin' interest in a woman at that time. I just wanted to be left alone. I quit gambling. I was doing all right for myself. Yes, I was having a desire to go gambling, but I didn't because I was trying to turn my life over. But somehow she spotted me. Out of all the fucking people in the world, she spots me."

Ginger Gasaway had been attending Gamblers Anonymous meetings at St. Mary's Catholic Church, and after a couple of weeks of running into Joe Brown, she finally asked him out for a cup of coffee. She had no idea that she was inviting the end of her life when she met him.

Brown had moved out of the mission and found himself a room at the Alpine Motel. Ginger was having marital problems with her husband, Hobert, and sometimes spent the weekends with Brown.

"I was like a boy toy to her. I was really like forty-two years old, but I was like thirty inside, and she was like a sex freak. She was seven years older than I was, so I guess I exceeded all her expectations, you know what I mean.

"She showed her affection more than, probably more than. . . . She was more of a mother to me than anything," Brown said.

Eventually, Ginger and Hobert invited Brown to live with them, and then in spring 1998, Brown convinced Ginger to move away from her husband, and the two of them got an apartment on Tippecanoe Avenue in Evansville.

Ginger liked to gamble almost as much as Brown, but her weakness was the slot machines, while Brown preferred the blackjack tables. They began to go to the Queens Casino on Admiral Expressway in St. Louis. Joe said that he began to pick up prostitutes there. He said that was where he met his next two victims.

"Were you with Ginger when you met either of these?" Mayhew asked.

"No, no, I . . . uh . . . probably in '98 she (Ginger) supported me pretty much. All I done was gamble, you know what I mean. That was fine with her. She didn't care."

"So in '98, these two prostitutes, are these the next two victims you had?"

"Yeah."

"Number seven and eight?"

"Yeah."

"When did you meet number seven?"

"Probably around the last part of July, first part of August. I know it was on a Saturday. She always worked on Saturday and, uh . . . that's about the best time period I can put on it, you know what I mean.

"I went there to gamble too—don't get me wrong—but I found out when I used to go to Tunica, that it was easy to pick up prostitutes. I mean I gambled too. You gotta gamble. They like that. They see the money pass hands and stuff, the chips and all that. That's what attracts them.

"So like I said, I was coming back from the Queens Casino and got back on Admiral Expressway. Before it cuts onto I-64, there's a strip joint called Déjà Vu or Showgirls. I used to go there sometimes, but I never picked nobody up there, you know what I mean. That was too fast of a place. I can show you exactly where it was at."

Brown was handed a blowup of St. Louis, Missouri, and the surrounding area, and he pointed to a casino near Horseshoe Lake. After showing the detectives his path of travel, Brown decided that he must have driven on Kings Highway, and not the Admiral Expressway.

He pointed out where he thought the strip club was located and the Motel 6, right down the street from it.

Brown said that he went to Queens Casino specifically to pick up a prostitute.

"So what happened there?" Reed asked.

"I met a prostitute. She wanted five hundred dollars for a night and she was worth it. She was classy. She looked nice. She just handled herself well. I don't know how else to say it.

"I gave her the five hundred bucks right off the bat. I knew I was getting it back anyway, you know what I mean. But that set the stage. I gave her a twenty-five-dollar chip to play with, and I played a few hands of blackjack. I wasn't really interested in playing, but I did just to pass the time. We were only there for about an hour or so, and then we left and went to the Motel 6 down the street," Brown said.

Brown said the woman was probably in her late twenties and described her as five feet seven inches tall, about 120 pounds, with "big tits."

"Fake?" Mayhew asked.

"No, they wasn't fake. I know what you're talking about, silicone."

"Silicone," Mayhew repeated.

"No, they wasn't fake. She had slender legs and a small ass. That's the way I like it, you know what I mean. She had—"

"What was she wearing?" Reed asked before Brown began drooling over himself. Brown said that she had on a brown pantsuit that zipped up, a very nice pair of shoes, and a choker around her neck.

"She wore it around her neck like a priest wears that white collar. It's like a ribbon, I think that's what it was made out of, ribbon."

"Long hair?"

"No, short hair, brownish. She might have been a redhead, you know what I mean."

"So then what happened?"

"We had sex all night long. Like I said, she was a classy girl. She was worth it."

"You tie her up?"

"Yeah. I don't think I taped her mouth, but I know I tied her hands behind her back. I don't know if she liked to let me do it, but she seemed to like it."

"Did she make you ejaculate?"

"Oh yeah. I didn't have any trouble with her, but I

went there for one reason and one reason only. I wanted to pick up a prostitute, and I knew I was gonna kill her afterwards.

"She went along with anything I wanted to do. I think that sometimes I had trouble getting an erection or ejaculating, but other times. . . . You gotta realize I was locked in prison for twenty years and I was forty years old when I got out.

"I think that's what attracted Ginger. I might have been forty, but I acted like I was twenty-five, you know what I mean. I was trying to make up for the years I lost. That's about the best way I can explain it. Yeah, I tied her hands behind her back."

"How'd you kill her?"

"After we got done having sex, she laid down and I went and took a shower. I most always took a shower except with the whores I picked up on Fares Avenue. I didn't trust them enough to leave my pants there, you know what I mean. After I got out of the shower, she was already asleep on the bed."

"Was she still tied up?"

"Heck no. I just tied her up for the sexual thing. But I did climb on her back when I strangled her. I got a hard-on when I strangled her, but I didn't do nothing about it. I, uh . . . well, I sort of fucked her. It really caught me off-guard. I mean, there were times I strangled them and I got gratification out of it, but it never was like this one before. It actually excited me sexually," Brown said.

"This is kind of an evolving thing, you know. You're progressing where you need more and more each time," Reed said.

"I didn't proceed any further after fucking a dead woman. I never done . . . Well, I will probably take that back. I did try. I did Sandra."

"Okay. Getting back to this one, though. Did you have to dress her then?"

"She was already dressed. She was just lying on the bed. I spent five hundred bucks for the whole fuckin' night. She was exactly what I was looking for. She just didn't realize that."

"After you strangled her, did you take any of her stuff?"

"I took her ID and I took my money back. That's all I ever took back off those prostitutes, just the money that I gave them. I took everybody's ID. Out of the fourteen women, the only ones I didn't take was Slick's and Ginger's. I didn't want their IDs. I didn't want to have to look at their pictures, because there's times that I took the damn IDs out and looked at them, you know what I mean.

"I just looked at them. I didn't give a fuck what their names were or nothing. It made me tingle when I looked at them pictures, 'cause I know I had power over them. I took their lives. I took something from them."

Brown said that he took his seventh victim's body and loaded her into the trunk of the Mustang that Ginger had bought for him to use. Then he drove to the Déjà Vu strip club and threw the body in the Dumpster behind the building.

"Okay. Let's go ahead and do number eight," Mayhew said.

THIRTY-NINE

"It seemed like every time that Ginger kicked me out of the apartment, I'd go kill somebody. Now that I sit back and look on it, I guess the reason I went to St. Louis and killed them two women was because I never trusted Ginger.

"I loved her with all my heart, I mean that. But I never trusted her because I seen how she did her husband. I was brought up old-fashioned, and that's why it was hard for me to accept them being swingers. I was never brought up around that environment, so I can't honestly say I ever trusted her. I never trusted her. So it seemed like every time she kicked me out, I'd go kill somebody else," Brown told Reed and Mayhew during his confession.

He had already described his part in the murder of seven women in addition to Ginger Gasaway. His last account was of a prostitute that he had picked up in St. Louis, Missouri. His alleged eighth victim was also from St. Louis.

"Ginger kicked me out probably ten times. I ain't gonna sit here and say I didn't deserve it; I mean, a compulsive gambler, an alcoholic, a drug addict . . . they are very . . . I can't think of the right word."

This was the first and only time that Brown

mentioned any problems he may have had related to the use of drugs and alcohol.

"Vulnerable?"

"No, she was the one that was vulnerable. I was always trying to play on people to get money."

"Manipulating?"

"Yeah, I was very manipulating to everybody, especially to her. She was so gullible. We went to other casinos, but she liked going over to St. Louis. This was during the time that I started having anxiety attacks. I'd just cry. I'd be sitting at the table eating, and I'd just start crying. It was really hard on her, but I couldn't understand why. Hobert was an alcoholic. He used to go through them . . . what they call blackouts.

"She felt like I was doing the same thing, but I couldn't tell her why I was crying, you know what I mean. So she kicked me out just before Christmas, and I went back to St. Louis. I went there to find a prostitute. I had to fucking kill her, you know what I mean. I went through the same old ritual of buying some new chips and sitting at the blackjack tables. I was going up to the bars with a handful of black-and-green chips, twenty-five-dollar chips."

"Queens Casino?"

"Yeah, it was the Queens and I caught one. The usual small talk. 'How you doing? All right, how about yourself? Oh, kind of looking for some action,' you know what I mean.

"I knew exactly what she was talking about. Five hundred bucks for one night, yeah, play a little blackjack. I could say that I wasn't even interested in gambling at this point. I just went there for the sole purpose of having sex and killing her."

Joe described his eighth victim as a woman who stood about five feet eight inches tall, weighing approximately 125 pounds.

"She didn't have no big titties; in fact, none of the

gals I picked up had them fucking air bags in their tits. But she was a classy girl. That's why I liked going there.

"Although I killed them afterwards, I felt that when I picked them up, I gave them that much more respect for them feeling a little crappy about themselves instead of just wanting five or ten bucks to go out and buy a hit of crack. I know there's not much difference, but in my eyes, it was a big difference."

"What was she wearing?"

"Jeans and a pullover sweater. I believe she wore glasses. She had short brownish hair, but it was probably black underneath. She had black pubic hair, so I assumed that's what she was, but her hair was kind of tinted brown.

"I paid her the money. We went back to Motel 6, and went through the same old ritual, you know what I mean."

Brown said that he took this woman to the same motel as his seventh victim, but he checked into a different room on the first floor.

"I got a little carried away on this one. Sex was a . . . it wasn't enough for me. I couldn't ejaculate at all. She tried to get me sexually excited. She was good-looking and had a really nice figure. I just couldn't ejaculate, you know what I mean."

"Did you get frustrated?"

"Oh yeah. I guess she realized I was kind of having a problem."

"Was this rodeo sex?"

"Yeah, almost all of them were. I fucked like that, doing them from behind with their hands tied behind their back. That's the way I liked it. I didn't want to look at their faces."

"What happened after you were done having sex?"

"This one I faced. I think she was the first one that I turned on her back, and I strangled her that way. I wanted to look her in the eye, because to me, I felt like she let me down. I felt like it was her fault that I couldn't get my nuts off or whatever, you know what I mean. I took my frustrations out on her. I smacked her a couple of times," Brown said.

"Did you beat her or just slap her a couple of times?"

"Slapped her a couple of times. The only one or two that I actually . . . um . . . no, there was three that I actually hit with my fists."

"Did this girl struggle at all?"

"She struggled a little bit."

"Were her hands tied?"

"Behind her back, just like Ginger. I can't exactly explain the feeling that I was having when I was strangling her, looking her in the eyes."

"Were you mad?"

"I don't know whether I was mad. I felt like it was her fault that I couldn't get sexual gratification out of it. I figured that if I pay that much money, she should be able to help me, but it wasn't really her fault at all. I didn't see it that way. I only saw it as her fault and strangling her from behind wasn't enough for me. The only way I felt like I was completely satisfied was looking her in her eyes."

Brown told Reed that he choked this girl with shoestrings and that it took a minute or two for her to die. He said that he liked using shoestrings because their elasticity allowed them to tighten up enough to collapse the arteries in the neck that led to the brain.

"So when this girl died, did you have to dress her?" Reed asked.

"Yeah, she was still naked. I was sitting on her when I got done. I felt, I don't know how to quite say how I felt. I felt like I was Rocky running up them steps in Philadelphia. I felt like I not only took a life, but I took something else. I felt like I finally got even.

"I didn't have what you'd call a hard-on, but I felt gratification. It's hard to explain. A couple of times I got sexually excited and got a hard-on, but other times, I just got the satisfaction of like I conquered something. Can you understand what I'm trying to say?"

"Yeah" was all Reed could respond with, knowing that he could never understand the satisfaction that Brown received from killing other people.

"Every time this happened, went on, did you feel gratification? Was it the same or . . . ?"

"No, it wasn't the same. I think, yeah, I got more rougher with them. I'd have to say that."

"Where'd the body go, this girl here?" Reed asked.

"I took her to a Dumpster. It wasn't at the Déjà Vu. I came to the first place I saw a Dumpster. It might have been an apartment complex. It might have been a business. It was the first Dumpster I came to that dumps overhead. That's where I put the body."

"Is it on the same street as the Motel 6?"

"No. I was going west, I think, back toward I-64 and past Déjà Vu. I made the first left and went down a few blocks. That's where I threw the body. Once I got out of St. Louis, I got off the nearest exit and got rid of her purse and stuff."

At first, Brown didn't have much to say about his ninth victim—except that he met her by calling Savage Entertainment again. He said that he tried to have sex with this woman but was unable to stay erect, so he became frustrated. Brown said that the woman just kind of lay there and was unresponsive to his touch. He blamed her for his inability to ejaculate. He said that he became very angry and beat her up with his fists before strangling her to death with a shoestring. Then he put her body into the passenger side of the Mustang and drove to a Dumpster at the Green River Village Apartments, where he disposed of her.

In other statements, Brown said that his ninth victim was Andrea Hendrix-Steinert, the prostitute that he frequented and eventually befriended. He sometimes mixed her up with the account of his sixth victim. Andrea became one of the most controversial parts of the entire Joe Brown case because hers was the only body—other than Ginger's—that was actually found.

FORTY

During Brown's confession, he said that he killed his tenth victim after he beat up Ginger and fled the state.

On April 23, 1999, Brown's on-again, off-again girlfriend, Ginger Gasaway, filed a petition for a temporary protective order against Brown after she kicked him out of her apartment. One month later, on May 25, she filed a petition to dismiss the order, which the court quickly approved and finalized on June 9.

On July 19, 1999, Ginger petitioned the court again for a temporary protection order against Brown. On August 9, the court entered a permanent protective order in favor of Ginger's petition, but Brown came back on Labor Day Weekend and beat her nearly to death.

She was living at Embassy East Apartments then, and had rented the apartment in her name alone. Joe Brown had never lived there. He walked into the community laundry room and found Ginger talking to another man, who was doing his laundry.

"She kept talking to this guy and ignoring me. She didn't even acknowledge that I walked in. I don't know what I was thinking at the time. I just . . . lost it, you know what I mean. I just started whaling on her," Brown confessed.

"I don't really remember exactly what was going

through my mind. It's like I couldn't stop hitting her. She said something like 'Smokey, if you ever loved me, please don't hurt me no more,' and there was blood everywhere. I thought I had killed her. She was just lying there, not moving. Her face was all swollen up and she was covered in blood. I was covered in blood. This guy just watched the whole thing, and he didn't even try to stop it. That's when I saw that what I'd done was wrong and I took off," Brown said.

It was September 5, a date that continued to come up throughout Brown's violent life. The police report was filed by Evansville police officer Brad Evrard. The report stated that Ginger was talking with Brown outside the laundry room at the Embassy Apartments and then he followed her inside. He asked her for some money, and she told him that she only had $5, which she gave to him.

The report stated that it was at this time that the other unknown male in the laundry room left. Ginger told police that Brown asked for more money. She told Brown that they were no longer a couple, and that he would have to look somewhere else to find support.

Ginger said that Brown became angry, and he began to strike her repeatedly with his closed fists. She told police that Brown said "You brought this on yourself," while he was beating her. Then he told her that he had to attend a Gamblers Anonymous meeting in Newburgh and left in her car.

Brown fled the scene in Ginger's Mustang before police arrived. He drove to Terre Haute to see his sister Jennie, but she was in Evansville on business. Her teenage son and young daughter were at home, and the sight of Uncle Joe standing there, covered in blood, scared them. Joe told them he'd just killed someone and that he needed money.

Not knowing what to do, and fearing for their safety, the boy called his mother and asked what he should do. After hanging up, Jennie's son gave Joe what little money he could find, and then asked him to leave. Joe wanted more, but he figured that at least he could buy gas for the car, so he left without further incident.

Brown drove out of Terre Haute and he traveled along I-70. He was heading to Las Vegas, Nevada.

"I tried calling Ginger collect for, like, three days along the way to Las Vegas, but I never got no answer. I was up in the mountains now, and it was cold, but I liked driving with the top down, so I'd roll up all the windows and just crank up the heat," Brown said.

Just outside Denver, Colorado, Brown said, he picked up a girl who was hitchhiking near a rest area. He described her as a white female between eighteen and twenty years old, with an athletic body. He said she was very pretty, with long blond hair, and she might have been around five feet ten inches tall.

Brown said that the girl wore a San Diego State University sweatshirt and blue jeans. She told him that she was from Denver, and that she was on her way back to school.

Feeling a bit uncomfortable, Brown turned on the car stereo to fill the awkward silence in the car.

"I played some Twisted Sister, Tesla, and all that crap. The younger kids seem to like that music, so we just sat back and listened to it. We didn't have a whole lot to say to each other anyway. Hell, I was twice her age. She kind of reminded me of my daughter. I never had a chance to raise my daughter, so I didn't know what to think or say. She didn't look anything like my daughter, but she looked real innocent. She wasn't dressed wild, with earrings hanging out of her nose or wherever," Brown said.

After driving a short while on I-70, Joe said that the girl had fallen asleep, and that he turned the car into a small rest area that consisted of no more than a park bench and a place to pull off for the view.

"I shut the car off and made my seat go all the way back. I can't say exactly what was going on in my mind at the time, but I was . . . uh . . . I didn't want her to wake up scared, so I put my hand on her leg to tell her that I was going to get out to make a phone call. She took it the wrong way, thinking I was trying to molest her. The last thing I heard her say was something like, 'Get your hand off me, pervert!'"

Brown said he didn't even think about it, he just started beating her with his fists. She fought back, and this surprised him. None of the others had fought him, and he said he never understood how they could just "let me kill them."

"She didn't scream for help, but she fought back. She might've even scratched my face up a little bit. This one was different. I can't say why, but I just thought it was good. She managed to get out of the car and then she fell down on the asphalt. I got on top of her and pulled her pants down," Brown said.

He said that he wasn't able to get an erection, and that he strangled her to death trying to control her. He even tried to have sex with her after he knew that she was dead. He put his fingers inside her still corpse, but that didn't excite him either.

Brown pointed out the location of the rest stop on a map. He said it was on a sharp curve on I-70, just east of Vail, Colorado.

"I carried her over the rail and threw her down the ravine. I don't know how deep it was, but I didn't hear her hit bottom," he said.

Brown thought her name was Sandra.

At this point in the questioning, Brown broke down and cried like a baby. Over and over, he said that he was sorry for the things that he had done. He kept repeating that he never intended to kill anybody, and that he couldn't explain the reasons for his actions.

"I really need to get this off my chest," he said as he wept.

Brown's tears did not make Reed feel compassion for the murderer, and he pressed on with the questioning. Both Brown and Reed were anxious to end the interview process, and so they moved on to murder number eleven.

FORTY-ONE

Brown told Reed that after killing the San Diego State University girl in Colorado, he drove to Las Vegas, Nevada. He said that he only spent one day there and that he gambled most of his money away.

Out of cash and almost out of gas, Brown said that he managed to find a job helping a man roof his house. It only lasted a day, but he was paid in cash, and he was ready to move on anyway. He decided that he needed to see Ginger again, and so he headed back toward Indiana.

The money he earned was burning a hole in his pocket, so he stopped at Mesquite, Nevada, to gamble a bit. He pulled into a truck stop near the casinos, and got himself a cup of coffee. That's where he said he met his next victim.

Brown described her as a white female in her twenties, and not very pretty, but full of life and excitement.

"She had that 'I just don't give a fuck' attitude, but with class. She reminded me of Slick in a lot of ways," Brown said.

She told Brown that she was traveling to Colorado from California, and that she had a complimentary room at one of the casinos in Mesquite.

Brown told her that he was driving to Indiana along

I-70 and that he would be happy to give her a ride. She seemed to be very impressed with the convertible Mustang, and that made Brown feel important, even though he knew that the car really didn't belong to him. He didn't tell the woman that he had taken the car from Ginger Gasaway after beating her almost to death in a laundry room. Instead, he acted like he did own the Mustang, and they drove back to her room at the Oasis Casino.

"She told me that she was going to show me a time that I'll never forget, and she did. I've been to a lot of strip clubs and stuff, and I've seen a lot of things, but she gave me more sexual thrill than anyone ever did before. I could tell by her voice that she was for real, the way she was saying, 'Come on . . . come on . . . come on, baby,'" Brown said.

"Still, I couldn't get off, and it was very frustrating. She put her hand on my shoulder and told me that it was all right. After we were done, she fell asleep and I took a shower. Then I went out to my car and got my gloves and a pair of shoestrings. Walking back in was like walking down a corridor where you know that when you get to the end, that they're going to kill you, but you've got to keep walking anyway. I knew what I was going to do. I got on top of her, and I just strangled her right then and there.

"Killing her was as hard, if not harder, than signing the adoption papers for my daughter. Even when I was chopping up Ginger, I didn't feel any emotion, but this one was hard.

"I put her in the Mustang. There was a truck stop across from the casino, but I can't honestly remember if I put her in a Dumpster there. I know it was somewhere in that town, though," Brown said.

He then drove through Utah and picked up a few odd jobs along the way to keep gas in the Mustang. As each day passed, he became more determined to get back with Ginger again.

Ginger filed a report with the Evansville Police Department on September 10, 1999, saying that Brown had been harassing her, sometimes calling her more than thirty times a day by using a calling card that he had stolen from her.

The police report stated that Ginger had received numerous phone calls from Joe Brown between August 20 and September 9 and that she had a permanent protective order against him. The report also stated that Ginger told police that Brown showed up at her place of employment as well, but no further information surrounding that incident was included.

On September 18, Brown pulled the Mustang into the parking lot of a Moto Mart at I-64 and US Highway 65 in Vanderburgh County, just outside of Evansville. He was afraid that there might have been a warrant issued for his arrest for beating Ginger in the laundry room at Embassy East Apartments thirteen days earlier.

Ginger agreed to meet Joe at the Moto Mart. As soon as she hung up the phone, she picked it up again and called the sheriff's department. She told them that Brown would be waiting at the Moto Mart in her red Mustang.

When two sheriff's cars pulled into the parking lot, Brown knew right away that Ginger had betrayed him. He started up the Mustang and floored the accelerator pedal. He sped along the highway with the sheriff's cars in hot pursuit for nearly an hour. Finally, he was able to elude his pursuers and escape.

Brown planned to reunite with Ginger when he came back to town. Now he would get back at her for her betrayal. He realized for the first time that he wanted to kill her. That maybe, he had wanted to kill her all along. He went to the small town of Owensboro for a short time and lay low.

For more than a week, he stalked Ginger, trying to keep out of sight. He watched her every move. Ginger called the Evansville police on September 27 because Brown was at her door trying to get in. She feared that he would cause her harm. The next day, a bench warrant was issued for Brown, for the battery incident against Ginger that took place at the Embassy East Apartments three weeks earlier.

Exactly one month later, on October 27, 1999, Evansville police arrested Brown for public intoxication. He later told Reed and Mayhew that he wasn't drunk, but that he had taken a bunch of pills in an attempt to commit suicide.

While in custody, he pleaded guilty to one count of battery against Ginger Gasaway, and one count of invasion of privacy, both misdemeanors. The court imposed a fine of $50 plus court costs, and 180 days for each count, but suspended the time on both counts under the conditions that Brown agree to have no further contact with Ginger, and that he would attend classes at the Drug and Alcohol Intervention Program.

The court noted that a protective order against Joe Brown was already in place, and because Brown had no money at the time, his fines and court costs were deferred until November 24 and he was released on his own recognizance.

"When I was released, I didn't have no place to go, so as usual, I turned to Ginger. I always turned to her when I needed help, whether she would help me out or not. I always promised her that I'd never put my hands on her and I meant it when I said that. But she wouldn't help me out that night. She was still angry with me, and she wanted to punish me. She knew that it would be cold that night.

"I just spent the night outside walking with nobody

to talk to, and feeling colder than hell. I finally ended up at Ginger's apartment at about three-thirty in the morning. I knew that she'd be up getting ready for work. When she answered the door, I got on my hands and knees and begged her to let me in. She ended up taking me back, like I knew she would," Brown said.

Ginger was gullible. She didn't take Brown back out of love, but she was the kind of person who couldn't turn away anyone in need, regardless of the cost to herself. There were conditions set, however. Brown would sleep on the floor. Anytime that Ginger left the apartment, Brown would have to leave as well. She wasn't going to trust him alone with her things, and she didn't let him have a key to the place. She even made him hide out of sight when someone came over to visit her.

Brown was determined to win back Ginger's trust, and maybe even her love. He quit gambling and worked several jobs laying brick for various contractors. Hobert began to call Ginger when he found out that Brown was back in her apartment. He was concerned for her safety and tried to convince her to throw Brown out for good. She finally agreed to meet with him for a cup of coffee. Eventually they would begin to see each other secretly.

Ginger decided that the only way that she would ever rid herself of Joe Brown was to help him become self-sufficient. When he expressed an interest in starting his own masonry business, Ginger decided to help him succeed. She used her life's savings, cashed in her 401K account, and used the money to purchase all the equipment that Brown would need. Her only stipulation was that she would take care of the business's finances because she knew that Brown couldn't be trusted with money.

Brown began to procure some jobs and actually started to bring in some money. After he received a check for $25,000, Ginger decided it was time to let go of his hand. She told him that he had to continue on his own. She never asked to be repaid and even encouraged him, telling him that she was proud that he had worked so hard, and she was confident that he would succeed. But it was time for him to move out for good and that she wanted him to stay away from her.

Brown couldn't deal with the situation. Instead of being grateful for all that Ginger had done for him, he became angry that he had been kicked out once again. He went on a gambling spree and lost all of his money. He kept Ginger's Mustang, but he sold all the equipment from his masonry business and borrowed money from anyone who would give it to him. In a matter of weeks, he went through tens of thousands of dollars and had nothing to show for it. Joe Brown was right back where he started.

FORTY-TWO

Brown said that he decided that he would go back to Tunica, Mississippi, and revisit the city where he had committed his first murder. He wanted to try and recapture the thrill that he experienced when murder was new and exciting.

He traveled through Tennessee along I-24 and claimed to have picked up a woman whose car had broken down north of Nashville. Brown said that she told him that she was heading to Memphis, so he offered to give her a ride.

In a videotaped recording of his interrogation, Brown said that it was just before he reached Clarksville that the road was shut down because a tractor-trailer had crashed and caught on fire.

"They shut the whole interstate down, so I'm sure there has to be a record of that. It was a pretty big accident, so it ought to be easy enough to verify it and pinpoint the exact date," Brown told the detectives.

Brown said that because of the accident, he pulled the Mustang off the interstate at the nearest off-ramp and stopped at the first hotel he saw. He was tired from driving all day and needed the rest anyway.

"She was hesitant about sharing a room with me, but I told her, 'Do you want a ride or not?' I could sleep on the floor or whatever. It didn't matter to me. I was used to sleeping on the floor at Ginger's. I didn't have any intentions to do anything to her. I just wanted to get to Mississippi," Brown said.

Brown said that he slept on the floor while she slept on the bed, and that at some point during the night, she told him that he could get up on the bed with her if he wanted.

"Sometimes I can be naive when it comes to knowing what a woman wants, so I took that to mean that she was expecting to have sex from me. I decided that I was going to tear that shit up, you know what I mean. She said, 'Don't hurt me,' and I thought, 'How can you hurt that?' If they can have babies, there's no way you can hurt them. I went through the rigmarole of trying to have sex with her, and it was a disaster, so I just killed her. All I wanted to do was get to Mississippi, so I got the hell out of there," he said.

Brown described this woman as early thirties, five feet five inches tall, and about 130 pounds.

"She was a little plumpy, but I like plumpy. It was all I could do to pick her up and put her into the Dumpster. I guess that I got kind of angry at her because she was a dead fuck, and because she gave me that bullshit about 'Don't hurt me.'"

The next day, Joe arrived in Tunica, Mississippi, in the early afternoon, and he rented a room at the Holiday Express. He gambled for a while at the Horseshoe Casino, and then decided that it was time to reclaim the thrill he felt from killing his first victim. He called Cupid Escort Services, then waited in the parking lot for his thirteenth victim to arrive.

Brown told Reed that she was a good-looking woman, and the shortest one that he had ever been with. He said that she had brownish hair, and couldn't have weighed more than 115 pounds. Joe said that she had a creamy complexion with spots of freckles.

"I knew this would be the last one. I just had a feeling in my mind that this was it. I thought that I'd show her a good time, and hoped that I would get the gratification that I was looking for. I didn't know what I was going to do afterwards if I did get it. I wasn't thinking that far ahead. All I could think about was killing her," he said.

"I took her back to the hotel room. She was willing to do anal or anything else I wanted. I pushed the gas pedal to the floorboard. I figured, whatever happens, happens, and I wasn't going to stop," Brown said.

He told Reed that he tried everything humanly possible that he could think of with this one, including masturbating himself, but he was not able to achieve ejaculation. He resigned himself to the fact that he would never achieve the gratification that he desired, and so he strangled her to death, remaining dissatisfied.

It was at this point that Brown said he decided that nothing mattered to him any longer. He didn't care if he got caught for killing. He didn't care if he lived himself. One thing he did know was that if life was over for him, he was going to take Ginger with him.

Brown said that he tossed the prostitute's body in a Dumpster somewhere along Elvis Presley Boulevard; then he headed back to Indiana.

"Within a day of returning, I caught Ginger and Hobert together. I saw her kiss him outside of her apartment, but they didn't see me. I left to go gamble at Caesar's, and after I ran out of money, I returned to kill Ginger," he said.

Brown raised his hands in front of him and shook his fingers.

"I was nervous," he told Reed.

Brown's account of Ginger's murder was much different now than it was three years ago. In 2000, Brown said that he tried to reconcile with Ginger, and that she let him into her apartment of her own free will. He told detectives that they had been intimate with each other, and that it wasn't until Ginger told him that she had slept with Hobert, that Brown decided to kill her.

Now, Brown told Reed that he went to Ginger's apartment with a premeditated intention to kill her. Brown knew Ginger's routine well. He knew that she would wake up at three o'clock in the morning to get ready for work. She would make a pot of coffee and then take a hot shower. He said that he waited outside on her porch, crouched down next to her front door. He waited until he heard the safety chain slide free from its channel and the dead bolt turned open.

Instead of being invited in, like Brown had told police earlier, now he said that he slammed his body into the door just as Ginger opened it. He told Reed that Ginger's body flew back and landed on the floor. He said that she must have been scared because she tried to spray Mace in his face.

"She always carried that Mace around in her purse. I just grabbed the can out of her hand, and I wanted to shove the whole thing down her fuckin' throat," Brown said.

Brown said that he tied up Ginger and had sex with her several times. He said that he taped her mouth shut and tied her hands behind her back. He told Reed that he tortured Ginger for hours by repeatedly strangling her, or covering her head with a plastic bag until she would pass out.

"I wanted that bitch dead, but I was going to take my time and enjoy doing it," he said.

At 7:10 P.M., on September 18, 2003, Detectives Rick Reed and Tony Mayhew concluded their recording of the confession of Joseph Weldon Brown.

FORTY-THREE

During the interrogation, Joe Brown said that he kept identification cards from all his victims except for Andrea Hendrix-Steinert and Ginger Gasaway. Sometimes he would pull them out and look at their pictures. He said that it gave him a "sense of power over them," knowing that he had been able to take away their lives. He said that when he looked at them, it was almost a sexually stimulating experience for him. Brown also told police that he had hidden all the identifications inside a tire of Ginger's Mustang, in which he used to transport her dismembered body.

The same day that Brown made his taped confession, Officer Gary Gulledge was assigned the task of locating the Red 1993 Mustang. He contacted Ginger's daughter and ex-husband, but neither of them owned the car. They said that the vehicle went back to the dealership shortly after the EPD released it, which was nearly three years earlier. They could not remember the dealership's name.

With the help of a Henderson County, Kentucky, dispatcher, Gulledge was able to locate the current owner, Michael Stevenson, of Leitchfield, Kentucky. He purchased the car two months earlier, in July 2003. He said that the vehicle had two different types of tires on it when he bought it, and two of them appeared to be new. He had not replaced any of the tires since he owned it. Mayhew and Detective Alan Brack drove to Leitchfield and asked Stevenson to drive the car to a nearby tire shop, where the vehicle and tires were searched. The carpet in the trunk was missing and there was a brown stain on the passenger seat that may have been blood, but nothing was found inside the tires.

Stevenson reported that he purchased the vehicle from Donnie's Used Cars. Gulledge contacted Donnie Willis, the owner of the dealership, next. Willis stated that he had owned the car twice, once in August 2002, and again in May 2003. He said that he did not remember ever replacing the tires, but that he did send the car to Big O's tire shop, in Leitchfield, to have a wheel replaced for one of the owners. The owner of Big O's said that he remembered the vehicle because he liked the Mustang 5.0 rims. He said that he did not see anything fall out of the tire when he replaced the wheel.

Gulledge then tracked down previous owners. Gene Gibbs, of Millwood, Kentucky, purchased the car in April 2003 and only owned it for about a month before Willis bought it. Gibbs said that he never replaced the tires. Tim Williams, of Clarkson, Kentucky, purchased the car in February 2002. He said that he didn't believe that he changed the tires, but if he did, he would have remembered if anything fell out of them.

Ever persistent, Gulledge then located Doug Daniels, owner of McDaniel's Auto Sales. He was an untitled owner of the Mustang who obtained the vehicle from an Indiana dealership before selling it to Williams. He only had the car for a few days and did nothing to it. Daniels stated that before he owned the Mustang, it was in a minor accident. He said that the father of the driver took the car away and sold it to the Indiana dealership. Daniels still had a copy of the vehicle title that showed he purchased it from Birdie's & Paul's Auto Sales in Tell City, Indiana. Further investigation revealed nothing new.

EPD detective Alan Yeager assisted in the investigation to find Joe Brown's former 1979 Chevy yellow pickup truck. The VIN CCZ149S187175 was checked in a title search through the Indiana Data and Communication Systems. It was discovered that in 1996 a matching title had been returned to the then-named National City Bank.

Yeager called Gary Fein, the bank's security officer, who was able to find information about the truck. Fein reported that the bank had repossessed it in August 1996 from Joe Brown. The truck was then sold at Wolfe's Auto Auction to a place called South Side Auto Sales. Yeager checked in Zeus, and in the telephone book for a listing on the business, but it appeared that South Side Auto Sales was no longer in operation. Zeus had an old listing for the business and provided a contact name.

Yeager also contacted Wolfe's Auto Auction, and he spoke with the general manager. He was told that the vehicle had only been sold through the auction once on December 12, 1996, which was four months after the date that Gary Fein had said that the bank repossessed it.

The VIN was checked for registration in several states, including Illinois, Kentucky, Michigan, Ohio, and Tennessee. All inquiries were returned with a "not on file" status. Several other states were then checked for information, also with no results. The truck was never located.

FORTY-FOUR

After two days of interrogation by Reed and Mayhew, Brown was able to find time to write back to the reporters at the *Evansville Courier & Press*. In his letter, he wrote that he had been completely honest about his confession. He also wrote that he would be allowed to call reporters Maureen Hayden or Leigh Ann Tipton collect, and that it would cost $6.25 to accept a twenty-minute phone call.

In his letter, Brown seemed hungry for media coverage and promised to keep writing.

"Answer this letter as soon as you can," he wrote.

EPD assistant chief Burnworth was advised that the *Evansville Courier & Press* and Channel 25 were going to run a story about Brown's interview, so Reed immediately contacted Ginger's husband, Hobert Gasaway, and their daughter Lisa, to warn them that old wounds might be reopened.

The next day, the *Evansville Courier & Press* published the headline KILLER CLAIMS HE HAS SLAIN 13 OTHERS. It was the first of many articles that would fill newspapers for months to come. News of Brown's confession was also run on the Associated Press state and local wire that same day. His story was fast becoming of interest nationwide.

Local and state police from Pennsylvania to Utah began to dig up files of unsolved murders hoping to be able to close some cold cases, and the Federal Bureau of Investigation (FBI) began to profile Brown, hoping to connect him to some of their cases as well.

One of the broadest criminal investigations in the country was under way, and the suspected murderer was already behind bars without a chance of ever becoming a free man.

It didn't take long until reports of murdered prostitutes filtered into the Evansville Police Department. Detective Larry Nelson received a call from Captain Bill Tucker, of the Union County Sheriff's Department, in North Carolina. He said that they had an unsolved murder of a prostitute, Sharon H. Pressley, from Charlotte, who was last seen in the area of I-77 and I-85 in mid-September 1997.

Tucker said that he believed that she was hitchhiking at the time and that her body was found in Monroe County, twenty miles east of Charlotte. The woman was shot five times and then her breasts were cut off postmortem. Two pieces of rock cocaine were found shoved into her throat. Witnesses reported that she was last seen with a white male in a pickup truck.

Nelson checked the file on Joe Brown and found that it was around that time that he had been staying at Whitey's Motel near Owensboro, Kentucky. This was also when Christie Beaven stated that Brown had disappeared for a few days, and that when he returned, he was covered in blood.

Brown told Beaven that he was ripped off by a prostitute in Tennessee and that he got even with her. Nelson searched MapQuest, an electronic directory on the Internet, and found that the driving time from

Owensboro to Charlotte was only nine hours, and that the quickest route went right through Tennessee.

Nelson also discovered that the Kansas City Police Department was also investigating a series of murders that involved the use of shoestrings from women's shoes. Those murders ended abruptly in 1993, so it was suspected that the murderer was either dead or incarcerated.

Because Brown was in prison during that time, detectives suspected that he might have received information about those murders from another inmate and then incorporated it into his own story.

Detective Mayhew went to Whitey's Motel on US Highway 60, west of Owensboro, Kentucky. He searched the rooms that Brown had stayed in during part of 1997. Room number four was occupied, and Mayhew was given consent to search the premises. He found nothing of value. Room 5 had been converted into a storage area. Hidden in the ceiling tiles, Mayhew recovered a Crown Royal bag that contained a spoon and two hypodermic needles as possible evidence. He called Christie Beaven, who lived near Brown at Whitey's in 1997, and she told him that she had read a letter that Brown wrote to her girlfriend. In it, he wrote that he used to hide things in the ceiling of his apartment at Whitey's. Mayhew contacted Beaven's former boyfriend Mendel Shank, who lived next door to Brown at Whitey's. Shank said that he did not remember the letter that Beaven spoke of.

Mayhew received a call from Lieutenant Goodwin, of the Beaver City Police Department in Utah, reporting an unsolved homicide from February 1998. The victim was thirty-eight years old and a loner. She was described as heavyset and unattractive, the kind of woman that Brown had a history of developing relationships with.

She had been dead for several weeks when she was finally found in her apartment, and the cause of her death was never established, although it was ruled a homicide.

Reports of unsolved murders from all across the nation soon ended up in the lap of the Evansville Police Department.

FORTY-FIVE

During Brown's confession, he said that when he was arrested and taken to Lebanon, Ohio, for Ginger's murder, he had a pair of women's size-eight shoelaces in his pocket. On September 21, 2003, Reed called Ohio State Police sergeant Jim Brown to inquire about this. Sergeant Brown told him that if Joe did possess shoelaces when he was incarcerated, they would have probably been thrown away, and would not have been recorded on the prisoner booking sheet because they had no value.

Reed placed another call to the Henderson County, Kentucky, jail, where Brown had been incarcerated for theft in 1996. The prisoner booking papers there showed a wallet, shoes, and a set of keys were in Brown's possession when he was booked. There was no record of shoelaces.

Joe's sister Jennie called Reed on September 22 to confirm Joe's claims that he was abused by his father, was alone with his mother when she died, and she also said that Joe claimed he was molested as a child.

Reed also spoke to Joe's younger brother, David, who reported that he hadn't seen Joe since he was a teenager, except for one visit that Joe made to him in Ohio in 1996. David said that he let Joe spend the night at his house, and that he even thought about trying to find Joe a job. After he heard that Joe was incarcerated in Kentucky later that year, he had nothing further to do with him.

A meeting was held with Evansville detectives and agents from the FBI. It was decided that Brown would be given a polygraph test if he would consent. Afterward, Reed obtained a search warrant for Brown's blood, and then he drove to the Wabash Valley Correctional Facility to obtain the sample, which was sent to the state police lab to be used for DNA comparisons.

Reed and CSU officer Jim Myers visited Joe in jail on September 24 to reinterview him. This time, they videotaped the confession. The details in this confession remained fairly consistent to his previous one.

Mayhew contacted a Motel 6 in St. Louis and found that someone registered a room under the name of Joe Brown in August 1998. The address listed proved to be the home of a Joe Brown, but it was a different person. Caesar's Casino in Elizabeth, Indiana, also had a record of Joe Brown at their establishment in March 2000.

Susan Laine, a lab technician with the Indiana State Police, contacted Evansville detectives on September 26 to tell them that Joe Brown's DNA sample was compared to samples collected from Andrea Hendrix-Steinert. She said that Brown could be excluded as a match.

Laine added that sometimes, if there is a large amount of female DNA material and a minute amount of male DNA, the female DNA will mask the presence of the male. She said that there were two separate DNA samples found under Andrea's fingernails and that one of them was her own. Laine also said that there was a more accurate and more expensive test that could be conducted that sought out only the male material and ignored female DNA. This Y-chromosome Standard Tandem Repeat (YSTR) test was never conducted.

Laine told the detectives that fibers from a red carpet

were in the body bag with Andrea's body. Gibson County sheriff Dave Knowles checked all the motels along Fares Avenue in Evansville and reported that none of them had red carpeting at the present time. It was not known if any of the carpeting in these motels was replaced since 1997 when Andrea was murdered.

Dr. Mark Lavaughn, of the Vanderburgh County Coroner's Office, met with Reed on October 1, 2003, and together they examined crime scene photos of Andrea. Lavaughn admitted that in 1997 he hadn't noted the mark across Andrea's neck. He said that it was possible that the mark could have been made by a shoelace of some sort.

The next day, Reed contacted the public welfare offices in Ohio and Pennsylvania to see if there was any record of food stamps being issued to Joe Brown. There was none.

Detective Mayhew went to the Evansville Rescue Mission and asked for dates that Brown may have stayed there. The records showed that Brown had been a resident there from April 1998 until May 1999. Mayhew was told that if Brown had not come back for even a single night to take his required breath test, he would have been discharged from the facility. Mayhew asked to get a printout of Brown's record at the mission and they told him that their printer wasn't working.

The next day, Mayhew visited several motels along Fares Avenue to inquire about red-carpet fibers. He had no luck, so he tried to contact the National Personnel Records Center in an attempt to find records of previous carpeting at the motels. The fax machine did not work.

Mayhew gathered a list of all the escort services listed in the Yellow Pages of the Memphis, Tennessee, phone directory. He could not find a Cupid Escort Services, which Brown claimed to have used to contact one of his victims. Mayhew did find a listing for a Valentine's, but every time he attempted to call, he got a busy signal.

FBI agent Mary Williams contacted Reed on October 17 to tell him that he had been in contact with authorities in St. Louis, Missouri, and San Diego, California. St. Louis officials were searching records for any abandoned vehicles in the Queens Casino area, and would follow up to see if the owners were missing as well. In San Diego, a program was set up to identify any missing persons that fit the parameters of Brown's profile. In Brown's confession, however, he said that the girl who wore the San Diego State University sweatshirt was from Denver. There was no record of a similar search being conducted in Denver, but Detective Mayhew did call Sergeant Kirk Dunham, with the Denver Homicide Unit, to ask for a list of missing persons that might fit the profile of Brown's alleged tenth and eleventh victims.

A statement was taken on October 21 from Sharon and Harold Matthews, Andrea's aunt and uncle. They said that reports in the local newspapers that Brown had met Andrea in 1995 weren't true because Andrea was incarcerated in Little Rock, Arkansas, for prostitution, until Thanksgiving, 1995. The Matthewses said that before Andrea spent a year in the Arkansas jail, she gave birth to a black baby, who was addicted to crack cocaine, and that she just abandoned the infant at the hospital.

The Matthewses told Reed that Andrea visited them on Christmas, 1995 and then went to Ft. Lauderdale, Florida, where she had a husband and a boyfriend. They said that she also had a twelve-year-old daughter there who lived with her husband. They said that she returned to Evansville in 1996 and continued her life of prostitution and drug addiction.

Andrea gave birth to another black child in spring 1997 and gave the baby up for adoption to the Van

Husen Church. The Matthewses said that Andrea was dating a black Evansville police officer at the time, and they thought that he was the baby's father.

When Reed asked if there was anything else that they might be able to tell him to help with the investigation, Sharon Matthews said, "I was trying to tell you about a girl named Carla Lewis, who is supposed to be a sheriff's daughter. She told Andrea's now-deceased uncle, Paul Hendrix, that she was at Wolf's house, and she saw Andrea's purse lying on the sofa. Carla went to the house to buy drugs and she said that she heard moaning coming from the bedroom. When she asked about it, she was told that it was the cat, and they turned up the stereo real loud. Later, Wolf supposedly destroyed a mattress."

The Matthewses were shown photos of Evansville police officers, but they could not identify anyone as the man they claimed to have thought to be the father of Andrea's baby.

As far as Carla Lewis, Wolf, and the other names mentioned by the Matthewses, Reed said that they weren't able to verify that the names were correct, and that the information in the statement was sketchy, and not reliable.

Phone calls about unsolved murders from across the country continued to spill into the Evansville Police Department. One of them was from Detective Mike Luster, of Kansas City, Missouri. He reported an unsolved string of murdered prostitutes between 1977 and 1993. He said that four of the seven girls still had shoelaces tied around their necks when their bodies were found and several of them still had their hands tied behind their backs.

Joe Brown was in prison during this period, but Reed decided to contact Michigan City to find out if someone from the Kansas City area may have been incarcerated with Brown after 1993. He thought that Brown might have met someone there who may have talked to him about these murders.

Luster also told Reed about unsolved murders that took place in the summer of 1998 when two prostitutes' bodies were found in the Missouri River. They had been strangled also and their DNA was still in the national database. In Brown's statement, he said that he killed two prostitutes in St. Louis during that same period, so Luster ran a comparison with Brown's DNA, but they did not match.

Detective Rick Wilkinson, from the Ogle County Sheriff Department in Illinois, called about a prostitute that was murdered in July 1998 and her body was found in a gravel pit. She was a thin brunette in her thirties. Her name was Pam White. Her throat was cut, and she was stabbed twenty-two times in the back along her spine. Her wrists were cut postmortem. It is believed that she was on her knees at the time that her throat was cut from behind by a left-handed person. Samples of White's DNA were also on file, but because the violence of this murder was not consistent with what Brown confessed to, the matter was not pursued.

Another detective, John Beggs, from the Illinois State Police, called to report the body of a prostitute named Leticia Bolen found in April 2000 in a remote wooded area. Some boys found her buried under a pile of trash. She had been severely beaten and was set on fire, so there was no determinate cause of death.

Beggs said that Bolen could have been strangled, but the beating or the fire could have also been responsible for her death. He said that they had DNA samples on file. Reed received two photos of Bolen and decided to show them to Brown the next time he saw him.

Detective Barbara Mannix, of Hollywood, Florida, called about an unsolved homicide involving a prostitute that was strangled. She described the victim as a white female that was about five feet six inches tall and weighed only ninety pounds. She was a crack-cocaine addict with no teeth and mousy brown hair. Mannix said that the body was found on May 16, 1999, in a Dumpster. She was clothed only in a tube top and her body was cut in half by a sharp electrical saw. The victim also had been beaten in the head and face with some type of impact weapon similar to a hammer. There were also two stab wounds that appeared to have been made with a round object, like a Phillips head screwdriver. She had lived three blocks from a casino on a Seminole Indian Reservation.

To keep from having to check each and every call that came in, Brown's DNA sample was entered into the national database. Now any police department in the country could compare it to samples from victims that Brown might be suspected of being in contact with, and Evansville would not have to get involved unless there was a match.

Reed suggested that Detective Nelson and Agent Williams should interview Brown again, in November. He also suggested that Brown be allowed to show detectives the route that he took and the locations of where he dumped the bodies. It was decided that Brown would not be taken out of the prison. Like with all the other calls that came in, nothing further ever developed. Brown was already serving a life sentence without chance of parole. To Reed, the shared sentiment seemed that nobody wanted to pursue the investigation with vigor. Why spend the time and money when Joe Brown was already going to spend the rest of his life behind bars?

Reed became increasingly frustrated with the investigation. He felt that the lack of support was due in part to a case he solved in 2002 involving the murder of a young man named Monte Doss. In that investigation the current chief of police, Dave Gulledge, was still a motor patrol sergeant and was touted by the news media as a suspect. Reed never believed that Gulledge was involved except as a witness, and his instincts proved true. But during the time of that investigation in 2002, Evansville Mayor Russ Lloyd Jr. wanted to make Gulledge the chief of police, and Reed was being used as a pawn in a political battle. To make matters worse, the Fraternal Order of Police, or FOP, wanted the mayor to give them an unthinkable 21 percent pay hike, and some within their ranks saw this battle as a bargaining tool.

Reed was never supposed to solve the case, but he did the unthinkable and proved that Gulledge was innocent. But to do so, he had made some powerful political and departmental enemies.

As a result of that case Reed was transferred from Bunco-Fraud to the Violent Crimes Unit and Gulledge was appointed chief of police. Gulledge would end up being replaced in a year. The FOP never got their raise.

Enmity grew inside the Detectives Office until finally the newly appointed captain of detectives, Bill Welcher, told Reed that his presence was making the other detectives unhappy. Reed was asked and declined an offer to transfer to Burglary or Motor Patrol.

Later, Reed was promoted to sergeant and then was transferred to Motor Patrol. When he received the letters from Brown confessing to the thirteen murders, he was put back on the case. He found himself back in the Detectives Office, but this time without a desk, computer, or even a place to put his case file as it developed. Requests for DNA tests met with delays, and some tests were never performed. He said that even though he was pivotal in bringing Brown to justice along with Detective Larry Nelson, his suggestions now seemed to have no impact. The FBI offered to let Mayhew and Reed use an office in the Federal Building next to theirs with free phone lines and use of their computer, but this offer was turned down by the police department.

This was a city election year, and while Reed and Mayhew were attempting to unravel the string of murders claimed by Joe Brown, there was a second investigation overshadowing this one.

Voter fraud is a misdemeanor crime, but this investigation became top priority. Five detectives were assigned, and they were given the keys to the chief's conference room where computer and telephone lines were installed to give them complete privacy.

"They were untouchable. No information got out of that room that they didn't release directly to the press themselves, while information from the Joe Brown case was leaking like a sieve," Reed said.

At the same time, Reed and Mayhew were still working out of a hand-carried file, without Reed having a regular desk to use.

Reed finally asked to be taken off the case. Detectives Nelson and Mayhew visited Brown in prison for one last interview but nothing further developed at the time. The two detectives decided Brown was lying and the case was closed. But it would not be the last they heard of Joe Brown.

PART IV

DIGGING UP A COLD CASE

FORTY-SIX

September 2004

Reed was surprised when a letter from Joe Brown, dated September 25, 2004, was delivered to his house. It had been nearly a year since he had heard from him, but that wasn't long enough. The short message was scrawled on three-hole, college-ruled notebook paper. It read:

> Rick,
>   I am now willing to show you and Tony Mayhew where three bodies are buried in Indiana. I will take a lie detector test first. I need you to do something for me in return. All honesty, take care.
>
>   Joe Brown
> P.S. You knew I would eventually come back.
> NO PRESS THIS TIME!!!

Reed could feel his chest tighten. He threw the letter across the room and uttered a short profanity. He wondered when this would end. He knew that this short letter would cause him months of meetings, reports, search warrants, court orders, and false leads.

He was torn by feelings of both excitement and great sadness. It was sad that this case might end with the discovery of several decomposed bodies of women, who—for all their faults and mistakes—had lived, had loved, and had families, maybe even children. Their fatal mistake was meeting Brown.

The other way this case could end would be with the discovery that Joe Brown was nothing but an attention-seeking liar who hadn't killed anyone other than Ginger Gasaway. This was the ending Reed hoped for.

The tossed letter was lying on the floor. The envelope landed on top of some filing cabinets. Reed stared at them for a moment, and then with a sigh, he rose from his chair and collected the letter and envelope. They may be needed as evidence. That's what they were now, evidence. With a bit of hesitation, Reed picked up his phone and dialed the Internal Affairs office of the Wabash Valley Correctional Facility. He needed to tell them about the letter.

The last time Reed had to deal with Brown, Detectives Mayhew, Nelson, and himself tried to follow up on leads that poured into Evansville from all over the country. None proved to be productive.

In addition to Ginger, Andrea Hendrix-Steinert was the only body found, and not one missing persons file matched any of the women that Brown had confessed to murdering. If all of the missing women were prostitutes, it would have been easier to believe Brown's stories. However, he stated that several of the women were hitchhikers that may have been on their way to or from colleges. It was hard to believe that none of these young women had been reported as missing, or had been found in a Dumpster.

Now Brown was saying that he was ready to show where three of the bodies were buried. These were three of the women that he previously had claimed to have murdered and disposed of in dumpsters. Now he wrote that he buried them. Reed cringed at the idea of bringing the letter to the attention of the Detectives Office.

Deputy Chief Dave Fehrenbacher and the recently appointed police chief, Brad Hill, both agreed that there was no other choice but to follow through with an investigation into the new claims. Even if Brown had lied in the past, they had an obligation to investigate his strange admission, regardless of whether anyone believed him or not. Reed was elected to go to Wabash Valley Correctional Facility and conduct another interview with Joe Brown.

September 30, 2004, 11:40 A.M.

The gate guard at the Wabash Valley prison spotted Reed's car in the line of vehicles that waited for admission. As he leaned out of the guard shack, he waved at Reed and motioned for him to drive around the other cars. The guard recognized Reed from the many previous visits he made a year ago. Reed pulled forward and then stopped on the gravel shoulder of the road.

"I heard you'd be here today. Remember where to go to?" the guard asked.

Reed nodded that he did, and the guard waved him through the gates. He parked in front of the administration building, emptied the contents of his pockets into a gym bag, and stored it in the trunk of his car. Taking only an Indiana county road map, a small tape recorder, a spare set of batteries, and a notebook, he headed for the main entrance. Carl Lemmons, the prison's Internal Affairs officer that he regularly worked with, waited for him by the front doors.

Reed hadn't seen Brown since October 2003, but

things apparently hadn't changed much for Joe. He was
back in administrative segregation for causing problems,
and had been isolated in the prison's Segregated Housing Unit since December 2003.

Lemmons explained to Reed that the prisoners had
to earn their way back into integration. He told Reed
that even the harshest killer would be put in population when he first arrived at the prison, and would stay
in population as long as he didn't screw up. But things
like fighting, gambling, or any other prohibited activity would result in the inmate being moved to the isolation cells of the SHU. The most violent and crazy of
these individuals would go into a special wing of the
SHU called "B" East. The inmates and guards just
called it "the Beast."

The Beast is where the prisoners take great pride in
hurling not just insults, but also human excrement at
anyone who comes within target range.

After Lemmons and Reed signed in to the SHU, two
prison guards led them to a prison counselor's office
in the hub of the segregation wing known as "A" West,
where Brown waited for them. A cacophony of catcalls
and screams echoed down the range. Just inside the
doorway of that unit were two tiny cells with iron bar
fronts. Brown stood in one of these, facing Reed.

In addition to ankle chains, Brown wore the familiar leather belt around his waist that secured his wrists
with handcuffs. Lemmons took Brown's leash from the
guard, and he sat in a chair behind the prisoner. Reed
positioned himself across the counselor's desk.

"Hello, Joe," Reed said.

"Hey, Rick," Joe responded, flashing a huge, tooth-
less grin.

Reed noted Brown's appearance, comparing it to
when he had seen him a year before. His skin color had
drained from a fleshy pink to that pasty paraffin color
of a cadaver. His scraggly mustache was untrimmed and

covered his entire mouth. His hair had grown back out from the Charles Manson buzz cut he'd affected on Reed's last visit. He no longer looked intimidating, just piteous and almost sickly.

"Before we get started, here Joe, I have to read you your rights," Reed said, to which Joe nodded, yawned, and rubbed his face.

With the Miranda rights form signed, it was time to see what Brown had in mind. Reed pulled out the letter that Brown had sent to him.

"Are you ready to show me the locations of the three bodies?" Reed asked.

"I can take you right to them, but I want to tell you something first. I don't want to die. When you find these, you know they'll give me the death penalty. This time, they'll put me to death," Brown said.

"You know that I have no control over that. You still want to do this, Joe?" Reed asked.

Brown swallowed hard and nodded. "I would've told you before, but I was afraid."

The last contact that the Evansville Police Department had with Joe Brown was in late October 2003. Detective Tony Mayhew and Detective Larry Nelson visited Brown to deliver an ultimatum. They demanded that he give them the names of the girls he had killed, or they would no longer visit him.

Brown had supplied them with several names. None of the names checked out as people who were reported as missing or deceased, as far as the detectives were able to determine. The decision was made to end the investigation.

Reed asked Brown about those names, and asked directly about the veracity of statements made to the other detectives after Reed had left the case.

Brown admitted that he had gotten angry with the other two detectives because he felt that they didn't believe him, and that they wouldn't try to find out the truth. So he said that he just gave them the first names that popped into his mind.

Brown was adamant about keeping the identifications of the women that he claimed to have murdered, and he even said that he had carried them with him in a toolbox for a while. He said that he would sometimes look at the identifications, and that he would often return to the locations where he said he buried the three local ones. Brown said that looking back, he guessed that he discarded Ginger's body parts where he did, so that all the girls could be together.

The *Indiana Atlas & Gazetteer* is a large road atlas that depicts road and topographical map information of each county in Indiana. The detail was good enough to pick out individual farm roads, so Reed opened to the map of Gibson County and placed it in front of Brown. Joe was given a felt marker with instructions to put a check on the map corresponding to the locations of the two bodies he claimed to have buried there.

On page 61 of the map book, Brown put an X at the intersection of County Roads 800 South and 330 West, about a mile west of the small town of Fort Branch. He said that wasn't exactly right, but the location was within a quarter mile of there.

Reed took the felt marker back and closed the map.

"Joe, I was told by the chief that you would have one chance to prove your story. One chance. If you can't be more specific, we're done here. I had to move heaven and earth to even come up here and see you."

Reed waited a long moment. It was a bluff, but Brown wouldn't know that. Brown blinked first.

"Both of the bodies are within ten feet of each other. I buried them close to where I threw Ginger's head. Probably twenty to fifty feet at the most."

Reed gave the map and pen back to Brown, and this time he made his mark on the map at a location that was near the location where Crime Scene officers had found the skull of Ginger Gasaway in September 2000.

"You find the spot where you found Ginger's head, and the bodies will be right there."

Brown told Reed that he would sometimes drive around and find himself at the grave and dump sites in Gibson and Posey Counties. He didn't know what made him return to those areas, but it made him feel kind of peaceful when he visited them.

Reed turned on his tape recorder and began to ask Brown questions about the victims that he supposedly buried. The first one that he talked about was a prostitute that he claimed to have killed in October 1996. Brown's description of this victim remained true to the description that he provided in the confession he made in 2003. He also remembered that he was living on South New York Avenue at the time, and that he was working for Bryan Brown, his cousin, which coincided with the facts that investigators were able to verify.

In a letter Brown wrote to the *Evansville Courier & Press,* he said that he strangled this victim with shoestrings, but in his 2003 confession, Brown said that he strangled her with his bare hands. He stuck with that story during this interview as well. He was able to provide many more details of the events of the evening now.

Joe stayed with his aunt and uncle when he was first released from prison in 1995. His cousin, Bryan, gave him a job and tried to help Joe fit back into society. To do that, Bryan had talked Joe into going to church with him and his family. It was a Tuesday or Wednesday night, not a regular church night, so Joe thought the service would be short. But that wasn't the case, and the service lasted until late in the evening. After a full day of carrying hod and laying brick, Joe's patience was wearing at the edges.

Joe didn't have a religious inclination, and he didn't care for Bryan's church or any of the people Bryan had tried to introduce him to. He felt that they only pretended to accept him. He still felt like an ex-con. It was with that deep resentment still on his mind that he found himself driving home in the wee hours of the morning.

Brown said that he drove his old yellow Scottsdale pickup north on Kratzville Road and turned east on Diamond Avenue, heading for home. His thoughts were jumbled as he took the ramp that led from Diamond onto Fares Avenue. He said that a young white female appeared in his headlights. She flagged him down, then motioned for him to pull over on the side of the ramp.

Brown pulled over to the side of the road as she hurried up to the passenger side and jumped in. She wanted to know if he had some money, and he knew what she was offering. Brown said that he frequented the prostitutes of Fares Avenue since his return to Evansville, and at the time, they were so plentiful that he hadn't been with the same one twice. He said he didn't know what made him kill this one and not some of the others, or all of them.

Brown told her he only had a few dollars, but she enthusiastically agreed to go to his apartment anyway. They headed south to Columbia Street, cut over to US Highway 41, and continued south to Walnut Street. His apartment was only a few blocks away.

Brown said that this particular prostitute must have taken a shine to him, because she had removed her dirty blue jeans, in his apartment, and allowed him to enter her from behind. According to Brown, the sex was short-lived, and so was she.

While she stood with her back to him, pulling up her jeans, he landed a hammer blow with the side of his fist on her temple. The stunned hooker collapsed in a tiny heap at his feet. Brown said he then got on top of her and pinned her back to the floor while he strangled her.

Brown said that his petite prey went limp in his grasp, at which time he stopped applying pressure, to allow her to come to. When she regained enough consciousness to open her eyes, he bore down once again, this time taking her life. After she was dead, he took back the money he had paid her. She wouldn't need it anymore, Brown said. He added that she was just a crack whore who didn't have anything to live for anyway.

The entire incident from picking her up to the act of murdering her had taken less than thirty minutes. Brown said that he sat on the edge of his bed wondering how to dispose of the body. He wasn't in a panic. The act of taking a life with no provocation, and so easily, didn't disgust him. In fact, he felt that she had brought it on herself. After all, he wasn't out looking for a hooker. She flagged him down. She had asked him for money. She should have known the danger, so she got what she deserved.

Brown said that he carried the body to his truck and placed her on the floorboard in front. At first, he wasn't sure what he was going to do. He thought about just shoving her out in a ditch, or maybe dragging the corpse into the woods, but as he headed north on US Highway 65, he decided to bury her.

Since he was a construction worker, he always had a shovel in the back of the truck. It would be better to put her in the ground so she wouldn't be found right away.

He said that at about County Road 525 West and County Road 900 South there was an old Boy Scout camp, where he used to go. This was just inside the Gibson County line from Posey County. He thought about burying her there, but he decided against it, because Scouts did camp there occasionally. They might discover a fresh grave.

He began to think of his childhood, and he thought of the perfect place to dispose of the body. Taking back roads that only a local would know, he drove to a site in Gibson County, where he knew he could do what needed to be done in perfect isolation. This was a place where he would later dispose of Ginger Gasaway's severed head.

When asked if there was some reason that he picked this site, Brown responded that when he was a child, his grandfather had brought him out there to hunt squirrels. He said the area was so deserted that he knew he wouldn't have to worry about being discovered as he went about the task of digging a shallow grave. The spot he had picked was uninhabited, and was far enough away from any road so that his truck wouldn't be visible.

Closing in on the Gibson County site, Brown drove by a set of oil well pumps, and then back to the edge of a farm pasture where it met with woodland.

Brown said there was a cut in the thick brush at the edge of the woods, where he was able to carry the body through. She was fully clothed when he set her on the cold earth about ten feet back in the woods. He said the soil was soft for several feet deep, which made digging easy. The makeshift grave was about two feet wide and three feet long, and just deep enough to shove her in and cover her. When he was through, he looked around and was satisfied that the grave wouldn't attract attention from anyone at the edge of the woods.

Reed told Brown that there were coyotes in that part of the county, and he asked if Brown was worried about an animal digging her up. Brown said that he didn't care if coyotes got to her. He only wanted to keep other people from finding her.

FORTY-SEVEN

Brown said that he was living in a trailer park on St. Joseph Avenue, north of Mill Road, when he killed another prostitute in April or May 1997. This was the last location of Joe's cousin, Bryan Brown's, residence but this was the first time that Brown had ever mentioned living at this location. Although Reed was skeptical of Brown's statement, no attempt was made to verify his claim that he resided there at the time.

The area Brown said that he lived at was within blocks of the Browning Ferris landfill, and Reed made a connection with Brown's earlier claims that he had thrown the murdered prostitutes in Browning Ferris Incorporated (BFI) Dumpsters. In statements made to Reed and Mayhew in October 2003, Brown had remarked that the police should be able to get the records of the landfill to find out where those Dumpsters were emptied. They were not able to obtain that information.

Once again, Brown's description of this victim coincided with the account that he delivered a year earlier.

He said she was willing to have sex with him for whatever money he would give her. He promised her less than $12, but she eagerly got into his car. He had gotten rid of the Scottsdale truck and was now driving a black Nissan Stanza XE compact car.

He said that he gave her the money, then took her to his trailer, where he killed her in the same way as the one he had killed in October 1996, by striking her in the side of the head from behind, then strangling her. That was where his story changed. In Brown's 2003 confession, he said that he took this prostitute to the Royal Inn Motel and strangled her from behind with shoestrings.

Now that he no longer owned his truck, it was much more difficult to transport a body. The compact car barely had enough space on the front floorboard and seat to hold the body of this small woman, and he had trouble putting a shovel in the car as well.

Reed interrupted Brown to ask where he came up with the shovel, since he no longer had a truck. It didn't seem plausible to carry a shovel around in a small car.

Brown explained all this away by saying that he worked construction, and always had tools around. That didn't make sense to Reed, but he wanted to hear the rest of the story, so he didn't pursue this detail.

In Brown's 2003 statement, he said that he disposed of this body in the Diamond Valley Apartments garbage Dumpster. Now he was saying that he took this victim to the same site in Gibson County where he had taken the first prostitute in October 1996. At the site, he was able to drive the car off the road, across the field, and up to the edge of the woods. The car was set low enough to the ground that the growth in the field hid his actions from sight. When asked what was growing in the field, Brown said that he couldn't remember, but he thought it might have been corn or wheat. He said that it was no problem to drag the body from the car and into the woods, where he buried her in a shallow grave near his last victim.

Turning back to the Indiana atlas, Reed asked Brown to locate the other site in Posey County where the third victim was purportedly buried. This time, Brown didn't hesitate. With the felt pen, he marked a location near where Reynolds Road and Pumpkin Run Road intersected. He said it was March 1999 when he killed this one.

Brown stopped the narration of his purported murders with a loud clearing of his throat. Always the manipulator, he asked Carl Lemmons if he could have a cup of coffee before he continued.

Lemmons had worked at the prison long enough to know a con when he saw one. He told Brown that coffee was not possible. As an added incentive to continue, he told Brown that the interview was almost over, and that he had business elsewhere in the prison.

Brown was disappointed, but continued anyway.

Regarding the third body he buried, which was supposedly his ninth victim, Brown said she was buried in Posey County in a farm field. He said that he picked this prostitute up in March 1999 on Fares Avenue. A year earlier, he had said that he met this woman through Savage Entertainment.

Brown claimed that he strangled this victim just like the others. He always approached them from behind while they were preparing to leave and would strike them in the side of the head, stunning them, and then strangling them to death. The blow to the head was a new addition to his modus operandi.

At the time of this murder, Brown was driving the red 1993 Mustang convertible that Ginger Gasaway had purchased for his transportation to work. Brown said that he drove the Mustang to the area in Posey County that he marked on the map, and buried her near a huge oak tree that had a brush pile pushed up to it. This was at the edge of a farmer's cornfield and close to the road.

Brown remembered very few details about this victim

when interviewed by Reed on September 30, 2004. But in September 2003, he had expressed vivid memories about this slaying to both Reed and Detective Mayhew.

A year ago, he had described this prostitute as "pretty," five feet three inches tall, 120 pounds, with shoulder-length brown hair. In his current description, she was five feet six inches tall, 130 pounds, and blond. Even the clothing descriptions were extremely different now. In 2003, Brown said that she was wearing a sweater over a turtleneck and khaki pants. In his current description, she was wearing blue jeans and tennis shoes.

Also, during his confession a year ago, Brown had consistently mixed this murder up with the murder of Andrea Hendrix-Steinert. He thought he had murdered Andrea in March 1999, and was certain of snow being on the ground at the time that he threw her nude and lifeless body onto the side of the road. In that same erroneous thinking, he would say that he had murdered this prostitute from Savage Entertainment sometime in October 1997.

It was apparent that the order and descriptions of Brown's alleged victims were changing with each retelling of the story.

After the tape recorder was turned off, Reed asked Brown again if he could remember anything else that might help him find the graves or the identifications of the murdered women. Brown just shook his head and looked at his feet.

As Reed and Lemmons got up from their seats, Brown made a request. He asked if Reed would try to do one thing for him after they found the bodies of these three prostitutes. He asked if Reed would contact Tunica, Mississippi, and let them know that he could show them where he buried the very first prostitute that he killed, the one he called Candy. Brown said that that murder still bothered him, and that he still had nightmares because of it. He didn't elaborate any further than that. Reed made no promises.

As Brown was being led away by the prison staff, he turned to Reed and said, "This is my last chance. I know that, Rick. I'll never get out of here again if you don't find what you're looking for. But they're there."

The interview with Joe Brown hadn't taken long, but it wasn't expected to. Much of the information was simply a rehash of his 2003 confession, with the exception of the burials. At least now, it would be a simple matter of proving or disproving his claims. Not like in 2003 when Brown presented volumes of information, including where he picked up his victims, their descriptions, murder locations, dump sites, what he was driving, and possible locations of evidence. Those interviews of necessity had been exhaustive.

Outside, Reed sat on the lip of his open car trunk staring back toward the razor wire that surrounded the prison grounds, where he had just been. He bid Lemmons and the helpful ladies in the Internal Affairs office a temporary good-bye, and they had good-naturedly teased that they were going to put a desk for him in their office.

As he collected his personal items from inside his trunk, Reed remembered Brown's last word, "This is my last chance." It hadn't meant anything to him inside the walls of the prison, but under the sunny blue sky and fresh air, it took on an exaggerated importance.

Reed took a deep breath, enjoying the rich smell of pine that drifted in the breeze. He wondered what it would be like to be locked in a concrete cell for twenty-three hours a day. Brown's only activity outside of the tiny cinder block room was an occasional short walk to the shower facility, and maybe a five-minute phone call if he knew someone willing to accept the charges to talk with him. Even these things were done under the close scrutiny of prison guards. Reed asked himself,

"What would he be willing to do to experience the outside again?"

Add to this Brown's propensity for attention, and there was only one answer: Joe Brown probably would be willing to do anything. Just because the long hours of interviewing and investigation had been grueling for the detectives in 2003 didn't mean that it was exhaustive for Brown. On the contrary, he was probably revitalized by the attention. The isolation was probably what was exhaustive for him.

None of this really mattered, though. Reed knew that he would have to follow this through because it would be devastating to the reputation of the Evansville Police Department if Brown was telling the truth, and they didn't attempt to investigate. He imagined a scenario where the areas that Brown described as "burial sites" were one day zoned for a residential subdivision and bodies were found during excavation.

The nobler of reasons, of course, was closure for the family of any possible victim. To the EPD, the fact that Brown had described all these women as prostitutes meant nothing negative. They were citizens, and it was the sworn duty of the police to safeguard their lives and freedoms. If they had failed in protecting them while alive, at least they were owed the dignity of a proper burial.

Reed headed back to Evansville. His report to the police chief and to the commander of the Detectives Office would be that he had doubts as to Brown's veracity, but would recommend they continue the investigation.

The next week was a busy one for the Internal Affairs office of the Evansville Police Department. Heavy workloads usually came in spurts like this, with a calm period followed by a "blue light special" on complaints against police officers. The strange thing Reed had discovered while working Internal Affairs was that people didn't often complain about excessive force issues. The most frequent complaint was about officer rudeness. Apparently, you can beat a perpetrator with a nightstick, pepper-spray them, or shock them with fifty thousand volts from a Taser gun, but don't call them an asshole while doing so.

In between his regular duties, Reed made the connections to other resources that would be needed to complete this investigation. The first call was to Stan Levco, Vanderburgh County prosecutor. His assistance would be needed if Brown was taken out of the prison to show investigators the exact locations of the burial sites.

Levco was out of his office for the day, so Reed called the other important players. The dispatcher put through his call to Posey County sheriff Jim Folz. Folz was a retired marine gunnery sergeant. He had joined the Posey County Sheriff Department immediately after retiring. He was a ball of fire on the county streets, and in a short time, he had earned the respect and loyalty of many of the county residents. In 2002, he ran for sheriff and won almost two-to-one against the Democratic incumbent. What was unbelievable about that was he ran as a Democrat against a Democrat incumbent and beat him even without party support. Folz promised that his department would assist the EPD if needed.

The next call was to Gibson County sheriff Alan Harmon. Gibson County had gone automated, and Reed reached a voice recording instructing him to punch buttons to navigate their phone system. Frustrated that he couldn't get through to anyone, he finally gave up and left a message asking Harmon to contact him.

The local Federal Bureau of Investigation's special agent in charge, Tom VanWormer, happened to be in the police department on October 4 and Reed recruited his assistance as well.

If special equipment was required, such as ground-penetrating radar, the FBI's assistance would be vital. Even if their far-reaching resources were not needed, just invoking their name would help get the investigation moving past obstacles. Everyone wanted to cooperate with the feds.

Reed wanted VanWormer to meet Brown for himself, and they scheduled it for the afternoon of October 6. While Reed completed the arrangements with the Wabash prison, Sheriff Harmon returned his call. Harmon sounded skeptical when Reed explained that Brown claimed to have buried victims in Gibson County. Reed gave him the location that Brown had marked on the Indiana atlas, and Harmon said he remembered that was close to the area where Brown had disposed of Ginger's remains in 2000.

Harmon said he instructed Detective Chuck Finnerty to find the exact spot and take photos of the area. These would be helpful when Reed and VanWormer visited Brown in prison the next day.

The Gibson County Sheriff Department had been extremely helpful in September 2000 during the investigation and recovery of human remains from the Gasaway case. Reed hoped they would be as helpful in this new investigation.

FORTY-EIGHT

Reed received another letter from the Wabash Valley Correctional Facility. This time it wasn't from Joe Brown, but from another inmate, who shared the cell block with him. This inmate wrote that he had gained Brown's confidence and spoke with him about the murders. He wrote that he was sure that he could get a detailed map from Brown that would lead the investigators to the locations of several of the murder victims. In return for his assistance, he asked to be moved to a prison of his choice and to have his case reviewed by the courts again.

Reed met with Levco on October 6, 2004, to request a transport order so Brown could be taken from prison to identify the areas that he claimed to have buried the three women. When he arrived, Levco pointed to a seat and leaned back in his own chair. His first words: "Do you believe this guy?"

Reed respected Levco's acumen as a prosecutor and trial lawyer, and he began to doubt his own persistence in this case. He had to admit that he had his reservations, but he was determined to see it through. The police department was under an obligation to prove or disprove Joe Brown's confession. In the end, Reed left the office without a firm commitment on the transportation order.

He would need the backing of Police Chief Hill, but he knew that would not be a problem.

After the meeting with Levco, it was time to pick up Special Agent Tom VanWormer. Reed drove back to his office to pick up a binder that contained information about the case and maps of the area. Then he drove to the Federal Building on Martin Luther King Jr. Boulevard. He rode the elevator up to the third floor, then walked down the royal blue carpeted hallway to a heavy wooden door emblazoned with the emblem of the FBI. Reed met VanWormer and the two men left to go to the correctional facility in Carlisle, Indiana.

During the hour-long drive, the men used the time to get caught up on the case. VanWormer asked what services the police department might need of his agency. Reed explained that he was running this investigation at the request of Police Chief Brad Hill. Any official requests would need to be approved by him first, but Reed said that he would like to explore the possibility of using the FBI's forensic services and obtain the use of a ground-penetrating radar unit and operator. To have the equipment and an operator flown into Evansville, and then to prepare the area to be scanned, could cost as much as $20,000. At times, the FBI has provided this service at no cost to the requesting agency. VanWormer said that given Brown's lack of credibility, the use of the ground-penetrating radar was not likely.

Reed and VanWormer also discussed the letter that Reed received from Brown's fellow inmate, and the two men dismissed its contents as nothing more than a jailhouse con.

At the prison, Reed introduced VanWormer to Internal Affairs investigator Carl Lemmons, who ushered the men over to the SHU. Lemmons was also advised of the letter that Reed had received, and he left to prepare the other inmate for a clandestine meeting, in case the investigators desired it.

When Brown was led into the counselor's office, the initial smile on his face dissolved into a look of confusion at the presence of FBI agent VanWormer. But his hesitance abated after hearing that he was in the presence of the head of the local FBI office.

Brown knew this was his last chance to prove his claims, and in his demeanor, it was apparent he was going to try and impress VanWormer. Without prompting, Brown was able to give an almost verbatim account of the information that he had delivered on September 30 to Reed. He gave details of the three murders that he claimed to have committed in Evansville and the locations of where he buried the victims in Gibson and Posey Counties.

Before ending the interview, Reed asked Brown if he remembered anything else that might be helpful to the investigation. This is a standard question, and he hadn't really expected a response.

Brown said he only buried the three women in Indiana and the one in Tunica, Mississippi. He said he just tossed Slick (Andrea Hendrix-Steinert) on the side of the road. Brown added that it might still be possible to find the one named Sandra in Colorado, because he threw her over the guardrail, but the rest of his purported victims were thrown in Dumpsters, like he originally told investigators.

Then Brown made a comment that took both men by surprise.

"Maybe I shouldn't talk about the other one."

Reed and VanWormer exchanged a puzzled look. Reed asked Brown what he meant by "the other one."

Brown said he remembered the name of a girl he had killed in May 1998 in Flagstaff, Arizona, and it was Catherine Ferguson. This was the first time that Reed had heard of this.

According to Brown, Detectives Mayhew and Nelson told him in a 2003 interview that he must have had blackouts during some of the murders, and that while he was at Whitey's Motel, near Owensboro, he had come back to the motel covered in blood.

Brown said that he didn't remember any incident like that, but Mayhew told him that he had abducted a woman named Ferguson and killed her.

Brown was now admitting to crimes that he didn't even remember committing.

VanWormer and Reed left the prison and stopped at an Applebee's to eat and discuss how to proceed with the investigation. They decided that the next step would be to put Joe Brown on a polygraph. Agent VanWormer would supply the operator.

On October 27, 2004, Sergeant Reed and FBI agent Marty Williams drove to Carlisle, Indiana. FBI agent Rich Osborne drove to the Wabash prison from Indianapolis and was already waiting in the parking lot when Reed and Williams arrived. Osborne would operate the polygraph for them.

The men expected that Brown would fail the test; that is, the results would indicate that he was lying about the murders. What they were worried about was that the test would show "inconclusive," meaning that Brown could be lying or telling the truth, and the machine couldn't tell the difference. In any case, the results would not be admissible in court because polygraphs are not infallible.

The group still had to determine the right questions to ask Joe. They decided on the most pertinent questions: "Had Joe ever killed anyone besides Ginger Gasaway?" and "Did he kill Andrea Hendrix-Steinert?" Agent Osborne said he would ask about Andrea first, since that was the case that seemed the most likely to be true. If the test showed that Brown was lying about Andrea, the rest of the test would be inconsequential, since they didn't have any bodies or missing persons to go with the other supposed murders.

Inside the prison, the men were directed to the Education Department, where a special room offered the quiet solitude required to run a polygraph test. Osborne brought his own equipment with him and soon he had it set up. The guards went to retrieve Brown from his cell. Agent Osborne would be alone in an almost soundproof room with a known killer. There would be no handcuffs and no restraints.

Brown was brought in and introduced to everyone, looking even more haggard than on Reed's previous visit. His pasty complexion was now blotched with red spots, and he looked as if he had just gotten up from sleeping with his face buried in a pillow.

Brown said he was on a heavy dose of Prozac now because he was having a lot of trouble sleeping. Osborne later advised them that this medication would affect the polygraph, but it would be more prone to show him as being truthful instead of deceptive. The reason being that the drugs relax the physical responses to threatening questions like, "Did you murder thirteen women?"

Two guards, Agent Williams, and Sergeant Reed all waited anxiously for over two hours outside the small room where the polygraph was administered. Finally the door opened. Osborne stepped out and two large prison guards went inside and took Brown back to his cell.

After the guards led Brown away, the other men met in the room where the polygraph equipment was still set up. Osborne said that he talked to Brown for a long time to try and calm him. He said Brown swore that he was telling the truth when he said that he had killed Andrea, but Osborne's equipment told a different story.

The first chart he ran on Brown was all over the place. There was no way to score it for truthfulness or deception. But after Brown calmed down a little, the second and third tests both showed that Brown was deceptive to the question "Did you kill Andrea Hendrix-Steinert?" Osborne admitted that this could be because Brown didn't know her by that name, or at least he only knew that name from the investigation.

Brown had told Reed that he didn't know Andrea's name and never asked her. She was just a prostitute to him and he never got that involved with them. He said he only knew her by Slick because she thought she was being slick when she tried to steal his money.

In any case, the test results were the test results. The only thing left to do was search the two areas where Joe Brown said he had buried his victims. If these came up empty, this investigation would be over.

FORTY-NINE

Vanderburgh County Circuit Court judge Carl Heldt issued a prisoner transport order on November 12 to allow investigators to take Joe Brown out of prison for the purpose of locating the three grave sites. Vanderburgh County chief deputy Eric Williams was contacted and provided with a copy of the transport order. The original would be taken to the prison. Williams said he would make the arrangement with his transport unit and they would contact Reed. It was decided that they get this over with as soon as possible.

On November 16, 2004, at 7:00 A.M., Reed and Deputy Rob Lutz drove to the corrections center to take custody of Joseph Brown. Reed handed over the signed transport order and Brown was brought down the hall in full restraints. Deputy Lutz put his own restraints on Brown, trading cuffs and chains, and though this would be humiliating for most men, Brown was beaming. He was getting what he wanted: a little bit of freedom. But his joy was short-lived.

In order to secure Brown's release, Reed had to assure Levco and Chief Hill that this would not be a pleasure trip for Brown. When he saw the prison transport van, Joe Brown grunted in disbelief.

"This is what you're taking me in?" he asked, and

nodded toward the plain white panel van. "I thought I was going to ride with you."

The van had no windows on the sides and only one on the back, which was almost completely covered by the cage system inside. In the back were several compartments where prisoners can be shackled individually to avoid any contact and most conversation. The heat and a/c were controlled by the driver. There was a small sliding window behind the driver that could be used for communicating, if necessary. This would not be a pleasure trip, as agreed.

Brown was read the Miranda rights warning from an Evansville Police Department form. Reed held the form down so Brown could sign it with his restraints in place. Reed made a point to explain that this was being done because anything Brown said, or any evidence found, could be used against him in court in criminal proceedings. Reed wasn't going to take any chances in the event they found bodies. A defense team wouldn't rake him over the coals like they had done when Brown was arrested before.

In the guard shack, Deputy Lutz had been given possession of Brown's medication and advised that the men were responsible to see that he was fed and took his medication that morning. Opening the paper sack revealed a pharmacy of medications. Brown was taking six pills at one time, three times a day, and most of them were antidepressants.

Brown was loaded into a compartment in the back of the van—with a promise that they would stop somewhere and get him water, coffee, and maybe a doughnut.

"Did you bring any smokes?" he asked.

"It's against the law," Reed responded.

Deputy Lutz took them back the way they had come, and before long, the razor wire and guard towers of the prison faded out of sight.

The first stop was a gas station, where coffee, a bottle

of water, and a pack of cigarettes were purchased for Brown, who remained inside the van. Before he was given these items, they gave Brown his medications. The men watched to be sure Brown didn't hide any pills. It would be embarrassing if he was searched when he was brought back to prison and found to be hiding contraband.

The stop took less than five minutes and they were once again headed south on US Highway 41 toward Fort Branch. In another thirty minutes, the van was bumping down the dirt lane of the farm pasture at the Gibson County site. This was the place that Brown had indicated with the photos as the burial site of two of the victims. Assistant Chief Burnworth, of the Evansville Crime Scene Unit, was already waiting for them when the van arrived.

Brown stretched and yawned as he came out of the back of the cramped space. "That's it. Right over there," he said, nodding toward an area just to the south of where Burnworth stood with a handful of marker flags.

With an officer or two nearby at all times, Brown was allowed to take the orange marker flags and place them in the ground, marking a boundary of the area where he believed the bodies were buried.

Brown said that the area had changed a lot since 2000 when he had been there with the remains of Ginger Gasaway, but he was confident that he had marked the correct areas.

"Yeah. This is the right place," he assured the men. "I didn't bury 'em very deep."

The area that Brown marked with the flags was about ten feet across at most, and maybe only five feet wide. It would not take much digging to check his story here.

But the digging would have to wait for another day. Reed had not been able to make contact with the property owner to obtain permission to dig. Since the news media had not been alerted to the fact that Brown was going to be taking this trip today, there wasn't much of a hurry to get this done. Once they found out, it would be a different story. Every scoop of dirt would be documented for the newspapers and television cameras, and Brown would once again be gracing hundreds of thousands of television sets.

Brown was loaded into the back of the van, given a smoke and some water, and the trip resumed. This time, the Crime Scene vehicle followed the van west on I-64 toward Poseyville.

After the van started moving, Reed contacted the Posey County sheriff's dispatcher and had her contact Sheriff Jim Folz to let him know of their position. Folz had been made aware of the pending trip, the night before.

Sheriff Folz advised the dispatcher to have the van meet with his deputy at the Poseyville Road Exit, off I-64. Reed called Burnworth by cell phone and told him of the location.

As they drove west on I-64, they once again passed the Moto Mart at US Highway 65. A few miles beyond that was the exit to Poseyville. Looking off to the north, Reed found that the land was flat farm fields bordered by sparse lines of trees, which Reed guessed were wind and erosion barriers. Winter wheat was planted in some of the fields, but mostly there were the remains of the harvested corn crops jutting from the brown clay. Most of the ground was still soaked from the recent rains.

Before they turned north on the exit, two marked sheriff's units could be seen on the side of the road. At that location, they met with Deputy Beth Wire and decided to take Brown from the transport van for a look around. He had advised that he was not positive about the next location, but that it was at the same spot where he had disposed of Ginger Gasaway's legs in 2000. Wire hadn't been part of that particular search and was unsure of the location.

Brown advised the officers to drive north on Poseyville Road to the first gravel road and turn west. Then they would go to the next farm access road and turn south. He said to look for a "big-assed" oak tree with a deep drainage ditch, just to the west of it. He said the tree was very large and old and that there was a cornfield on the east side of that road when he buried this girl in April 1997. He also said that next to the oak tree would be a fairly large pile of brush and refuse.

With the sheriff's units leading the way, they followed Brown's directions. Within a mile, they arrived at the big oak tree with the brush pile. The farm field stretched out beside the road. It was exactly as Brown had described it.

Brown was once again taken from the back of the van and allowed to survey the area. He confirmed they were in the right place and that he had buried the prostitute about ten to twelve rows of corn in from the edge of that farm field. This was almost directly east of the oak tree.

Brown accompanied Burnworth and Lutz into the farm field. It was now growing young plants of winter wheat. Brown said that when he buried this prostitute, it was in early April and there was corn in that field. He said the plants were only about five to eight inches high at the time. He said the ground was very soft and that he dug a hole about four feet deep so that she wouldn't be pulled up by a farm implement when they plowed the field with a disc later.

Brown said this victim was fully clothed, wearing blue jeans, white tennis shoes, and some type of cotton blouse, but he couldn't remember the color. She had light brown hair and was about five feet four inches tall and very thin. He guessed her age at about twenty-five to thirty years old.

He said he was living in a trailer court on St. Joseph Avenue, near the BFI landfill, when he killed this girl, and he killed her inside his trailer by strangling her with his bare hands. This was about 9:30 to 10:00 P.M. and he waited until about midnight before he put her in his car, the black Nissan Stanza XE, and drove to the Posey County site. He said he had trouble getting both her and the shovel in the car.

Once again, Joe Brown put orange flags out to mark the boundaries of the area where he believed he had buried this girl.

FIFTY

November 16, 2004

In September 2000, when Ginger Gasaway's remains were found in this same area, the corn had been head-high, and it had been pitch-black. Standing in this field in 2004, with the young winter wheat barely raising its head, even Joe Brown was having a difficult time getting an exact measurement from the roadway to where he had disposed of the remains of the prostitute.

When he had buried her, the corn was less than a foot high, and it was pitch-black again. Reed made a few calls on his cell phone. He wanted to find someone with a GPS unit to get an accurate position of the site from September 2000.

Brown had just placed his last orange flag into the soft ground when a sheriff's department vehicle turned onto the gravel farm lane, with a white pickup truck following close behind. As Sheriff Folz parked along the soft shoulder of the gravel road, Brown lit up another cigarette. It was obvious that he wasn't going to be good for any further information.

Folz spoke to Brown for a few moments and then approached the Evansville officers. He asked the same question that everyone involved with this case had asked for the past year: "Do you think he's telling the truth?"

This was Posey County. The Evansville Police Department had no jurisdiction there. The moment Folz arrived on the scene, this had become a Posey County matter. Of course, if a body was discovered, both departments would share joint jurisdiction until it was decided where the crime took place. But according to prosecutor Stan Levco, even though a murder was committed in one county and the body was dumped in another, either county can prosecute the case. If a body was found in the field, it wouldn't matter to Reed who prosecuted Joe.

Most of the history of this case already had been exchanged between the Posey County and Evansville officers, so there wasn't much for Reed and Burnworth to do except stand by and watch the scene.

Folz assigned Deputy Wire to prepare and keep a scene log, a running document of anyone and everyone that came and went from the scene. He then called for the Vanderburgh County EMA Search and Rescue dogs to come to the scene.

While they waited for the arrival of the cadaver dogs, two men took GPS readings to find the exact location where Ginger Gasaway's remains had been disposed. When the men finally stopped and declared that they were standing right on top of the coordinates, they looked around. They were standing dead center in the area that Brown had marked with orange flags.

The area marked was at least fifteen or twenty feet square now, and Folz made the decision to widen that by another ten feet. Using his cell phone and his deputies, he contacted the owners of the property and located a backhoe to be brought to the scene. This would greatly speed things up. To dig up by hand an area that large would take weeks, but it would have also left very little room for error when it came to preserving the integrity of any evidence they might find.

All of the officers at the scene agreed with the decision to use the backhoe, and in fact, they brought in a second backhoe an hour later to work the opposite side of what turned out to be a dig site large enough for a regulation-size swimming pool.

Before the backhoes were brought into position, Brown finished off most of a pack of cigarettes and another cup of coffee. He was entertaining those that would listen with jokes. It was time to go.

Burnworth agreed to stay at the scene while Reed and Lutz took Brown back to prison. It was almost lunchtime, and since they were responsible for Brown's meals, the men stopped at a McDonald's and bought Brown three cheeseburgers, fries, and a soft drink. There was barely room for Brown to balance the sack on his legs in the confined space of the van's cargo area, but this wasn't supposed to be a picnic.

When they arrived back at the prison and opened the back of the van, a thick cloud of smoke billowed out. Brown had attempted to finish off the entire pack of cigarettes before being taken back to the smoke-free confines of his cell. The men had to let him sit for a moment to regain his bearings. He had been smoke-free for the last three years, and now he was dizzy and nauseated.

"Will you let me know something?" Brown asked as he was shuffled into the secured area of the prison.

Reed assured him that he would be back to see him if they found something. Brown nodded and was whisked away by two guards.

After returning Brown to the custody of the prison guards, the van headed back toward the Posey County dig site. They were curious to see how the dig was going. In no time at all, they were pulling back onto the gravel drive leading to the dig site in Posey County. Now there were several more vehicles lining the sides of the road. There was also a full-size van sporting a telescoping dish antennae. The media had arrived in force.

Finding a place to park was more difficult now, and the edge of the roadway had become muddy and rutted deep enough to bottom out a car on the chassis. What had started as a small dig had turned into an enormous gaping wound in the earth.

The Vanderburgh County EMA K-9 handler was taking her cadaver dog around the edges of the dig, letting the dog's sensitive nose play over the loose earth. The backhoes would dig for a little while and then stop periodically to allow the dog to search. In this way, they hoped to scent something prior to digging into it with the metal teeth of the backhoe.

So far, the dog had shown only a mild interest in one or two locations. Further digging had dispersed whatever it was the dog had scented, and it lost interest in those areas.

As the day wore on and the sun began to hide behind clouds, the digging seemed to slow to a crawl. Occasionally, one of the officers scattered around the edges of the pit would yell for the backhoe to stop because they spotted something.

The "something" would inevitably turn out to be a piece of an old cornstalk that had been disced into the ground, and not a bone, not a skull, not a leather belt, as they appeared in the shadows. Each new exclamation from a worker brought an onslaught of reporters and cameras jockeying for a better shot of whatever it was that had been spotted. Each new disappointment didn't make the dedicated news crews any less swift the next time.

Deputy Lutz had to leave at 6:00 P.M. and Reed went with him. Burnworth agreed to stay until Reed could go to Police Headquarters and fill in Chief Hill about the events of the day. When Reed arrived at the station, he retrieved his own vehicle and called Hill on his cell phone. He listened attentively to what had so far been a futile effort, but he was committed to seeing it the rest of the way through.

Before going home, Reed made arrangements for someone to relieve Burnworth at the dig site. The digging had ceased at about 7:00 P.M. and the area was secured for the night by Posey County deputies. Digging would begin again in the morning.

The next day, Reed, armed with hot coffee and two boxes of doughnuts, headed back to Posey County. A single backhoe was digging. The media had thinned out, having gotten their story from the night before. By noon, Folz called it quits.

November 19, 2004

The best chance of finding any evidence to support Joe Brown's claims had been with the dig site in Posey County. Continuing on to Gibson County was a fool's errand, but it had to be done.

The excavation of the Gibson County site didn't take long, even counting the time used to run the cadaver dogs through the area. The results of the search were the same as in Posey County. They found nothing. Not even a bone for the dog.

Reed was somewhat disappointed that after so much time and effort, they were not able to find any evidence to support Brown's claims. However, when looked at from the proper perspective, Reed decided that this was a happy ending to a case that had consumed several years of his life. He felt that no one could claim that a thorough investigation had not been completed, and most important, there was no evidence to show that these women were killed or even existed to begin with.

The death of Andrea Hendrix-Steinert has remained

an open case in Gibson County. The sheriff there said that he was pretty sure of who was responsible for her death, but he did not have enough evidence to accuse the culprit, who, he said, still lived in southern Indiana. Even if enough evidence was collected to make a case against Joe Brown for that murder, it could now be refuted by a defense attorney as the ramblings of a madman.

The next time that a letter from Joseph Weldon Brown, of the Wabash Valley Correctional Facility, lands on Reed's desk he can file it without an accompanying feeling of guilt, into the trash. Reed expects to hear from him during some September, a month that Joe Brown always seems to emerge. After all, it is a time that begins the season of death.